The History of Policing America

The History of Policing America

From Militias and Military to the Law Enforcement of Today

Laurence Armand French

ROWMAN & LITTLEFIELD
Lanham • Boulder • New York • London

Published by Rowman & Littlefield
A wholly owned subsidary of The Rowman & Littlefield Publishing Group, Inc.
4501 Forbes Boulevard, Suite 200, Lanham, Maryland 20706
www.rowman.com

Unit A, Whitacre Mews, 26-34 Stannary Street, London SE11 4AB

British Library Cataloguing in Publication Information Available

Library of Congress Cataloging-in-Publication Data

Names: French, Laurence, 1941– author.
Title: The History of Policing America : from militias and military to the law
enforcement of today / Laurence Armand French.
Description: Lanham : Rowman & Littlefield, [2017] | Includes bibliographical
references and index.
Identifiers: LCCN 2017040643 (print) | LCCN 2017051500 (ebook) | ISBN
9781538102046 (Electronic) | ISBN 9781538102039 (cloth : alk. paper)
Subjects: LCSH: Law enforcement—United States—History. | Police—United
States—History.
Classification: LCC HV8138 (ebook) | LCC HV8138 .F734 2017 (print) | DDC
363.20973—dc23
LC record available at https://lccn.loc.gov/2017040643

∞™ The paper used in this publication meets the minimum requirements of
American National Standard for Information Sciences—Permanence of Paper
for Printed Library Materials, ANSI/NISO Z39.48-1992.

Printed in the United States of America

To the vast majority of law enforcement personnel who diligently serve to protect the public's safety regardless of race, color, creed, age, or sex/gender—*The "Good Cops."*

Contents

Part IV: Twenty-First-Century Concerns

I

ORIGINS OF U.S.
LAW ENFORCEMENT

Militias, Military, Marshals, and Sheriffs

Introduction

Colonial Roots in Policing America

GENESIS OF STATUS ACQUISITION AND
MILITARY STATUS IN COLONIAL NEW ENGLAND

The 2016 presidential elections attest to the fact that America is as divided a society as it has been since the mid-nineteenth century and the War between the States (Civil War). Two hundred and forty years since its declaration of independence, the United States has yet to resolve its racial, sectarian, gender, and socioeconomic divides. Much of this divisiveness is rooted in its perception of social injustice, where the rich 1 percent get richer while the rest of the populace's quality of life seems to be in decline. Here, social justice is measured by the gap between ideal versus the actual implementation of constitutional guarantees. Both camps, right and left, claim they are championing the Bill of Rights (the first ten amendments to the Constitution enacted in 1791) in their interpretation of laws and other forms of social control, including police and military use of force, incarceration, and the death sentence. Even taking that as an ideal, the Bill of Rights, when initiated, had a very restrictive definition of what constitutes a citizen's eligibility for these rights. Herein lies a major factor in the administration of justice, notably *social justice*. Judicial ideals are vested in laws and statutes constituting *procedural* or de jure justice while the actual administration of these laws constitutes *distributive* or de facto justice. The divide between procedural and distributive justice constitutes the *social justice index*, reflecting the difference between America's judicial ideals and its actual practices. Much contention surrounds the interpretation of the Bill of Rights, which is vested in the federal court system, making presidential appointments (and Senate confirmation) to federal courts, notably the Supreme Court, the august body that interprets the United States Constitution, such an important matter in elections.

THE BILL OF RIGHTS

First Amendment: Freedom of religion, speech, and the press; rights of assembly and petition. Provides and protects freedom of religion, speech, assembly, and the press.

Second Amendment: Right to bear arms. Allows and protects the right to bear (own) arms (guns).

Third Amendment: Housing of soldiers. Prevents the army from moving into your home.

Fourth Amendment: Search and arrest warrants. Prevents unlawful searches and seizures, meaning the government cannot search or take your property without good reason.

Fifth Amendment: Rights in criminal cases (right to remain silent). Guarantees due processes, requires proper indictments, and prevents you from being tried for the same crime twice.

Sixth Amendment: Right of a fair trial. Guarantees a speedy trial, allows the accused to confront witnesses, and requires you to have a lawyer.

Seventh Amendment: Rights in civil cases. Concerns common law and guarantees a trial by jury.

Eighth Amendment: Bails, fines, and punishment. Guarantees punishment will be fair and not cruel and very large fines will not be imposed.

Ninth Amendment: Rights retained by the people. Promises your rights will not be violated even if you don't know what they are.

Tenth Amendment: Powers retained by the states and the people. Declares that powers not held by the federal government belong to the states or to the people.[1]

1. Library of Congress Cataloging In-Publication Data, *U.S. Constitution Pocket Guide* (2015), 21–35

The social justice divide in contemporary America is reflected not only in the widening economic gap between the ultra-rich and the rest of the country, but is also reflected in the perception of unfair entitlements doled out along racial lines, leading to animosities between whites and minorities of color; the working and middle classes versus the extremely rich ("1 percent"); "Christians" versus other religions and/or nonbelievers—all contributing to the current divisions fueling both "White Right" (alt-right nationalists and white supremacists) racist and anti-immigration fervor, at one end of the continuum, and the "Black Lives Matter" movement at the other end of this contentious divide. Ironically, Donald Trump, a billionaire who is clearly a member of the "1 percent club," was elected by many of those who fall into the "have not" economic category. And while the economy may have played a role in Trump's election, a racist, vitriol backlash to having a black president, Barack Obama, seems to be a major contributing factor in this divide. It is imperative to look at the original, colonial foundations of American justice in order to better understand how this situation has played out over 240 years.

The law and order issues plaguing America in the twenty-first century clearly have their roots in the unique Puritan society that emerged in the New England colonies. First and foremost is the concept of *Manifest Destiny* and its major tenet, the superiority of privileged whites. America's sense of social justice, selective morality, and entitlement emanates from this theological foundation, most notably its decentralized law enforcement agencies; social status hierarchy; and double-standards of justice. While the Puritan influence was predominate in the New England colonies, the ideal of white supremacy extended to the Southern plantations as well. The American version of the Protestant ethos was also designed to distant itself from the British aristocracy with its lineage of privileged status. By subscribing to the Calvinistic concept of divine predestination, the thirteen British colonies saw the opportunity to grow its own aristocracy, based on wealth and, to a lesser degree, military status. Military status, in turn, justified the exploitation of America's resources for their personal wealth, thus emerged America's version of capitalism.

THE PROTESTANT ETHIC AND THE SPIRIT OF CAPITALISM

Max Weber, the noted German social philosopher, articulated the relationship between Protestantism and capitalism in his work, *The Protestant Ethic and the Spirit of Capitalism*. Weber associates the emergence of capitalism with the Protestant concept of *predestination*, a marked contrast with the Catholic concept of *original sin*. This change in the Christian worldview, notably the concept of a god-chosen elite, was associated with the introduction of Calvinism, Pietism, and the Methodist and Baptist sects. Briefly stated, Catholicism, especially the doctrine practiced during the Middle Ages, posited that humans were predisposed with original sin and that life was a trial of good versus evil challenges, with a preponderance of one over the other, along with the appropriate sacraments, determining one's place in the hereafter.

With the Reformation, especially the works of Calvin and his brand of Protestantism, *Calvinism,* a new worldview perspective emerged, based on *moral predestined superiority,* a phenomenon based on divine selection before birth. Accordingly, those selected to the moral elite would be readily evident not only to these individuals, but to all by virtue of their earthly successes. In its religious conception, the *Protestant ethic,* a predestined individual would be identified by certain virtues: elevated social status, private wealth, and asceticism. The element of social status and private wealth provided the seeds for capitalism. Here, the long-held concept of inherited lineage—whether it be from religious or monastic elites—was debunked and replaced by the myth of predestination. With this new God-given authority, the earth's resources became the medium for establishing the new capitalist elite. Soon, the sacred element of asceticism was greatly diminished, paving the way for a secular mode of capitalism based on material wealth, social privilege, and conspicuous consumption. Fierce competition soon became the primary vehicle for these desired attributes. An associated feature of secular capitalism was the norm that the "means justifies the ends." Deceit, cheating, and corruption soon became the mainstay of American capitalism within the government and business community, eventually leading to a double standard of justice in America—white-collar crimes for the privileged elite and harsh criminal recrimination for the lower classes. In assessing American capitalism, Weber noted that it maintained a moral ethos as well; one that provided justification for expansionism at any cost.[1] This moral ethos, the proclaimed *Covenant of Divine Providence,* became the foundation of the U.S. policy of Manifest Destiny. Manifest Destiny fostered the idea of special favors from God, as well as a justification for both extreme wealth and discrimination.[2]

Not to be ignored are the works of Adam Smith, the Scottish economist and philosopher, whose manifesto, *The Wealth of Nations,* raised the main elements of Calvinist and secular capitalism into natural law, a philosophy that went on to drive Western-style market economies, especially in the United States. Smith's work was published the same year the United States declared its independence from Britain, hence providing the resulting justification of wage labor and class division within emerging industrialized societies at this time. Here, Smith linked a nation's wealth to the wage laborer who, as a class, would generate greater purchasing power that would fuel the society's industrial/capitalism base—thereby creating an upward cycle of improved living standards for all. Smith alluded to the New England colonies in illustrating the success of the progressive model of capitalism and its tenets of labor satisfaction and its resulting shared trickle-down wealth.[3] Conservative Calvinistic Protestantism and its belief in predestinated moral superiority existed from the beginning in the New World American colonies in both New England and Canada.

Max Weber noted that American capitalism, as espoused by Benjamin Franklin, went beyond secular capitalism by attaching a moral ethos as justification for its expansionistic designs: "Now, all Franklin's moral attitudes are coloured with utilitarianism."[4] This sense of religious and ethnic superiority, supported by the colonists self-proclaimed *Covenant of Divine Providence*, paved the way for the moral justification of expansionism and ethnic cleansing under the mandate of Manifest Destiny. Contrary to popular mythology, the Puritans did not come to the New England colonies to escape prosecution per se, but rather as part of a capitalist endeavor with the intention of establishing a colony based on their particular conservative and exclusive brand of Protestantism. The Massachusetts Bay Colony (originally including most of the current New England states) was chartered as a business corporation with legal authority to exercise law and order among its inhabitants. Charters were managed by a governor, deputy governor, and a board of eighteen stockholders, also known as *freemen*. The latter constituted the general court that met four times a year in order to admit new members, elect officers, and make regulations, hence a model for the current general courts in the New England states.

British settlements, often called plantations, consisted of thirteen colonies along the Atlantic seashore, with Georgia being the last settled in 1732. While initially predominately Anglo-Saxon, other white European emigrants began to emerge in the late 1600s, including the Scots-Irish, German, Huguenots, and Swiss, challenging any attempt for a theocracy outside of the New England section of British North America (the thirteen colonies were eventually divided into three groupings—New England, Middle Colonies, and Southern Colonies). The religiously conservative, hence intolerant, Massachusetts Bay Colony was initiated during the British Civil War between the Crown and Oliver Cromwell's Commonwealth, thus the term the Commonwealth of Massachusetts.

The genesis of John Winthrop's plan for a colonial settlement in New England began with a group of prominent Puritans who controlled a trading company and were successful in acquiring commercial rights to a large land grant in the new world. Winthrop and company were also able to transfer their corporate headquarters to their new home in New England, an unusual move at this time. Essentially, this became the first offshore business corporation, which is commonplace today. Moreover, this corporate charter would also serve as the basis for a civil government. The Crown's charter defined their legal landholdings and their civil government while corporate officers served as magistrates and stockholder's meetings served as legislative sessions (General Court). Within this Calvinistic capitalist system, the corporate chairman, John Winthrop, became the de facto governor. Some 20,000 Puritans soon joined Winthrop's New England Corporation, including many from the educated gentry, providing the foundation for the new White Anglo-Saxon Protestant (WASP) aristocracy. Winthrop's initial Massachusetts Bay charter was good for sixty years. Provincial governors were later appointed directly by the English Crown with the authority to authorize land grants to settlers. After the American Revolution, provinces became states.

What was lacking in the Massachusetts Bay Colony was religious freedom. Indeed, the Puritan leaders held an elitist view of Protestantism, an attitude similar to that held by their British counterpart and mentor, Oliver Cromwell, the Lord Protector of the Commonwealth of England, Scotland, and Ireland. Initially, in New England only church members were enfranchised with membership, strictly restricted so that most colonists were not part of the ruling elite that became the foundation for the U.S. aristocracy. The Puritans were bent on establishing an intolerant religious milieu in the Massachusetts colony instead of the opposite—coming to America to avoid religious persecution. Until 1630, church membership required a minster's endorsement, creating a strict social stratification even among the free whites. Indentured whites and people of color (blacks and Indians) suffered even more within this social milieu.

Kai Erikson illustrated the extent of religious intolerance among the Puritans in his book, *Wayward Puritans*: "God has chosen an elite to represent Him on earth and to join Him in Heaven. People who belonged to this elite learned of their appointment through the agency of a deep conversion experience, giving them a special responsibility and a special competence to control the destinies of others."[5] Intolerance toward "outsiders" grew, even among fellow whites, as the Puritans became more isolated from their home base in England and gained dominance in their section of the New World. Cromwell's Puritan forces not only defeated the King of England, it also split the group into two general groups, the Scottish Presbyterian moderates and the Congregational Independents. The latter eventually represented the New England colonies, becoming the recognized church of state.[6]

Other religions that challenged the New England Puritan theocracy were met with brutal force, including the Quaker persecutions of 1656–1665 when the anti-Quaker law carried the death penalty for anyone professing to be a Quaker within the Puritan colonies. Other forms of religious intolerance existed in New England following the *Revolutionary War* and the Declaration of Independence from Great Britain by the Rebels (Patriots). The legislation of morality was a common practice in the colonies. These restrictions on public and private behavior, most notably on the Christian Sabbath (Sunday) were known as the *blue laws*. While the term is obscured by history, some sources attribute the name to the color of the paper on which the laws were written.

Sections of these laws continued to be enforced in New England well into the twentieth century.[7]

Clearly, the Puritans were adamantly anti-Catholic, a Cromwell prejudice that contaminated the New England colonies and continued into the creation of the *new republic*. In his "God and Country" article in the October 2010 issue of *Smithsonian*, Kenneth Davis noted:

> Throughout the colonial era, Anglo-American antipathy toward Catholics—especially French and Spanish Catholics—was pronounced and often reflected in the sermons of such famous clerics as Cotton Mather and in statutes that discriminated against Catholics in matters of property and voting. Anti-Catholic feelings even contributed to the revolutionary mood in America after King George III extended an olive branch to French Catholics in Canada with the Quebec Act of 1774, which recognized their religion.[8]

Social control in the New World was manifested through parochial education where the group's moral imperative was inculcated through compulsory education. Here, education and state were closely linked during the colonial era. The Puritans followed Calvin's thesis that the church was supreme in establishing moral standards, with the obligation of the state to enforce the church's dictates. Indeed, the Calvinist view held that the church was superior to the state and that the state was the primary tool for enforcing church authority. Hence, colonial Puritan New England operated as a Protestant theocracy.[9]

Education within the New England colonial theocracy existed at three levels: 1) elementary Bible school; 2) classical Latin schools; and 3) colleges. Elementary Bible education was established by Puritans under the direction of the Calvinist Resolution—*the Synod of Dort* (1618–1619). The instruction was for all children, with Bible instruction being taught both at home and at school. Thus, while the Puritans included females within their elementary schools, the purpose for this education was for them to be better prepared for further instructions in the scriptures under male guidance. However, both the classical Latin high schools and colleges were exclusively for males, a select elite of males at that. The colonial elite, while dismissive of the established European nobility, were bent on creating their own unique system based on Calvinist doctrine of predestination. Toward this end, they created their own elite educational system, one to rival that in England—Harvard, Yale, Columbia, Dartmouth—designed to produce the American aristocracy. These institutions, in turn, were richly endowed by the privileged elite, so as to maintain the semblance of superiority vis-à-vis "lesser colleges and universities"; hence, a self-filling prophecy that continues to the present.[10]

In 1647, the Massachusetts Bay Colony required towns to establish and support their own schools in order to provide apprenticeship training and elementary Bible training for all children. This law required communities of fifty families or more to maintain an elementary school and a Latin prep school for every community of at least one hundred families, which was patterned after the British common laws relevant to local control. Those elite males selected to attend the Latin prep schools were among those then selected to attend Harvard College, which was established in 1636. In 1650, Connecticut passed a similar law, and soon this educational system became the norm in colonial New England. The Puritan education system provided the foundation for the common school system in the United States. In this sense, the U.S. public school system was initially established as a Protestant school system. Even then, the poor whites were absorbed into society via apprenticeship training, a system based upon the 1562 British Statute of Artificers and the 1601 Poor Laws. The charity school concept, initiated in the Middle Colonies by the Society of Friends, also contributed to the colonial school format that eventually was adopted by the new republic following independence.[11]

Education in the Southern Colonies differed greatly in that it was a private affair, with the plantation elite providing tutors and special schooling for their children. Few resources were available for plantation laborers, indentured whites, and black and Indian slaves. Little attention is paid to the fact that the South enslaved both Indians and blacks. Indeed, the Indian slave trade continued for over a century, with Indian slavery credited with building Charlestown, South Carolina.[12] The absence of a middle class not only restricted the development of public schools but also forced poor whites, black slaves, and indigenous peoples to rely basically upon the charity of the plantations owners for whatever education or training they received, if any. Some researchers noted that some slaves were afforded a limited education within the Southern caste system, with these "educated" blacks later providing the foundation for the black bourgeoisie that emerged during the early republic era and following emancipation. Ostensibly, education in the South, from the colonial era up until the Civil War, was specifically for the purpose of providing the small number of professions needed for the plantation economy. Within this system, public education was clearly discouraged during the antebellum era even within the South's most progressive communities.[13]

Manifest Destiny was a unique ideology vested in the conservative Protestantism concept of predestination and divine rights that not only endorsed excessive wealth and ostentatious lifestyles, it also provided license to exploit "lesser" peoples and denude the New World resources along with its indigenous peoples. The unique American WASP aristocracy subscribed to the ethos that not only were they predestined by divine rights to a heavenly superiority in the afterlife, but they were also destined to enjoy the best that a worldly life could provide. Part of this theology was the need for others to recognize their superiority, leading to America's societies based on class and caste stratification. These tenets of classism were promoted by the educational system that posited these values to everyone, including the "lesser" people who were destined to help the American aristocracy exploit the untapped riches of the New World. For this to happen, a creed of "us" versus "them" needed to be promulgated, justifying the exploitation that was to occur, including slavery and the ethnic cleansing of American Indians. An enforcement agency needed to be created in order to carry out these plans—one clearly controlled by the privileged elite.

THE COLONIAL MILITIA

During the colonial era, the thirteen British colonies maintained militias (the Provincial Defense Force) to assist the British army in protecting settlements from French and Indian forces. This was part of British common law (Statute of Winchester) that provided for a constable to be in charge of the one hundred families in his district. In the British colonies, the leaders of the corporation vested responsibilities such as collecting tithing and taxes and providing basic community security, such as fire watch to the Committee of Safety, which also was responsible for raising and equipping the provincial militia. And while the British Army had garrisons throughout the thirteen colonies, they were often spread thin, thereby relying on the locally armed defense force. The fact that British troops were often imbedded in private homes, with the homeowner having little recourse to these arrangement—hence, the Third Amendment to the Constitution, forbidding the housing of soldiers in private homes without the consent of the owner. Martial law trumped this provision, as was noted during the Civil War.

Militia officers were part of the privileged colonial elite who often were selected for regular commissions into the British military. George Washington, a slaveholding, wealthy Virginia aristocrat, was made a major in the Virginia militia at age twenty-one during the French and Indian War. The following year, he was promoted to full colonel, leading a force against Fort Duquesne in Pittsburgh under British General Edward Braddock, who died in battle. Due to this military success, Washington, at age twenty-three, was made commander of all Virginia troops. Following General Braddock's death, Governor William Shirley of Massachusetts, the architect of the Acadian Expulsion, assumed command of all British troops in North America. Discouraged by his failure to obtain a commission in the British military, Washington resigned his militia commission and returned home to serve in the Virginia House of Burgesses.[14]

The Provincial Defense Force consisted of all able-bodied, Protestant males between the ages of sixteen and sixty. They were required to own their own musket, bayonet, knapsack, and cartridge box, with one pound of black powder, twenty bullets, and twenty flints. They mustered four times yearly and were on call the remainder of the time. Each regiment was headed by a colonel (commanding officer) and a lieutenant colonel (executive officer), with majors heading battalions and captains in charge of companies. These provincial forces were headed by a major general with a brigadier general as his second-in-command. This military structure provided the format for the Revolutionary War, along with the innovations adopted from their American Indian allies who taught the colonial forces "hit-and-run" commando tactics. A New England colonial militia captain (later major), Robert Rogers, created a "commando unit" patterned after the Indian fighters the colonists encountered in battle, with such tactics as living off the land and making hit-and-run strikes into enemy territory. More companies were added, forming a ranger battalion with Major Rogers in charge. Rogers's "28 Rules of Ranging" provided the foundation for both the Queen's York Rangers of the Canadian Army and the U.S. Army Rangers.[15]

In addition to protecting the colonies during the French and Indian War when France and England were battling for control of North America, the colonial forces, the *Blue Coats*, were heavily complicit in the infamous Acadian Expulsion, the model for ethnic cleansing that the new republic used to extricate American Indians from their traditional homelands. The Blue Coats consisted of colonial militia recruited from New England, notably Massachusetts and its former territories, New Hampshire and Maine. The enticements promoted for this expedition into the Maritimes were both sacred and financial (pay and plunder). The sacred motive was promoted as a Protestant crusade against both the French Catholics and the native Indians. The monthly monetary benefits for signing up, in addition to any bounty, were as follows: colonels, fifteen pounds; captains, four pounds, ten shillings; corporals, one pound, eight shillings; enlisted men, twenty-five shillings, plus a one-time enlistment bonus of one pound, plus a five-shilling weekly subsistence allowance and a daily ration of rum.[16]

THE RHETORIC OF HATE AND DIVISIVENESS

The Puritan colonies departed from the Native interaction standards dictated by European international laws established in the sixteenth century, whereby it was felt that indigenous peoples in conquered lands were entitled to sovereignty and property rights. These rights were expanded by the French and British to all tribes, even those that did not convert to Christianity. Under these rules, conflict with aboriginal groups was justified only when the local tribes refused Europeans the right to trade and to preach Christianity. Another element of this Christian capitalist colonial pact was the *Doctrine of Discovery*, a policy that gave exclusive rights of negotiation with tribes to the European colonial power that first claimed the territory. The Puritans, however, had their own view of things and did not feel that they had to comply with international rules. They felt that Old England was still corrupt in that it had not totally broken with the satanic ways of popery and Catholicism, feeling that their divine purpose could flourish only in this new, uncorrupted land once it was rid of the undesirable occupants—the indigenous tribes and French Catholics. Hence, the extreme animosities directed toward both American Indians and French Catholics, especially when these two populations were allied. This sentiment was articulated by Jonathan Edwards, the leading Protestant theologian of the American colonies during the Great Awakening of the 1730s and 1740s, who equated French Quebec with the Whores of Babylon.[17]

The roots of Manifest Destiny extend to the colonial era with the Puritan's concept of their God-given predestined supremacy over all others. This social philosophy played a crucial role in the Puritan's plan to exterminate Indian groups, as well as excluding other whites of different denominational affiliations. The principle of predestination that drove policies of discrimination and genocide was introduced into Nova Scotia, in the Canadian Maritimes, once control over the indigenous Mi'kmaq (Micmac) and French settlers was transferred to the British Colonial governors. The Acadian Expulsion began a hundred years after the Quaker persecutions of the mid-1600s when anti-Quaker laws sanctioned the death penalty for anyone professing to be a Quaker within the Puritan colonies. Less publicized was the systematic expulsion of the indigenous tribes in New England. Those who were not massacred outright were captured and sent to England as slaves. Those who could escape made their way to French Canada.

In the mid-1700s, the Mi'kmaq's original population was decimated by diseases, inadvertently introduced through European contact, reducing the tribe to several thousand Indians—a mere 10 percent of its pre-Columbian total. The Acadian French, on the other hand, were unique because these male fishermen and coastal farmers lived among the Mi'kmaq, adopting elements of their lifestyle and forming common law families with indigenous women and creating the first substantial *metis* population in Canada (mixed European/Indian heritage). Thus, the Acadian French differed from most other white colonial settlers in that part of North America that is Canada and the United States in that they integrated into the Mi'kmaq culture, forging a harmonious community of mixed Indian/white people—as well as the wrath of the Puritans.

The expulsion scheme was devised by the British colonial governors of Nova Scotia and Massachusetts (including what is now Maine), who in 1755 authorized the forceful removal of the Acadian French, citing their friendliness with the local Indians as a pretext for this exercise in ethnic cleansing. John Mack Faragher, a Yale University history professor, cited a September 4, 1755, article in the *Pennsylvania Gazette* that justified the expulsion order:

> We are now upon a great and noble Scheme of sending the neutral French out of this Province, who have always been secret enemies, and have encouraged our Savages to cut our Throats. If we effect their Expulsion, it will be one of the greatest Things that ever the English in America; for by all Accounts, that Part of the Country they possess, is as good Land as any in the World: In case therefore we could get some of good English farmers in their Room, this Province would abound with all Kinds of Provisions.[18]

Consequently, some seven thousand French-speaking, Catholic Acadians were forcefully removed from the rich lands and waterways along the shores of the Bay of Fundy so that English colonists could occupy them. This action also gave the British-American colonists an excuse to displace and disperse the Mi'kmaq Indians. And while the colonial black slave trade was evident mostly in the Southern Colonies, New England captains became wealthy in bringing these slaves to America. The success of the New England slave trade is evident in the ostentatious mansions along the Atlantic seaboard.

In 1763, the Treaty of Paris ended the Seven Years' War, also known as the French and Indian War. Here, France ceded their North American holdings to England (Canada and all territory east of the Mississippi River). The French that remained in Canada outnumbered the English by fourteen to one (70,000 French; 5,000 British), forcing Britain to delegate local control to the French Catholic hierarchy in Quebec. Ostensibly, this distraction played a role in activating Revolutionary plans within the thirteen colonies, a plan that would pit Colonial Loyalists against the Rebels. In a sense, this was America's first civil war. The Rebels subscribed to the concept of Puritan divine rights and its brand of exploitative capitalism. This is most evident in the forced expulsion of some 100,000 Loyalists, of which about 50,000 migrated to British Canada. Disillusioned with the Revolutionary mandate, those entering Canada did not attempt to replicate the Puritan standards in their new homeland, even when they were the majority. Canada was more inclusive and less racist than its counterpart that became the United States of America.

The Revolutionary War, regardless of its mythical origins, was a resource war where a segment of the colonies wanted to have total control over the virtually untapped New World resources. The Puritans, in particular, felt that this wealth was part of their divine rights, pitting them against those who wanted to remain loyal to Great Britain. The Italian sociologist Vilfredo Pareto termed this type of fighting for social dominance as the *circulation of elites*, hence more a civil upheaval than a revolution for internal structural changes. The Rebels felt distanced from the constant European colonial wars and were reluctant to be forced to fund them. At the same time, Great Britain was souring on the commonwealth, assembly type of governance that emerged in their thirteen colonies. Hence, the American Revolution was not for the purpose of extending rights to all adults residing in the colonies, but rather to consolidate these riches for an even smaller elite.[19] In fact, the American Revolution impacted greater change in Canada once Loyalists (Tories) were banished from their properties.

This process is illustrated by what happened in New Hampshire, the conservative outpost of the Massachusetts colony, headed by Governor John Wentworth. Following the Declaration of Independence, the Provincial Congress gave the Loyalists (Tories) three months to sell their property and leave the country. The Rebels employed the Committees of Safety (existing police forces) to enforce the banishment laws. Those forced out had their property sold and placed into the newly coined state treasuries. The banished were forbidden to return to their former colonies, often under threat of death. Governor Wentworth, born in New Hampshire, was among those banished and threatened with death.[20]

Some 50,000 Loyalist fled to Canada, both the Maritime Provinces and Quebec, forcing a considerable adjustment in the Indian, French, and English settlement, which led to the division of Nova Scotia into two provinces—Nova Scotia and New Brunswick—and the division of Quebec into French Quebec (Lower Canada) and Ontario (Upper Canada), along with defined reserves for both the Maritime Indians (Meliseek and Mi'kmaq/Micmac) and other Algonquin and Iroquois tribes in both Lower and Upper Canada. Moreover, the Loyalists, like their English and Canadian counterparts, were not inclined to follow the Puritan example of governance, relying instead on the British parliamentarian form of government, while the French Canadians continued with their autonomous feudal seigneurial system. Canada was a more tolerant and inclusive society than the American severe caste and class structure. Indeed, in 1793, Canada was the first to outlaw slavery in North America (Mexico was second, doing so with their independence from Spain in 1821). The then former New Hampshire colonial governor, banished to Canada during the American Revolution, went on to serve as the lieutenant governor of the newly created province of New Brunswick, serving nearly a decade. He soon was bestowed the title of Sir John Wentworth.[21]

The seeds of racism were nurtured during the American Revolution, setting the stage for both slavery and Indian extinction as foundations for America's development and expansionisms. The combination of white supremacy and local control set the stage for the unique form of policing in the United States. While the issue of slavery divided the nation and contributed to the War-between-the-States, the Civil War ended black slavery, even as it set into play another form of social division—segregation. Equally significant was the continued war against the indigenous peoples who had long occupied the New World. The Indian Wars not only continued in the new republic, but it also intensified, providing a model for ethnic cleansing that was replicated elsewhere, including Nazi Germany.

Treatment of American Indians during the Revolutionary War (1775–1783) provided the foundation for their treatment throughout the nineteenth century. This crisis was intensified with the flood of white settlers unleashed onto tribal lands. Calloway noted that the American Revolution elevated acquisition of Indian lands into a national policy:

> The new nation, born of a bloody revolution and committed to expansion, could not tolerate America as Indian country. Increasingly, Americans viewed the future as one without Indians. The Revolution both created a new society and provided justification for excluding Indians from it.[22]

• 2 •

Introduction to the Origins of
American Jurisprudence

It took four years between the Treaty of Paris ending the Revolutionary War in 1783 and the composition and signing of the U.S. Constitution in 1787. The Preamble reflected the regional and sectarian differences and interests that existed at that time within the three regions comprising the newly established states. New England and the South were more conservative than the Middle Colonies but differed on the issue of slavery. The Middle Colonies represented a more diverse sectarian mix, including Roman Catholics, which were despised by the Puritan elements in New England—the Congregationalist and Presbyterians. In an effort to appease the various elites comprising the new aristocracy; the preamble reads:

> We the People [free white males] of the United States, in Order to form a more perfect Union, establish Justice, insure domestic Tranquility, provide for the common defense, promote the general Welfare, and secure the Blessings of Liberty to ourselves and our Posterity, do ordain and establish this Constitution for the United States of America.[1]

With designs for expansion from the onset, the United States looked west, north, and south, gaining territory throughout the nineteenth century through purchase, treaties, and wars; exacerbating both the Indian and slave dilemmas. The third president, Thomas Jefferson (1801–1809), doubled the size of the United States with the Louisiana Purchase in 1802 (ratified by the U.S. Senate in 1803); the fourth president, James Madison (1809–1817), attempted to gain the Canadian Maritimes from Great Britain with the War of 1812; Florida was forcefully acquired from Spain under the administration of the fifth president, James Monroe (1817–1825); the infamous Indian Removal policy was enacted and implemented under the term of the seventh president, Andrew Jackson (1829–1837). The Mexican War (1846–1848) occurred under the stewardship of the eleventh U.S. president, James Polk (1845–1849); the Gadsden Purchase (1853) was obtained from Mexico under threat-of-war during the reign of Franklin Pierce, fourteenth U.S. president; the War-between-the States (U.S. Civil War, 1861–1865) occurred during Abraham Lincoln's administration (sixteenth U.S. president); the long Indian War era (1862–1892) also began during Lincoln's administration. Alaska was purchased from Russia in 1867 during the administration of Andrew Johnson (1865–1869), who became the seventeenth president following Lincoln's assassination in 1865; the Indian Wars intensified under Ulysses S. Grant's administration (eighteenth U.S. president, 1869–1877); and the United States acquired Puerto Rico, the Philippine Islands, Guam, Mariana, Carolina, and Marshall Islands from Spain during the Spanish-American War (1898–1899) during the administration of William McKinley (twenty-fifth U.S. president, 1897–1901). It became readily clear that more non-WASP, "lesser" peoples were needed to explore the newly acquired territories, at their own peril, so that the WASP elite could exploit the untouched riches these lands held. Clearly, these immigrants would be bait for discontented Indian tribes whose lands were being exploited.

John Isbister, in his research on immigration waves in the United States, noted that the first wave occurred during the colonial era through the early years of the republic (1607–1820s). Most of the first wave was English, followed by Scots-Irish, Dutch, German, Swedes, French, and African slaves. While the African slave trade was officially outlawed in 1807, a lucrative, illicit trade continued until the conclusion of the Civil War in 1865. The second wave of immigrants began in the 1840s and extended to the 1870s. During this time, some 15 million immigrants entered the United States—this time the majority being of other than British origin, mainly from Ireland and Germany, while the United States inherited hundreds of thousands of Mexicans following the acquisitions of new lands in the Southwest gained from both the Mexican War and the Gadsden Purchase. A significant number of Chinese, mainly males, also entered the United States at this time to work the gold fields of California and later to work on the intercontinental railroad. French Canadians also began their migration during the second wave to work in the textile industry in New England. The third, and largest, wave of immigrants, according to Isbister, accounted for some 25 million people entering the United States between 1880 and 1930, when the borders were closed during the Great Depression. This wave included substantial numbers from Southern and Eastern Europe, Poles, Italians, Russians, Greeks, Austro-Hungarians, who were either Roman or Orthodox Catholic or Jewish.[2]

It became clear the new republic did not view all men as being equal, not even white men. One of the first actions of the United States was to define what constitutes being an American Indian. This was a necessary step in order to provide whites an upper hand in dealing with indigenous peoples as new territories were being settled. The United States chose to restrict the legal status of both African slaves and American Indians to that of "lesser humans," hence not worthy of the broader constitutional guarantee granted "free white males." In its effort to determine the rules for representation to the House, the first census (1790) counted black slaves as three-fifths of a person, as specified in Section 2, Article I of the Constitution, giving white Southern plantation owners a disproportionate weight in their state's representation in Congress. Indigenous peoples, on the other hand, were not counted at all. This is not surprising given that of the first eighteen U.S. presidents (Washington to Grant), all but three were slaveholders. The exceptions were the Adams (second and sixth presidents), who were stanch elitist New England Puritans, and Abraham Lincoln, whose White House was the last to be staffed by black slaves. Regarding the social status of the twenty-five presidents from Washington to William McKinley at the turn of the twentieth century, fourteen held military rank prior to their presidency: Washington, Monroe, Jackson, Harrison, Taylor, Pierce, Lincoln, A. Johnson, Grant, Hayes, Garfield, Arthur, Harrison, and McKinley. Only Zachary Taylor and Ulysses S. Grant were commissioned as Regular Army (West Point Military Academy was created in 1802 under President Jefferson); the rest, including Washington, were commissioned as part of state militias. Further distinctions are made for George Washington, who rose to commanding general of the Continental army, and Chester Arthur, who served as Quartermaster General of New York troops during the Civil War.[3]

While an influx of immigrants was needed to occupy newly acquired lands, often at the peril of the settlers invading Indian Territory, laws were often enacted in order to both control their numbers as well as their degree of participation in the political, economic, and social elements of American society. This process, in a nutshell, is evident in immigration legislation. The first immigration law was the Naturalization Law passed in 1790, requiring that an individual needed to be both free (not indentured) and white to be eligible for U.S. citizenship—a stipulation that remained on the books until the Immigration and Nationality Act of 1952. Later, allowing the naturalization and citizenship for freedmen (former black slaves), the 1870 Naturalization Act excluded Chinese from citizenship, despite their role in exploiting mineral riches and working on the construction of the transcontinental railroad for wealthy whites. Chinese could not appear as witnesses in court, vote, or become naturalized citizens. Their children had to attend segregated schools, and they were assessed a special foreign tax. In 1882, Congress passed the Chinese Exclusion Act, barring most Chinese immigrants now that the dangerous work with mining and the railroad was completed. This act was the first law that specifically banned immigration by race or nationality. The Geary Act of 1892 required Chinese aliens to carry a residence certification with them at all times upon penalty of deportation. The 1917 Immigration Act, also known as the Asiatic Barred Zone Act, restricted Asians from any country not owned by the United States adjacent to the continent of Asia (limiting immigration to the Philippines). This act also played into the growing eugenics movement of the time, forbidding the entry of those with mental and/or physical handicaps and requiring an English literacy test.[4] The Immigration Act of 1917 reinforced elements of the 1914 Harrison Narcotics Tax Act, setting the stage for targeting Asians and Hispanics, as well as American blacks, for criminalizing cultural lifestyle that departed from that of the Anglo white status quo. This was the foundation for the eventual racial-biases of the U.S. War on Drugs, a phenomenon that extends into the twenty-first century.

A similar process occurred with Mexican migrants. Needed as farm laborers during the Second World War, a deal was forged with Mexico for seasonal laborers, a program known as the *Bracero Accord*. Instituted in 1942, this program allowed Mexican laborers to legally enter the United States as migrant farm workers, a program that was in place until 1964, when those workers, seasonal or not, earned illegal status, even as millions continued to enter the United States for jobs shunned by most Americans. On the other hand, Mexican families and subsequent generations absorbed into U.S. society by virtue of their residency at the time of the Louisiana Purchase, the Treaty of Guadalupe-Hidalgo, annexation of Texas, or the Gadsden Purchase were subjected to the same conditions forced upon freed blacks and their families following emancipation—that of enforced segregation along with unequal treatment under the law, a fate that both groups endured until the civil rights laws of the mid-1960s. American Indians gained federal citizenship in 1924 but continued to suffer tremendous hardships and abuse on reservations into the late twentieth century.

The fifty-years following the U.S. Civil War was a complicated and violent era, one requiring a strong police presence in order to control the onslaught of white settlers eager to occupy lands once comprising Indian Country. Social control was also required at the local level with an increased influx of immigrants, notably Irish Catholics fleeing starvation from the potato famine of the 1840s, and the emergence of large metropolitan areas like New York City. Clearly race and strata differential played a crucial role at both the federal and state levels, often providing contravening regional differences denoted by race-driven policies. The challenge was to balance federal versus local (state) control over an expanding United States. Toward this end, a two-tier system was developed: a federal and a local (state/territory) system of executive administration, legislative bodies, and courts. Law enforcement, whether by militia, the military, or police agencies, emerged to address these challenges.

THE GENESIS OF LAW AND ORDER
IN THE UNITED STATES

The Founding Fathers drafted a versatile Constitution, one based on separate governmental bodies with checks and balances; a system that has weathered both history and challenges—although serious questions concerning the Electoral College have arisen given the results of the 2016 presidential elections, when, for the second time within the twenty-first century, the candidate who won the popular vote did not win the Electoral College or the presidency. Clearly the strength of the Constitution is the separation of powers outlined in the first four Articles, with Article I providing the basis for a fluid representative government—one based on demographics and fluidity by forcing elections every two years. The Senate, however, can be seen as a carry-over from the British House of Lords, whereby each state would have two senators serving for six-year terms. Initially, these senators were chosen by their respective state legislatures, ostensibly from the aristocratic elites. This system did not change until 1913, with passage of the Seventeenth Amendment calling for the direct election of U.S. Senators. Article II created the executive branch with the president and vice president, each with a four-year term of office. In 1951, following F. D. Roosevelt's unprecedented four terms, the Twenty-Second Amendment limited the executive officers to two terms. Article III, in turn, created the third independent branch of the federal government—the judicial branch, vested in a Supreme Court and inferior appellate and district courts where jurists are appointed by the president and confirmed by the U.S. Senate. Article IV set the stage for the dual-system of government and justice in the United States by recognizing the sovereignty of states in making laws and establishing order within their boundaries, independent of federal intrusion other than in situations that involved national security or interstate issues. This system placed Indian matters within the federal jurisdiction while allowing the slave issue to be resolved by the states.

Article III of the U.S. Constitution was implemented with the Judiciary Act of 1789, creating the U.S. Supreme Court with a chief justice, John Jay, and five associate justices. It also created the office of the attorney general of the United States with Edmund Randolph's appointment. This same act created the U.S. district court system with each of the original thirteen states constituting a federal district. Three circuit courts were also created, one each for the eastern, middle, and southern states. Here, the Supreme Court justices resided in addition to their high court duties. This process ended with the creation of the U.S. Circuit Court of Appeals in 1891. The district courts also had a head prosecutor, the district attorney. Much of the federal legal system dealt with international relations, including interaction with Indian tribes, which initially held the status of independent nations that were dealt with via treaties.[5] States had their own court systems with the legislative bodies often referred to as the "General Court."

ARMY, MILITIAS, NATIONAL GUARD, AND MARINES

Federal law enforcement can be traced to the origin of the Continental army on June 14, 1775, which became the Legion of the United States in 1791 and finally the Regular Army in 1796. Article II, Section 2, of the U.S. Constitution notes that "the President shall be Commander in Chief of the Army and Navy of the United States, and of the Militia of the several States when called into the actual Service of the United States."[6] The U.S. Marine Corps, the military that was used to police the Americas under the Monroe Doctrine throughout the nineteenth century, credits its colonial heritage to November 10, 1775, as part of the U.S. Navy. The U.S. Coast Guard, from its beginning in 1789 as the Revenue Cutter Service, has long operated as both a civilian and military federal law enforcement agency. Today, it is part of the Department of Homeland Security. During the Revolutionary War (1775–1783), the de facto head of the army was George Washington, who held the rank of lieutenant general (three stars) and the title of commander in chief of the Continental army. Following independence, the senior army officer usually held the rank of major general (two stars) and the title of senior officer of the U.S. Army. The first with the title of senior officer was Henry Knox (1783–1784), who replaced Washington. But as the U.S. Army pared down from its Revolutionary strength, some officers of lesser rank headed the military: Brevet Major General John Doughty (1784); Brevet Brigadier General Josiah Harmar (1784–1791); Major General Arthur St. Clair (1791–1792); Major General Anthony Wayne (1792–1796; died in office); and Brigadier General James Wilkinson (1796–1798/1800–1812. George Washington continued to hold the rank of lieutenant general in the event he would be needed if another serious crisis occurred during his lifetime. Alexander Hamilton held the rank of major general while serving as the inspector general of the army (1799–1800). James Wilkinson was promoted to major general during his second term as senior officer of the U.S. Army at the beginning of the War of 1812. The title for the head of the army changed again in 1821, following the War of 1812, when it became apparent that a more substantial army was needed for the various insurrections and ongoing Indian conflicts as the United States continued its expansion and settlements throughout the nineteenth century.

Those holding the title of commanding general of the U.S. Army included Major Generals Jacob Brown (1821–1828), and Alexander Macomb (1828–1841). During the Mexican American War, Winfield Scott was the first since George Washington to hold the rank of lieutenant general (brevet; e.g., temporary). Scott led American forces during the Mexican American War and headed the U.S. military through Indian Removal in the late 1830s, serving over twenty years in this capacity until his retirement at the onset of the Civil War in 1861. He was the oldest serving commanding general, retiring from this position at age seventy-five. Like Washington and Eisenhower, he also ran for president, challenging Franklin Pierce in 1853. Scott was replaced by Major General George McClellan during the Civil War (1861–1862), who was subsequently removed by President Lincoln for incompetency, while his successor, Major General Halleck (1862–1864) was not much of an improvement. Union success came when President Lincoln chose Major General Ulysses S. Grant to head the Grand Army of the Republic, giving him the rank of lieutenant general and then making him the first four-star general in the army (1866–1869), a rank he held until the resigned to become the eighteenth president in 1869.

Grants's two favorite Civil War generals, William Tecumseh Sherman (1869–1883), and Philip Sheridan (1883–1888; died in office), followed Grant with the rank of four-star generals, leading the army during the long Indian Wars (1862–1892). Lieutenant General John Schofield (1888–1895) took over as commanding general of the U.S. Army during the Indian Wars, while Lieutenant General Nelson Miles (1895–1903), another noted Civil War and Indian War fighter, was the last to hold the title of commanding general. Following Miles's tenure, in 1903 the head of the U.S. Army was now titled chief of staff of the army. The United States did not have a permanent (non-brevet) four-star general until 1866 when this status was awarded to U. S. Grant. The Confederate army, on the other hand, conferred four-star rank to Robert E. Lee during the Civil War. And while President Grant made Sherman and then Sheridan four-star generals during the Indian Wars, this rank did not become permanent until 1919 when it was given to John (Black Jack) Pershing. The Second World War not only saw the proliferation of four-star generals and admirals, but the emergence of five-star generals and admirals. Even then, only nine men held this rank; four admirals and five generals (including Douglas MacArthur and Dwight Eisenhower). The five-star rank ended with the death of Omar Bradley in 1981. George Washington was added to the list posthumously on July 4, 1976. Indeed, General John (Black Jack) Pershing, leader of U.S. forces during World War I, was later named "General of the U.S. Armies"—the highest military rank in the United States (a status shared only with George Washington). This rank warrants four gold stars, outranking the silver five stars, created during World War II and ended with the death of Omar Bradley in 1981. Today, the head of the Joint Chiefs of Staff and the heads of the four military branches (army, navy, air force, marines), as well as the head of NATO forces, hold four-star rank, as do many of their subordinates.[7]

The National Guard is an outgrowth of the colonial militia, tracing its origin to the creation of the Massachusetts Bay Colony militia regiment created in December 1648. The U.S. Constitution, in Section 8, Article I, formalized the continuation of state militias, including the provision for their federalization. The U.S. Congress formulized the state militias with the Militia Act of 1792 that recognized the president's authority to activate the militia for federal use in times of national interest, such as times of wars and insurrections. The first use of this was during the War of 1812. The militias were federalized again in 1862 during the Civil War and even expanded to include free blacks and emancipated slaves within militia ranks. The post–Civil War Reconstruction era fostered another modification under Title 18 of the U.S. Code (section 1385) with the Posse Comitatus Act of 1878. The intention of this act was to restrict the role of the occupying Union army in the former Confederate states, especially in those areas deemed more appropriate under state's rights, including domestic law enforcement. This restricted use of federal, or federalized (National Guard/militias), military allowed for the emergence of the *Jim Crow* laws and forced segregation in the South, a process that was not adequately addressed until the Civil Rights Act of the mid-1960s.

The Militia Act of 1903 made the armed state and territorial militias the primary organized reserve forces within the military. This act also changed the name of these militias to that of the Army National Guard. In 1916, as war raged in Europe and Mexico, the National Defense Act of 1916 merged the National Guard and the Army Reserve along with Regular Army into a composite, Army of the United States, allowing for quick mobility without the cost of maintaining a large permanent military force. This new organizational structure prepared the National Guard for action during the Mexican Revolution (1910–1920), notably the Punitive Expedition against Mexican General Pancho Villa, hence preparing the armed forces for their entry into the First World War (1917–1918). The National Guard made up 40 percent of U.S. combat divisions during this war.

The proven success of the National Guard during the First World War as a ready reserve force led to the establishment of a federal chief of the National Guard under the 1920 amendment to the National Defense Act. The National Guard provided nineteen army divisions during World War II and over 140,000 guardsmen mobilized during the Korean conflict (1950–1953). The creation of a separate Air Force in 1947 led to the creation of the Air National Guard as a reserve unit of the Air Force. The navy and the marines do not have National Guard or militia affiliates. While 95 percent of National Guard funding is federal, the Guard remains basically a state militia under the direction of the governor. All fifty states have a National Guard component where the governor appoints an adjutant general (at either the rank of brigade or major general) with the state governor acting as the commander in chief unless the Guard is federalized. The National Guard is more political than the regular armed forces in that the state governor appoints the state's adjutant general along with general rank. Here, the governor can appoint someone whose regular or reserve rank is merely that of a lieutenant colonel (0–5) jumping at least two, often three, field grades.

Nonetheless, the president is the Guard's commander in chief. At the state level, governors can activate their Guard units for domestic emergencies, including riots, disasters, and rescue operations. The federally appointed chief of the National Guard Bureau now holds four-star rank. The 1987 Montgomery Amendment to the National Defense Authorization Act states that governors cannot withhold consent to the federalization of the state's Guard units for duty, including that outside the United States. Some states, like New Mexico, kept their state militia as a component of the Army National Guard. It is called the New Mexico State Guard (NMSG) and acts as a military reserve force under the direction of the state adjutant general. Formal military training, such as ROTC (Reserve Officers Training Corps) or some form of officers training is not required for appointments to the NMSG. It operates much like the early militia forces during the colonial and early republic eras when status determined one's military rank. While the NMSG functions as a reserve unit to the National Guard, it is also mandated to assist communities and law enforcement when required.[8]

The U.S. Marine Corps, *Monroe Doctrine Police*, like the U.S. Army, traces its origins to 1775 and Revolutionary War. Marines fought alongside General Washington's Continental forces at the Battle of Princeton. They were disbanded following the end of the war in 1783, only to be reauthorized by the U.S. Congress in 1798. The first foreign action of the marine corps occurred in 1805 against Barbary pirates in the Port of Tripoli. Marines also saw action onboard ships during the War of 1812 as well as being a component of General Jackson's army in the battle of New Orleans in 1815. They served in the Seminole War of 1836 and in the war with Mexico (1846–1847) and police actions in Panama (1852–1854) and the Fiji Islands (1855–1858). They were involved in the capture of John Brown at Harpers Ferry in October 1858 and participated in the U.S. Civil War on the side of the Union. The police action of the marine corps during the remainder of the nineteenth century included action in the Spanish American War (Cuba 1898) and the Philippine insurrection (1899). These police actions intensified during the twentieth century within the Americas as part of enforcement of the Monroe Doctrine; activities described later in the book.[9]

The U.S. military also has its own law enforcement component (MPs or Military Police) whose jurisdictional fiat is not the Constitution but rather the Uniform Code of Military Justice (UCMJ). Here, offenses outlined in the UCJM, committed by service personnel on or off government military facilities, can result in a criminal conviction such as an Article 15 (misdemeanor) or a court-martial (felony). These are federal offenses and are subject to any and all restrictions associated with a federal conviction. There are three types of court-martial—summary, special, and general, with only the latter able to recommend a death sentence. In 1948, the U.S. military was integrated, and this mix was reflected in the creation of joint military police forces, while integrated police in the United States did not become effective in many parts of American, specifically the South, until the turbulent 1960s and the passage of Civil Rights law in 1964 and 1968. Even then President Eisenhower federalized the National Guard in the late 1950s to provide protection for blacks integrating into former all-white Southern public schools. Interestingly, the main force of opposition and violence toward blacks at this time was the local law enforcement agencies. Today, this concept of training the National Guard to act in a law enforcement capacity is seen in Iraq and Afghanistan, as well as along the U.S.-Mexico border in the ongoing *War on Terrorism*.

Following the Second World War and the establishment of permanent international military consortiums such as NATO, the United States had to provide its own police forces in order to maintain law and order among its troops deployed both at home and abroad. These forces have been instrumental in maintaining security in the former Yugoslavia and in Northern Ireland with mixed results. However, these interventions are considered to be temporary solutions until local autonomy can be established with protection for all community members. The exception is the establishment of permanent and/or semipermanent military police forces. Toward this end, a number of military police forces emerged designed to police military personnel both in bases and in surrounding communities, doing so under the authority of a provost marshal. The army has the Military Police Corps, while the U.S. Air Force has its security police and the navy, marine corps, and the coast guard are served by the shore patrol. The shore patrol was initially designed as an ad hoc law enforcement force, deployed when ships docked at domestic and foreign ports. Due to this unique circumstance, law and order, including the operation of a brig, is the responsibility of each separate command.

The largest of these military police forces is the U.S. Army's Military Police Corps that provides the main law enforcement entity for the Department of Defense and manages prisoners of war and other confinement facilities during times of conflict, including the current War on Terrorism being conducted in Iraq and Afghanistan. When other military elements are also deployed (marines, air force), the military police corps hold primary jurisdiction, including that of federalized National Guard service personnel serving as "military police." Nonetheless, joint military police forces emerged in communities where there is a large, mixed military presence such as Hawaii and Okinawa. These combined military law enforcement include service personnel from all the participating services.

In Hawaii and Okinawa (the largest U.S. military force in Japan), this includes army, air force, navy, and the marines. Hawaiian Armed Forces (HAFP) operates in a multiethnic environment, compounded by both permanent and transitory military personnel. Sensitivity to various cultural orientations, including military subcultures, is a crucial part of HAFP training since its inception in 1948. Hawaii has one of the most diverse mixes of cultures in the United States with representation from many of the Southeast Asian nations, as well as from Polynesia. Add to this mix the integrated U.S. military forces from all branches and the multiethnic, multicultural mix becomes more complex. Until statehood in 1959, territorial laws and customs provided security to the various ethnic enclaves in Hawaii. The main central police force often was HAFP. In this sense, HASP trained its forces to become aware of the various subcultures operating within their jurisdiction, including the various military subcultures—navy, marines, army, air force, and coast guard. Clearly, HAFP was one of the first to practice *community policing* in the United States.

The Ryukyu Armed Force (RAFP), on the other hand, began with the U.S. military occupation of Okinawa as an effort to better police the large military contingency on the island. The RAFP was the main police force on Okinawa during the U.S. administration from 1945–1972, when the islands were returned to Japan. Okinawa was administered by a U.S. Army lieutenant general who held the title of *governor general* during these twenty-seven years of occupation. The complexities at this time included indigenous islanders who were fighting for a separate nation much like in Vietnam. In order to keep the peace, the main island of Okinawa was partitioned into zones A, B, and C. U.S. service personnel were restricted to the zones surrounding the military bases and the corresponding liberty (bar) zones. Here, the RAFP held sway. Local police operated in the local districts serving only the indigenous Ryukyuan population. Even then, the RAFP held original jurisdiction and could enter any segment of the partitioned island. Toward this end, the joint military police had to be cognizant of local cultures and customs—a lesson shared with the HAFP. The RAFP continued to police the numerous military bases following the return of Okinawa to Japan while the Japanese civilian police took over local community policing. The Japanese now holds original jurisdiction over criminal offenses committed by both locals and U.S. personnel off base. This is similar to the conditions now existing in Iraq. Military personnel and private contractors, including private security police, are no longer exempt from arrests and adjudication by local authorities.

U.S. civilians can be subjected to martial law, a situation whereby certain constitutional rights are suspended during a defined period of crisis, a process borrowed from British common law known as the writ of habeas corpus (due process of law; e.g., Bill of Rights). The Constitution states: "The Privilege of Writ of Habeas Corpus shall not be suspended unless when in Cases of Rebellion or Invasion the public Safety may require it."[10] Early in the republic, President Jefferson urged Congress to enact a suspension of the Bill of Rights (habeas corpus) in order to keep jailed members of the Burr conspiracy from being released. Congress declined his request. Later, during the Civil War, President Lincoln initiated the suspension of the writ of habeas corpus for Confederate sympathizers. The Union army carried out Lincoln's suspension over the objection of the chief justice of the U.S. Supreme Court. Congress defused the situation by ratifying President Lincoln's order. Following the Civil War, the Congress sided with President Grant in his suspension of the writ in his efforts to curtail the Ku Klux Klan during the Reconstruction era. But this action was nullified by passage of the Posse Comitatus Act, also known as the Knott Amendment to the 1807 Insurrection Act. The 1878 Posse Comitatus Act prohibited the use of federal troops (army, later U.S. Air Force) in policing domestic policies. This act does not pertain to the National Guard units (army or air force) when activated at the state level, but martial law would override these restrictions.

Ostensibly, the Posse Comitatus Act did much to set the stage for both racial and class divisions within post–Civil War America. Here, the privileges of whites continued following the Civil War, with political actions challenging the advances put forth by the Thirteenth, Fourteenth, and Fifteenth Amendments. These efforts to undermine federal authority and responsibility under Reconstruction began immediately with President Lincoln's vice president and successor, Andrew Johnson (1865–1869). Johnson was impeached by the U.S. Senate, but not removed from office, for violating the Constitution by removing Secretary of War Edwin M. Stanton from office, thereby obstructing the implementation of the Reconstruction Act. A Southern Democrat, born in North Carolina and representing Tennessee as both governor and, later, senator, his prejudice against blacks was well known. He served out the remainder of Lincoln's second term, following the president's assassination, and later returned to the U.S. Senate (senators were appointed by their state delegations until passage of the Seventeenth Amendment in 1913, which called for direct election by the voters).

Even then, de facto support for Jim Crow was actually an agreement between Republicans, who wanted to stay in office following Grant's administration, and Southern Democrats. Murphy, Fleming, and Barber note that Jim Crow discrimination emerged during the disputed Hayes-Tilden presidential compromise of 1877 that allowed the Republicans to retain the White House in exchange for ending Reconstruction in the South. This was done by transferring federal civil protection for the newly freed blacks to state authority, which would be run by whites. Thus, while efforts to undermine the rights of blacks were often associated with the dismal presidency of Andrew Johnson, the deal for Jim Crow discrimination was actually secured during the administration of President Rutherford B. Hayes (1877–1881), leading to confirmation in the 1896 the U.S. Supreme Court in *Plessy v. Ferguson* (163 U.S. 537, 1896). Here, the separate but equal *Jim Crow* laws in the South were upheld by the U.S. Supreme Court when it stated that racial segregation did *not* violate the Fourteenth Amendment's equal protection clause. The Jim Crow debacle was later reversed through the school integration rulings in *Brown v. Board of Education* (347 U.S. 483, 1954) and later with passage of the U.S. Civil Rights Acts of 1964.[11]

The problems associated with Jim Crow laws were further exacerbated under President Woodrow Wilson, whose presidency did more to legitimize segregation, including banning blacks from attending Princeton when he was the school's president. Wilson viewed blacks in condescending and paternalistic terms. His view of African Americans did not vary considerably from that of his opponents in the presidential election of 1912—Theodore Roosevelt (1904–1908) and William Howard Taft (1908–1912). The main difference was that Wilson formally instituted segregation at the federal level, transcending the mostly parochial practices of the Southern states. Once elected, Wilson appointed five conservative Southerners to crucial cabinet posts—treasury, agriculture, attorney general, secretary of the navy, and postmaster general. Clearly, these appointees were willing agents of white supremacists, notably the National Democratic Fair Play Association. Collectively, their actions resulted in the segregation of federal workers along with the removal of any blacks in supervisory positions over whites. Wilson's racist sentiments were expressed on February 18, 1915, when he held a private viewing for his cabinet members and their families of the inflammatory film, *The Birth of a Nation*, an anti-black film produced by two of his friends from Johns Hopkins University, Thomas Dixon and D. W. Griffith. The film celebrated the Ku Klux Klan as the saviors of Aryan culture over what the film depicted as inferior blacks.[12]

The conspiracy between Republicans and Democrats to maintain Jim Crow discrimination in the South continued through Wilson's presidency and through that of Franklin D. Roosevelt's administrations. André Schiffrin explained the evolution of the white Southern *redneck* in his book, *Dr. Seuss & Co. Go to War.*

> Because of the stranglehold of Southern Democrats in the Senate, legislation abolishing the poll tax, or even lynching, was blocked by the threat, and reality, of the filibuster. Roosevelt, for the most part, went along with this Southern veto, depending as he did on the electoral votes of the Southern Democrats, who were kept in power by a tiny fraction of the voters because of the very racist laws they were able to maintain. The poll tax, which Seuss and *PM* [New York City political tabloid] opposed continuously, completely distorted the American political scene. Not only were black voters in the South completely excluded, but so were a large number of the poorer whites. When the tax was finally abolished in Florida in the 1940s, Democrats calculated that 70 percent of white voters had also been excluded. . . . Others in Congress who actually represented the vast majority of Americans were thus stymied by a small number of racists, who, benefitted from seniority as well as the threat of the filibuster.[13]

During World War II, President Roosevelt suspended the writ for Japanese Americans living on the West Coast, an action that resulted in their internment in concentration camps. The most recent example of federal suspension of the writ of habeas corpus followed the terrorist attacks on the United States on September 11, 2001. Here, President George W. Bush issued an executive order stating that suspected "terrorists" would be tried in special military tribunals.[14]

Private security policing is another feature of social control in America. Private security agencies often carry the weight of public law enforcement agencies while usually operating outside the legal mandate regulating public police forces. They tend to operate under the radar of official regulatory oversight and often are seen as using extralegal authority to serve private interests. In the United States, private security played an important role as a special police force for industrial giants, notably railroad and mining companies, that needed strike breakers. The oldest surviving agency is Pinkerton Inc.—the agency that J. Edgar Hoover credited as the model for the *Federal Bureau of Investigation* (FBI). The Pinkerton National Detective Agency was an outgrowth of the North-Western Police Agency, established in 1850. The agency was established by Scottish immigrant Allan Pinkerton and his partner, Edward Rucker. It was a private detective agency that catered to businesses that needed extralegal control over their employees. In February 1855, they offered their services to six midwestern railroads and established their headquarters in Chicago. The North-Western Police (Pinkerton) agency gained national attention when it was credited with thwarting an assassination attempt on President-elect Abraham Lincoln. With this publicity, they changed their name to the *Pinkerton National Detective Agency*. During the nineteenth century, they also provided private militias to companies to control strikes.

In 1871, the newly established U.S. Department of Justice (DOJ) outsourced their investigative mandate to detect and prosecute federal law violations to the Pinkerton Agency. They are also credited with initiating *undercover* police work by infiltrating the Molly Maguires and other mine unions. They also created violence through spies and *agent provocateurs*. However, the bloodshed fueled by Pinkerton agents as strike breakers at the Andrew Carnegie Homestead Mill in 1892 led to laws in twenty-six states banning the use of private security agents during labor disputes. Nevertheless, Pinkerton agents continued to serve as de facto federal agents until the U.S. attorney general authorized the creation of a federal corps of *Special Agents* in July 1908. In 1909, the attorney general put these special agents within the new agency—the *Bureau of Investigation*—later called the Federal Bureau of Investigation (FBI).

Another private security agency with links to the federal government was the Burns Detective Agency, headed by William "Billy" J. Burns, which began in 1910. Billy Burns's *International Detective Agency* was created as an alternative to the *Pinkerton Agency*. Burns and his agents also served the DOJ when President Harding's attorney general, Harry Daugherty, hired his childhood friend, Billy, to head up the Bureau of Investigation. Burns and Daugherty were later caught up in the *Teapot Dome Scandal*, leading to jury tampering convictions for Burns. The Teapot Dome trials came during the Coolidge administration, forcing Attorney General Harlan Fiske Stone to clean up the Bureau of Investigation—leading to the appointment of J. Edgar Hoover as the director of the revamped agency—now known as the FBI. J. Edgar Hoover served from May 10, 1924, until his death in 1972 at age seventy-seven. Both the Pinkerton and Burns agencies were acquired by the Swedish security company—*Securitas AB*—forming the largest security company in the world. *Securitas*, founded in 1934, went international in 1989 when it merged with security agencies in Norway, Denmark, Portugal, and Hungry. It went public in 1991 expanding throughout most of Europe, including Great Britain.[15]

CIVILIAN LAW ENFORCEMENT

The oldest civilian federal law enforcement agency is the U.S. Marshals Office. George Washington appointed the first thirteen U.S. marshals on September 24, 1779, one for each of the states, making them the first "officers of the court" with the responsibility of carrying out the death sentence imposed by the federal courts. The marshals were also responsible for taking the census in their jurisdiction (state) every ten years for the annual tally. The federal marshal and his deputies were the major civilian police force during America's westward expansion, and they served as the forerunner to the U.S. Secret Service (created in 1865) when they were used to pursue counterfeiters. They were also used to pursue Whiskey Rebels, illegal moonshiners who dodged federal taxes, often working in conjunction with federalized state militias. In 1870, both the U.S. Marshals and U.S. Attorneys came under the newly created U.S. DOJ. Under the DOJ, marshals now assisted the Internal Revenue agents in enforcing whiskey tax laws. In 1880, marshals took over the responsibility of custody of federal prisoners, and in 1890, these duties were extended to the protection of federal judges. Together with the army, the marshals represented law and order in territories until they obtained statehood. U.S. Marshals were also deployed along the U.S.-Mexico border during the 1910–1917 Mexican Revolution. Each state and territory has a designated "U.S. Marshal" appointed by the president and confirmed by the Senate. He or she is head of the office and its deputy force, an established federal law enforcement force with career-based permanent personnel. Marshals continue to play a significant role in federal law enforcement, working with other federal agencies while serving as officers of the judiciary.

Perhaps best known worldwide today, the FBI is but one of many federal law enforcement agencies that have emerged over the past century, each with their own special jurisdictional authority established by Congress. While all four major branches of the military (army, navy, air force, marines) have their own law enforcement agencies under the Department of Defense, the coast guard acts as a law enforcement agent under the newly created Department of Homeland Security, following the September 11, 2001, terrorist attacks, along with numerous other law enforcement agencies, including Customs and Border Protection; Office of Border Patrol; U.S. Secret Service; and the Transportation Security Administration. Other federal agencies with law enforcement authority include: Department of Agriculture; Department of Commerce; Department of Education; Department of Energy; Department of Health and Human Services; Department of the Interior, with the Bureau of Indian Police, Bureau of Land Management, and U.S. Park Rangers; DOJ, which includes the U.S. Marshals Service; the FBI; the Bureau of Prisons; Bureau of Alcohol, Tobacco, Firearms, and Explosives; U.S. Drug Enforcement Administration and Office of Inspector General; Department of State; Department of Labor; Department of the Treasury; and the Department of Veteran Affairs.

The separate state system held primarily to the British common laws that prevailed in the thirteen colonies. This system was composed of county sheriffs and justices of the peace. The county became America's equivalent of the shire while the *shire-reeve* became the sheriff, the only constitutional law enforcement officer in the United States. The high sheriffs, in most of the counties (3,080), are elected by the voters in their jurisdiction and therefore are exempt from any state or federal legislative restrictions that may pertain to other law enforcement agencies. Louisiana is organized into parishes instead of counties while Alaska has boroughs. Some states also have municipal sheriffs while New York City's sheriff is an appointed position covering all five boroughs (Kings, Queens, Richmond, Bronx, and New York). Sixty-two of Colorado's counties elect their sheriff while the sheriff is an appointed position for the larger city-county entities, Denver and Broomfield. The sheriff and his deputies were considered to be "officers of the court," a system that continued after independence, making the county sheriff a constitutional law enforcement officer. This system, along with state militias, continued following independence. Originally, before the advent of state police, the high sheriff, along with the county attorney, represented the top state law enforcement officers. The sheriff and county commissioner still hold considerable power and authority in states with strong county government, mainly in the southern and western states. In the northeast, the sheriff's office serves mainly as officers of the court. The Los Angeles County Sheriff's Department is the largest in the United States. Forty-eight of the fifty states have sheriffs. There are 3,143 counties or county equivalents in the United States. Accordingly, the National Sheriffs' Association states that there are over 3,000 sheriff's offices in the country. An interesting historical footnote, Grover Cleveland, the twenty-second and twenty-fourth U.S. president, was previously elected sheriff of Erie County, New York.

State police forces trace their history to the Texas Rangers, created in 1835. While Texas was an independent republic, it lays claim to the title of the first state police department, given that is what they reverted to when Texas became a slave state in 1845. In 1865, Massachusetts created "state constables," which had statewide policing authority. Obviously, their mandate predated the automobile. Initially, they were used to enforce the Massachusetts's prohibition blue laws in Boston.

The foundations of the current state police agencies began with the advent of the interstate road system, a model based on military need that began following WWI with General John (Black Jack) Pershing's map for better military mobility. The 1922 plan was known as "the Pershing Map." Pennsylvania's state police, established in 1905, was created for statewide motor vehicle and other intercounty law enforcement. State police departments soon became the norm following the First World War and the advent of automobile travel and statewide roads. Later, General Eisenhower, impressed by the German Autobahn system developed by the Nazis, greatly expanded the post–WWI 200,000-mile highway system while U.S. president Eisenhower felt that the United States needed an uninterrupted, multilane, interstate highway system designed for the rapid mobilization of National Guard and regular army and marine corps units in times of crisis as the Cold War heated up following the Korean conflict. Hence, the 1956 Federal Aid Highway Act forged a stronger relationship between state police and the federal government—which had original jurisdiction over the new interstate highway system connecting all corners of the United States without local interference.

This new relationship between the state's top law enforcement officer, the attorney general, and the military generals actually provided the civilian police general (attorney general) original jurisdiction within the state, save for locally restricted jurisdictions such as county sheriffs and large municipal police agencies. The state police became the de facto law enforcement for the attorney general's office, a role that expanded well beyond policing the highway system (highway patrol). Most states now place major crimes under the attorney general's office and the state police. Consequently, the head of the state police holds a rank subservient to the attorney general (usually colonel) and is usually appointed by the governor with the agency having statewide jurisdiction, hence representing the highest level of law enforcement at the state level. Moreover, the attorney general's rank is usually seen as being comparable to that of the highest-ranking member of the state National Guard (brigadier or major general).

Municipal police also have British origins. England traces the origin of municipal police to 1829 when London established its system under the influence of Sir Robert Peel, hence British police being known as *Bobbies*. The term *cop* in the United States probably comes from the British "Constable on Patrol." Cities in the United States soon followed the British model for municipal police departments, adding another layer to the constable and sheriff system. Following the British model, municipal police adopted a military rank structure. Municipal police usually divide their jurisdictions into precincts with a ranking officer holding the rank of captain. Politics and political corruption has long been a problem within municipal police forces, as is evident in the nation's largest force—the New York Police Department. Established in 1845 as the Municipal Police, it soon became so corrupt that the state legislature in Albany forcefully took control of law enforcement in New York City in 1857, calling it the Metropolitan Police, modeled after London's Metropolitan Police Service. In fact, the emergence of municipal law enforcement agencies was to better address the riots and civil unrest that plagued America in the decades leading up to, and during, the Civil War. It was this era of riots and civil unrest that spawned independent urban police forces. Large municipal police forces coexist along with the sheriff's department, especially where the city and county share the same geographical area (such as Denver, Los Angeles, and the like) or exists within several counties (Houston).

· 3 ·

Growing Pains—1783–1865

Insurrections, Rebellions, and Indian Removal

As alluded to previously, American was born a violent society by virtue of its involvement in the European colonial wars that were rooted in sectarian and ethnic hostilities. Slavery and the ongoing onslaught on indigenous groups greatly added fuel to the flames of conflicts and divisions. The United States was never the ideal melting pot envisioned in the myth of the American dream. Richard Maxwell Brown addressed this premise in his selection, Historical Patterns of Violence in America (chapter 2), in the 1969 report on the causes and prevention of violence, *The History of Violence in America*; also known as the *Eisenhower Report*.

Our nation was conceived and born in violence—in the violence of the Sons of Liberty and the patriots of the American port cities of the 1760s and 1770s. Such an event was the Boston Massacre of 1770 in which five defiant Americans were killed. British officers and troops had been goaded by patriotic roughnecks into perpetrating the so-called massacre. The whole episode stemmed naturally from the century-long heritage of organized mob violence in Boston. The same thing was true of the Boston Tea Party, wherein the anciently organized South End Mob of Boston was enlisted in the tea-dumping work. During the long years of resistance to British policy in the 1760s and 1770s, the North End and South End Mobs, under the leadership of Samuel Swift and Ebenezer MacKintosh, had been more or less at the beck and call of Samuel Adams, the mastermind of patriot agitation, and the middle-class patriots who made up the "Loyal Nine."

With the decision in 1774 to resist the British by military means, the second round of Revolutionary violence began. The main goal of Revolutionary violence in the transitional period from 1774 to 1777 was to intimidate the Tories, who existed in fairly large numbers in the seaport cities and hinterland. The countrywide Continental Association of 1774 was drawn up to cause an interruption of all trade between the colonies and the mother country, but a related purpose was to ferret out Tories, expose them to public contumely and intimidation, and bring them to heel or to silence. Where exposure in the newspapers was not enough, strong-arm tactics were used against the Tories. The old American custom of tarring and feathering was mainly a product of the patriotic campaign to root out Toryism.

Aside from the regular clash of the Continental and British armies, the third and final phase of Revolutionary violence was the guerrilla strife that occurred all the way from the Hudson to the Savannah. Wherever strong British occupying forces were to be found—as in New York City, Philadelphia, and Charleston—in opposition to an American-dominated hinterland, the result was the polarization of the population and the outbreak of savage guerrilla strife, desperate hit-and-run forays, and the thrust and counterthrust of pillage and mayhem. Thus, the lower Hudson Valley of New York was the theater of rival bushwhacking parties of Whigs and Tories. The Hackensack valley of North Jersey, opposite the British bastion on Manhattan Island, was a sort of no man's land across which bands of Whigs and Tories fought and ravaged. South Jersey's bleak and trackless pine barrens furnished ideal cover for the "land pirates" of both Whig and Tory persuasion, spewed up by the British and American competition for the allegiance of New Jersey and the Philadelphia area.

South Carolina emerged as the great battlefield of the war after 1780. North Carolina and Georgia suffered at the same time from the scourge of guerrilla strife, but their casualties were light compared to the dreadful cut-and-thrust of the Whig and Tory forces in the Palmetto State where Andrew Pickens, Thomas Sumter, and Francis Marion led Whig partisan bands in their own particular sectors of the backcountry. Negro slaves were stolen back and forth, and baleful figures like the half-crazed Tory leader Bloody Bill Cunningham emerged from the shadows to wreak special bands of murder and massacre. Neither side showed the other any mercy. Prisoners were tortured and hanged. Virginia felt the destruction of Benedict Arnold's vengeful campaign (1781) but experienced nothing like the suffering of South Carolina. Still it was characteristic of the rising passions of the times that strife among Whigs and Tories in Virginia's Piedmont, as noted earlier, gave rise to an early manifestation of lynch law.

Two things stand out about the Revolution. The first, of course, is that it was successful and immediately became enshrined in our tradition and history. The second is that the meanest and most squalid sort of violence was from the very beginning to the very last put to the service of Revolutionary ideals and objectives. The operational philosophy that the end justifies the means became the keynote of Revolutionary violence. Thus given sanctification by the Revolution, Americans have never been loath to employ the most unremitting violence in the interest of any cause deemed to be a good one.[1]

What Brown's essay fails to address is the long-sanctioned violence against both blacks and American Indians, a policy readily adapted to other minorities, notably Hispanics, Asians, and non-Protestant whites. President George Washington set the stage for this process of aggression against American Indians early in his administration. In September 1783, Washington's policy statement on "Indian and Land Policy" referred to Indians as being less-than-human and equating them with wolves and other predatory animals. By referring to American Indians as simple-minded savages, President Washington set the stage for the *trickery by treaty* government policy that was to dominate U.S.–Indian relations during the treaty era from 1783 until 1947. This was in response to the fact that white settlers were encroaching on Indian lands and establishing unauthorized settlements from the beginning of the republic. The Indian land grab soon came under the exclusive authority of the U.S. Congress, which began the farce of treaty negotiations with those they selected as Indian leaders. These treaties were written in English, a language not common to all Indian groups at the time, and often after the Indians were sufficiently lubricated with alcohol. Thus, under President Washington's advisement the treaty process of deception officially began October 15, 1783. And in anticipation of its long war with the Indians, the War Department was established by the First Congress under the new Constitution on August 7, 1789.[2]

President Thomas Jefferson, prior to the acquisition of lands west of the Mississippi River following the *Louisiana Purchase* in 1803, offered a false hope to Indian groups still residing east of the former boundaries of the United States. The Jefferson policy was that these tribes could remain in their traditional homeland if they changed their cultural ways to those of the Anglo-Protestant model. Those groups that followed this advice became known as the *civilized tribes.* However, with the *Louisiana Purchase*, President Jefferson now felt that he had another solution to what he describes as the *Indian problem*—that of creating new homelands for Indian groups in the territory west of the Mississippi River, thus sowing the seeds for the United States' formal policy of Indian expulsion, or ethnic cleansing, known officially as the *Removal Policy.* President Jefferson initiated the *Lewis and Clark Expedition*, led by Meriwether Lewis and William Clark in May 1804 to explore the newly acquired *Louisiana Purchase*, mainly as a scouting expedition in order to gain a better knowledge of the Indian tribes residing in this new addition to the United States and how they may hinder opening up the territory to white settlers. The eighteen-month expedition mapped out the territory and made famous the Shoshone woman, Sacajawea, who assisted in this process. Indeed, she adorns the collectable, gold-colored U.S. dollar coin (2000–2008). What is often omitted is her French-Canadian husband, Toussaint Charbonneau, an interpreter with the expedition and the father of her Métis child also depicted on the coin.

The Louisiana Purchase doubled the size of the United States, with lands extending west of the Mississippi River, north to the Canadian border, and east of the Missouri River, setting the stage for the War of 1812, the War with Mexico in 1846, and the U.S. Civil War (second Civil War), as well as the bloody Indian wars of the nineteenth century. The moral justification for Manifest Destiny is articulated by the words of the sixth U.S. president, John Quincy Adams, a staunch New England Puritan, in a letter to his father, John Adams, the second U.S. president:

> The whole continent of North America appears to be destined by Divine Providence to be peopled by one nation, speaking one language, professing one general system of religion and political principles, and accustomed to one general tenor of social usages and customs.[3]

Clearly, Adams linked the destiny of the United States to the Old Testament's divine providence. From this perspective, providence had provided the North American continent for the United States to conquer, occupy, and convert. Here, the "finger of God" directed the Puritans to America for its domination.

The first of these battles for North American domination, the War of 1812, was unsuccessful, but it made the United States realize that it needed a permanent standing army to replace the state militias that to that point contributed to an ad hoc army, like the Continental army during the Revolutionary War and War of 1812. This resulted in the establishment of the U.S. Army under General Winfield Scott, as well as the creation of the U.S. Military Academy, West Point. The British blockade also made the United States realize that it needed to be more self-sufficient and reliant on domestic resources, notably slave labor in the South and the textile mills of New England. The War of 1812 was likely fueled by Jeffersonian policies, especially that which contributed to the legitimacy of violence in American's expansionist plans. Sheehan noted this in his works on Jeffersonian philanthropy and the American Indian:

> Indian-white relations approached a climax in the decades after the Revolution. The Indian now has few options. Retreat in the Northwest meant conflict with other, more hostile tribes. Retreat in the South meant that more sedentary peoples faced the prospect of abandoning lands long held and changing the very basis of their social life. Moreover, the influence of

civilization had taken effect. Many Indians, particularly the mixed bloods among the tribes, understood the white man's aims. Determined to stand their ground, they used knowledge acquired from civilization to resist him. . . . From the other side of the dilemma of cultural conflict, American society in the late eighteenth and early nineteenth centuries seemed likely to overwhelm any obstruction to its advance, particularly the comparatively feeble opposition offered by the Indian tribes.[4]

The *Indian Removal Act of 1830* put a cruel end to any pretense of President Jefferson's delusion that Indian groups would be welcomed as equals by their white neighbors once they adopted the Euro-American ways. This is evident by the dramatic transformation of the Cherokees, the largest southeastern tribe and one of the *Five Civilized Tribes* that altered their traditional ways in order to fit President Jefferson's assimilation model. In adopting the U.S. societal model, the Cherokee had to disenfranchise adult women who held equal status, including voting rights, under the traditional aboriginal system. They also had to adapt to a slaveholding society, given that they resided in the South where this was the norm in the early 1800s. A tribal police force was established in 1808; a bicameral legislature and judiciary system in 1817; they created their own written language and alphabet (syllabary) in 1821; a Supreme Court in 1823; in 1827, a National Constitution based on the U.S. Constitution was adopted; and they had a nationwide newspaper, *The Cherokee Phoenix*, in 1828. By 1825, the new Cherokee Nation consisted of successful farmers, herdsmen, and merchants, leading the supporters of Jefferson's philanthropic scheme of transforming aboriginal Indian cultures into Western-style societies as a remarkable feat. The Cherokee, with the encouragement of the northern liberal establishment, were able to successfully adopt a separate, yet parallel, cultural lifestyle similar to that of their white counterparts in the South. But this proved to be a shallow victory.

Unfortunately, the seeds of destruction were being sowed as the Cherokee Nation emerged and as Southern states demanded the removal of all Indian tribes residing within their state boundaries. Adhering to President Washington's "trickery by treaty" policy, the United States made 394 Indian treaties between 1778 and 1868, not including those made by tribes with the Confederacy during the Civil War. In 1871, the Indian Appropriations Act ended treaty making with American Indian groups. In ratifying the U.S. Constitution, the Southern states disregarded the existence of Indian groups within their avowed state boundaries, with Georgia, South Carolina, and Virginia doing so in 1788, followed by North Carolina in 1789 and Kentucky, Alabama, and Tennessee soon after. Evidently, President Jefferson played into this scheme when he promised Georgia that he would remove all Indian tribes from the state in exchange for clear U.S. title to all western lands formerly claimed by Georgia (1802 Georgia Compact). In the end, not even the U.S. Supreme Court could protect Indian tribes from expulsion.

Now that it was clear that the rest of British North America (Canada) would not be an easy target for expansion given Canada's aggressive response to the War of 1812, although efforts would continue in this vein until after the Civil War, the United States turned its focus to the Spanish territories and the Indian nations for its expansion. General Andrew Jackson, the first of many future U.S. presidents who gained fame as an *Indian fighter*, expanded the conflict, justified by the War of 1812, to include Spanish holdings in what is now Florida. In 1817–1818, Jackson ignited what became known as the First Seminole War when he unilaterally deposed the Spanish authorities and executed British subjects. These actions led to the U.S. acquisition of Spanish Florida in 1819, effectively eliminating the Spanish from the Florida peninsula and leading to the eventual war with Mexico. Spanish holdings in the Caribbean would not become subject to U.S. expansionism until the conclusion of its Indian Wars in the late nineteenth century with the initiation of the Spanish-American War.

This stark reality became evident with the administration of the seventh U.S. president, Andrew Jackson, yet another Indian fighter of Scot-Irish (Ulster Scot) descent. Indeed, Andrew Jackson was perhaps the most dangerous and racist president yet (the Trump presidency is still unfolding . . .). His election was a departure from the Virginia aristocracy and New England Puritan (Adams) control over the executive branch. Jackson's bitterness over Adams's 1824 election highlighted the intrigue associated with U.S. elections. Even though Jackson had the majority of the Electoral College votes with ninety-nine to Adams's eighty-four, he lacked a majority, and the House of Representatives gave the election to John Quincy Adams. With more and more states expanding the vote by enfranchising a greater proportion of white adult males by eliminating the property ownership provision, Jackson became the choice of the rank-and-file newly coined "Democrats." In their second matchup, Jackson came out with a resounding 178 votes to Adams's 83. Jackson was pro-slavery and an anti-Indian racist whose administrations (1829–1837) set the stage for the divisions that would lead the United States toward its most devastating war—the second Civil War—as well as for its protracted policy of physical and cultural genocide toward American Indians.[5]

The fourth chief justice of the United States Supreme Court, John Marshall, in a number of cases before the court acknowledged the federal government's exclusive role in making treaties with tribes relevant to tribal lands (*Johnson v. McIntosh*, 1823).[6] Justice Marshall, in his decisions, established the legal rights of Indian tribes to occupy their traditional lands, thus reinforcing the European colonial concept of *aboriginal title* or *Indian title*. However, matters deteriorated rapidly under the Jackson presidency when ethnic cleansing became the official doctrine of his Indian policy. Jackson's anti-Indian sentiments were well known, fostering strong support for the forceful removal of all major southern tribes west of the Mississippi River into what was then designated *Indian Territory*—later the state of Oklahoma. With the endorsement of the Removal Act, President Jackson effectively overturned the U.S. Supreme Court with little recourse for Chief Justice Marshall. Dealing with this new reality, one that clearly showed that American Indians were not, and could not be, considered the equal of white Americans, Marshall, in the 1831 *Cherokee Nation v. Georgia* decision, established that Indian tribes were to be considered henceforth as *domestic dependent nations*, essentially wards of the U.S. government and subject to its whims and fancies regarding their ultimate fate. The 1838 Cherokee removal depicts how the U.S. Army under the direction of its leader, General Winfield Scott, rounded up Indians and placed them into stockades with minimum provisions for a forced march to their new and strange land. This stage of *ethnic cleansing* became known as the *Trail of Tears*, resulting in the death of a quarter of the 20,000 Indians removed from their homeland to *Indian Territory* (Oklahoma).[7]

Canby noted that in the end, those favoring removal had their way and all but a few remnants of tribes remained east of the Mississippi:

> The journeys were often attended with extreme hardship and some became virtual symbols of imposed suffering, such as the Trail of Tears traveled by the Five Civilized Tribes (Cherokees, Choctaw, Creek, Chickasaw and Seminole) from the Southeast to what is now Oklahoma. In 1849, with the East nearly free of tribal Indians, the Bureau of Indian Affairs was moved from the War Department, where it had existed since 1824, to the Department of Interior.[8]

Feldman, in looking at the riots and disorder during Jacksonian America, noted how these earlier events differed from the turbulent era of the 1960s and 1970s:

> Americans who remember the urban unrest of the 1960s can readily identify with the crisis of violence that gripped Jacksonian American cities. The 1830s, 1840s, and 1850s produced a constant stream of riots reminiscent of the "long hot summers" of the not-too-distant past. Jacksonian cities were torn by fighting between immigrants and native-born Americans, abolitionist and anti-abolitionists, free blacks and racist whites, volunteer firefighters and street gangs, Mormons and "Gentiles," even rival factions of Whigs and Democrats. And like the 1960s, Jacksonian collective violence resulted in greatly enlarged and strengthened police forces better able to repress riots and disorder—either with or without death or injury to the rioters.[9]

The forced removals were known for their cruelty associated with these expulsions, including a high mortality rate. Gloria Jahoda documents the story of the American Indian removals of 1813–1855, along with the hardships these Indians suffered under U.S. authority. She noted that John Quincy Adams, one of the most adamant Puritans, while president, initiated treaties with the Dakotas, Osages, Kansas, Chippewas, Sacs, Foxes, Winnebagoes, Miamis, Ottawas, and Potawatomis through dubious, and clearly illegal, means. Here U.S. agents unilaterally created "chiefs" that, in fact, were not representative of their people, and then got them drunk and bribed them to make their "mark" on an English-written document, which most could not understand, and then claimed that these individuals signed-off on treaties for the entire tribal group.[10]

Leading up to the Civil War, President Franklin Pierce was complicit in bilking Indians of treaty-guaranteed lands when white men demanded them. In 1854, he authorized the stealing of 18,000,000 acres from Indians in Kansas and Nebraska, terming this new arrangement for these tribes *diminished reserves*. More land was taken during the continued Indian wars in the West and Southwest following the Mexican War of 1846–1848, while President Franklin Pierce extorted more lands from Mexico in 1853 with the Gadsden Purchase. It is within this framework that civil unrest occurred in the years leading up to the Civil War, a phenomenon also addressed in the *Eisenhower Report*:

In symbolic terms, the Great Fear on the eve of the Civil War was altogether fitting as a prelude to the decade and more violence and mischief that follow. The struggle between the Northern and Southern armies still stands as the most massive military bloodletting in American history, but almost forgotten is the irregular underwar of violence and guerrilla strife that paralleled the regular military action. In numerous localities throughout the North, resistance to the military draft was continuous and violent. The apogee of resistance to the draft occurred with the massive riots of 1863 in New York City when the city was given over to three days of virtually uncontrolled rioting. Related troubles occurred throughout the war years in southern Indiana, southern Illinois, and southern Iowa where widespread Copperhead feeling caused large-scale disaffection, antidraft riots, and guerrilla fighting between Union soldiers and Union deserters and other Copperhead sympathizers. The guerrilla war that took place along the Kansas-Missouri border has seldom been equaled for unmitigated savagery. Jim Lane and his fearsome Kansas Jayhawkers traded brutal blows with the Confederated guerrillas of Missouri headed by the band of William Quantrell that included Frank and Jesse James and the Younger boys. Kentucky, too, was the scene of frequent ambushes and affrays.

The Confederate South was bedeviled by pockets of resistance to official policy. The mountain regions of north Arkansas, north Alabama, and eastern Tennessee had important centers of Unionist sentiment that never became reconciled to the war effort. Even Mississippi contained one county (Jones) that was perorated with disloyalty to the Confederate cause, as did Alabama (Winston). The frontier areas of northern and central Texas were liberally dotted with Unionist sympathizers and antislavery Germans. At best the German-American never gave more than grudging support to the War and sometimes resorted to sabotage. The result was brutal retaliation by the "heel-flies" (Confederate home guards) who were often quite careless of whom they injured.

Perhaps no event in American history bred more violence than the Civil War. Racial strife and Ku Klux Klan activity became routine in the old Confederate states. Regulator troubles broke out in central Kentucky and the Blue Grass region. Outlaw and vigilante activity flamed in Texas, Kansas, and Missouri. Outbreaks of feuding scorched the southern Appalachians and Texas. As late as the closing years of the (nineteenth) century white capping, bald knobbing, and night riding, while spurred by particular social and economic causes, remained as legacies of the violent emotions and methods fired by the Civil War.[11]

· 4 ·

Post–Civil War Unrest and Social Control during the Nineteenth Century

De facto law enforcement, known as vigilantism, is generally directed toward outside groups and arises when traditional policing is either deemed inadequate or undesirable, such as the Union army occupation of the former Confederacy. While the Ku Klux Klan is a prime example of this form of extralegal social control, the *Eisenhower Report* notes its long existence in American society, extending to the colonial era:

> Vigilantism arose as a response to a typical American problem: the absence of effective law and order in a frontier region. It was a problem that occurred again and again, beyond the Appalachian Mountains. It stimulated the formation of hundreds of frontier vigilante movements. On the frontier the normal foundations of a stable, orderly society—churches, schools, cohesive community life—were either absent or present only in rough, immature forms. The regular, legal system of law enforcement often proved to be woefully inadequate for the needs of the settlers.
>
> Fundamentally, the pioneers took the law into their own hands for the purpose of establishing order and stability in newly settled areas. In the older settled areas the prime values of person and property were dominant and secure, but the move to the frontier meant that it was necessary to start all over. Upright and ambitious frontiersmen wished to reestablish the values of a property holder's society. The hurtful presence of outlaws and marginal types in a context of weak and ineffectual law enforcement created the spectre and, often, the fact of social chaos. The solution hit upon was vigilantism. A vigilante roundup of ne'er-do-wells and outlaws followed by the flogging, expulsion, or killing of them not only solved the problem of disorder but had crucial symbolic value as well. Vigilante action was a clear warning to disorderly inhabitants that the newness of settlement would provide no opportunity for eroding the

established values of civilization. Vigilantism was a violent sanctification of the deeply cherished values of life and property.

Because the main thrust of vigilantism was to reestablish in each newly settled area the conservative values of life, property, and law and order, vigilante movements were usually led by the frontier elite. This was true of the greatest American vigilante movement—the San Francisco Vigilante Committee of 1856—which was dominated lock, stock, and barrel by the leading merchants of the city. Again and again it was the most eminent local community leaders who headed vigilante movements.

"Vigilance Committee" or "Committee of Vigilance" was the common name of the organization, but originally—and far into the nineteenth century—vigilantes were known by the now obsolete term of "regulators." Variant names for vigilante groups were "slickers," "stranglers," "committees of safety," and, in central Texas, simply, "mobs." The duration of vigilante movements varied greatly, but movements which lasted as long as a year were long lived. More commonly they finished their business in a period of months or weeks. Vigilante movements (as distinguished from ephemeral lynch mobs) are thus identifiable by the two main characteristics of 1) regular (though illegal) organization and 2) existence for a definite (though possibly short) period of time.[1]

Brown went on to point out problems with frontier law enforcement and justice. Poor resources for hiring law enforcement officers at the local and country level, coupled with poor transportation and holding facilities, contributed to the sense of inadequate justice. Political corruption also played a critical role in the lack of faith in the judicial system, especially when a member of the "out-group" was on trial or a member of the "in-group" was accused of an offense against an "out-group" member. Post–Civil War neo-vigilantism went on to target "out-group" members, including Catholics, Jews, Blacks, immigrants, laboring men and labor leaders, political radicals, advocates of civil liberties, and nonconformists in general. Similar to vigilante groups was the emergence of para-police, like the Pinkerton National Detective Agency, who felt themselves above the law, using techniques now patently illegal such as the "third degree" and summary executions. Indeed, they set the stage for what is commonly known as "police brutality."[2]

Sectarian, ethnic, and class objects of judicial prejudices aside, the major targets of severe, often violent, discrimination and extrajudicial abuses during the nineteenth century were racial minorities—blacks, American Indians, Asians, and Mexicans, noticeably Mestizos. While Asian discrimination was mainly focused on Chinese coolies being brought here to engage in dangerous work in the West like the construction of railroads or to work in mines, and Mexican discrimination was focused on territories gained from Mexico in the 1840s and 1850s, discrimination and intimidation of both blacks (slaves and freedmen) and American Indians were more pervasive during the era following the U.S. Civil War. Indeed, the Jim Crow South, with its history of extralegal abuses stemming from the Ku Klux Klan and lynchings, was legitimized by the U.S. Supreme Court in 1896 in the *Plessy v. Ferguson* decision, upholding the so-called separate but equal Jim Crow laws and obviating the Fourteenth Amendment's equal protection clause for blacks.[3]

Terror was endemic within the former Confederacy, with lynching being the major tool of engendering fear among freed blacks—an extralegal social experiment that lasted a hundred years until the Civil Rights Acts of the 1960s. Again, the *Eisenhower Report* created following the civil unrest of the 1960s on violence in America provides a curt historical review of lynching in the United States:

> Lynch law has been defined as "the practice or custom by which persons are punished for real or alleged crimes without due process of law." The first organized movement of lynch law in America occurred in the South Carolina back country, 1767–69. It appeared again in the Virginia Piedmont during the latter years of the Revolutionary War near the present city of Lynchburg. The Virginia movement was initiated by Colonel Charles Lynch and was employed against Tory miscreants. Well into the 19th century lynch law meant merely the infliction of corporal punishment—usually 39 or more lashes well laid on with hickory withes, whips, or any readily available frontier instrument. By the middle of the 19th century, lynch law had, however, come to be synonymous, mainly, with hanging or killing by illegal group action. . . . By term "lynch-mob" is meant an unorganized, spontaneous, ephemeral mob which comes together briefly to do its fatal work and then breaks up. The more regular vigilante (or "regulator") movements engaged in a systematic usurpation of the functions of law and order.
>
> Lynch-mob violence (in contrast to vigilante violence) was often resorted to in trans-Appalachian frontier areas before the Civil War, but it became even more common after the Civil War. In the postwar period (down to World War I) lynch-mob violence was employed frequently in all sections of the country and against whites as well as blacks, but in this period it became preeminently the fate of Southern Negroes. From 1882 to 1903 the staggering total of 1,985 Negroes were killed by Southern lynch mobs. Supposedly the lynch-mob hanging (or, too often, the ghastly penalty of burning alive) was saved for the Negro murderer or rapists, but the statistics show that Negroes were frequently lynched for lesser crimes or in cases where there was no offense at all or the mere suspicion of one. Lynch-mob violence became an integral part of the post-Reconstruction system of white supremacy.[4]

Ralph Ginzburg, in 1962, documented accounts of lynchings in the South from 1859 to 1961. He documents those mutilated, tortured, hanged, and burned alive. His documentation includes a public statement of a Harvard College professor advocating for the legalization of lynching (Albert B. Hart, December 30, 1900), and the 1919 lynching of the mayor of Omaha,

Nebraska, when he tried to intervene with a lynch-mob hanging of a black prisoner. Ginzburg includes a February 29, 1904, letter to the *New York Tribune* from Booker T. Washington and his concerns over the extralegal lynching of blacks:

> These burnings without trial are in the deepest sense unjust to my race. But it is not this injustice alone which stirs my heart. These barbarous scenes are more disgraceful and degrading to the people who inflict the punishment than to those who receive it. If the law is disregarded when a negro is concerned, it will soon be disregarded when a white man is concerned, and, besides, the rule of the mob destroys the friendly relations which should exist between races, and injures and interferes with the material prosperity of the communities concerned.
>
> Worst of all, these outrages take place in communities where there are Christian churches; in the midst of people who have their Sunday schools, their Christian Endeavor societies and Young Men's Christian Associations; where collections are taken up for sending missionaries to Africa and China and the rest of the so-called heathen world. Is it not possible for pulpit and press to speak out against these burnings in a manner that shall arouse a public sentiment that will compel the mob to cease insulting our courts, our Governors and our legal authority; to cease bringing shame and ridicule upon our Christian civilization.[5]

Following the Civil War, more severe punishments emerged, most directed toward freedmen and other racial minorities, especially in the former Confederate states. A unique institution in the Jim Crow South was the chain gang. Prior to the Civil War, there were no state prisons, and all punishment was dispensed at the county or local level. Jails were used only as temporary holding facilities. Following the Civil War, the chain gang was developed. Here, prisoners were placed in enclosed, barred wagons, which could be transported from job to job. Shackles and chains, as well as the ship and sweatbox, were the normal and legal method of control. These controls were enforced by county officials, who originally regulated the chain gang system, and most of the convicts were convicted of misdemeanor offenses. Felons, on the other hand, were sentenced to the newly created state prisons. Barnes and Teeters referred to the Southern chain gang as "the American Siberia," stating that they were not only discriminatory but manifested some of the cruelest punishment and inhumane treatment ever recorded in American penal history. Transients were arrested for loitering and sentenced to the chain gang merely to supply the county with cheap labor. The guards were white while blacks made up the vast majority of offenders who were sentenced to the chain gangs.[6]

Jesse Steiner and Roy Brown, on the faculty at the University of North Carolina, wrote one of the earlier studies on the Southern chain gang, in 1927:

One of the most common types of movable prisons still in use in many of the counties is the wooden or steel structure mounted on wheels which is popularly spoken of as the cage because of its resemblance to the cages in which wild animals are sometimes confined. In size, these so-called cages are usually 18 feet in length and 7 to 8 feet in height and width, designed to provide sleeping quarters for eighteen men. When constructed of steel, the roof, floor, front and rear ends of the cage consist of solid steel of sufficient thickness to provide security, while the two sides are enclosed by a close network of flat steel bars, thus providing plenty of ventilation. In bad weather, the sides of the cage are covered with a tarpaulin which gives protection against rain and cold, but interferes with ventilation and leaves the interior in darkness. The cage is entered through a solid steel door in the rear made secure by a padlock on the outside. The interior of the cage is fitted up with three three-decker bunks on either side of a narrow passage way about two feet wide. A small stove is crowded usually in the front end or middle of the cage and a kerosene lantern is swung from the ceiling. Each bunk is provided with blankets and a cheap mattress ordinarily not covered with a sheet. A night bucket and a pail of drinking water complete the equipment. When the cage is filled to capacity, there is no place for the men except in their bunks which are too low for a sitting posture. Since the men are locked in these cages not only at night, but on Saturday afternoons, Sundays, and on days when bad weather makes work impossible, it is obvious that such cramped quarters are particularly objectionable.[7]

Steiner and Brown addressed the use of corporal punishment for minor infractions for chain gang inmates. The nineteen infractions included the use of profane or vulgar language, smoking during working hours, wasting food, or trading between convicts. The punishment for the first violation was solitary confinement in a dark cell for forty-eight hours, while a second infraction warranted flogging. It was noted that whippings were often severe, some resulting in death. The prisoners were chained to ankle shackles, some with spikes attached. Guards were allowed to shoot to kill any convict they suspected of attempting to escape. Steiner and Brown noted that this essentially was giving the death sentence for an individual convicted merely of a misdemeanor.[8]

POLICING INDIAN TRIBES: U.S. ARMY, BUFFALO SOLDIERS, INDIAN SCOUTS, AND U.S. MARSHALS

During the U.S. Civil War and immediately following, America was caught in an internal battle between military and civilian authorities over who would manage Indian Country. Racist leaders prevailed in both camps, with generals like Sheridan, Sherman, Crook, and (brevet) Custer eager to hunt down Indians deemed "renegades." They often competed with corrupt, politically appointed Indian agents and/or condescending religious zealots for control over the spoils that could be gained from federal contracts awarded for the care of Indian tribes forced (incarcerated) onto reservations that were virtual concentration/internment camps. Included in this mix were *agent provocateurs*, eager to ignite hostilities between Indians and whites, including those intruding into the so-called protected tribal domains in Indian Country. Militias often acted with considerable license in their pursuit of Indian groups, including nonhostiles. A glaring example is the Sand Creek Massacre of November 29, 1864. Looking for Indians to punish for an alleged attack on a white family near Denver, the territorial governor, John Evans, incited local whites to kill and destroy hostile Indians. John Chivington, a preacher and militia colonel in the Union army who viewed killing Indians as a God-given mandate, heeded Governor Evans's call to punish local Indians. The Indians at Sand Creek were on designated reservation lands and adorned their teepees with white flags denoting their peaceful intentions. Nevertheless, hundreds of cavalrymen under Chivington attacked without provocation, killing at least two hundred Indians, mostly women, children, and the elderly. Tony Horwitz noted that what distinguished this massacre from many like it was that the atrocity was reported by U.S. Army personnel who witnessed the wanton murder of these peaceful Indians, challenging Chivington's claim that he and his troops engaged some 1,000 fully armed warriors. Chivington and his men also had the scalps they took displayed in Denver where their attack was lauded as another great military success in the Indian wars. Chivington was allowed to resign from the army in lieu of a court martial.[9]

Neither the U.S. Army nor the Indian agents appeared interested in preserving the traditional cultures of the tribes they oversaw. By all appearances, the U.S. Army was bent on physical genocide while their civilian counterparts were engaged in cultural genocide. The idea of accepting American Indian culture and traditions as equal to those of the dominant white society was destroyed with the removal of the Five Civilized Tribes in the 1830s, a process that continued until the twentieth century and with new ramifications in the 1950s under termination and relocation. The use of Indian scouts by the U.S. Army and Indian police by civilian agents emerged during the second half of the nineteenth century, during the second phase of the U.S. Indian Wars—1855–1890.

U.S. Army and the Indian Wars of 1862–1898

As previously noted, Indian wars began during the colonial era and continued off and on up to the U.S. Civil War. Nonetheless, the United States longest official war were the Indian Wars that began during the Civil War and lasted until the 1890s. Interestingly, President U. S. Grant (1869–1877) played a major role in fueling the ongoing Indian conflicts that preceded his administration. Like the first president, Grant followed Washington's "Trickery by Treaty" policy of deceit while publicly promoting his so-called *Peace Policy* and, at the same time, clandestinely promoting war with the Western tribes, a program he delegated to his favorite Civil War generals, William T. Sherman and Philip H. Sheridan. The Indian Bureau, under the Interior Department, was complicit in this diabolic plan, writing bogus complaints against the Lakotas so as to justify labeling "non-treaty Sioux"—those who chose to maintain their traditional ways with the Great Sioux Reservation—as "hostiles," hence opening the Black Hills to white gold prospectors and settlers. According to Peter Cozzens:

> He [Grant] had no legal reason for seizing the Black Hills, so he invented one, convening a secret White House cabal to plan a war against the Lakotas. Four documents, held at the Library of Congress and the United States Military Academy Library, leave no doubt: The Grant administration launched an illegal war and then lied to Congress and the American people about it. . . . During four decades of intermittent warfare on the Plains, this was the only instance in which the government deliberately provoked a conflict of this magnitude and it ultimately led to the Army's shocking defeat at the Little Bighorn in 1876—and to litigation that remains unsettled to this day.[10]

Here, the army's official *Indian Campaign Medal* was awarded for service in enumerated campaigns or against hostile Indians or in any other action in which the U.S. troops were killed or wounded between 1865 and 1891. The eligible campaigns during the Indian wars include the following:

- Southern Oregon, Idaho, northern California, and Nevada between 1865 and 1868
- Against the Comanche and confederate tribes in Kansas, Colorado, Texas, New Mexico, and Indian Territory between 1867 and 1875
- Modoc War between 1872 and 1873
- Against the Apaches in Arizona in 1873
- Against the Northern Cheyenne and Sioux between 1876 and 1877
- Nez Perce War in 1877
- Bannock War in 1878
- Against the Northern Cheyenne between 1878 and 1879
- Against the Sheep-Eaters, Piute, and Bannocks between June and October 1897
- Against the Ute in Colorado and Utah between September 1879 and November 1880

- Against the Apaches in Arizona and New Mexico between 1885 and 1886
- Against the Sioux in South Dakota between November 1890 and January 1891
- Against hostile Indians in any other action in which U.S. troops were killed or wounded between 1865 and 1891

The Indian Campaign Medal was issued only once regardless of how many battles or campaigns a soldier was involved in, much like the current National Defense Medal. However, a silver citation star was attached to the medal for meritorious or heroic conduct. This was the predecessor to the Silver Star, currently the third-highest military award for heroism. Eleven troopers were awarded the silver citation between 1865 and 1891. The highest U.S. military award, the Congressional Medal of Honor, was also awarded during the Indian campaigns. Like many other military awards, the Indian Wars Medal was not authorized until 1907, the same time that the War Department created the Civil War Campaign Medal. These medals were awarded retroactively.

While the Indian Campaign Medal only covers battles and encounters between 1865 and 1891, the U.S. Army documents numerous battles between the Mexican War of 1846–1848 and the Civil War (1861–1865), including fights in the 1850s with the Apaches and Utes in New Mexico Territory; the Yakima, Walla Walla, and Cayuse in the northwest; Sioux in Nebraska; Cheyenne in Kansas; and Comanche in Oklahoma and Kansas. During the Civil War, the army pursued the Sioux in Minnesota in 1862 during the Great Sioux Uprising and in campaigns in the Upper Missouri River region in 1863–1864. The difference following the Civil War was the division of the western United States into combat regions like the U.S. military did a century later in Vietnam (1959–1975). The major structure for frontier defenses was the division of the western areas into the Department of Dakota; Department of the Platte; Department of the Missouri; Department of Texas; Department of Arizona; Department of California; and the Department of the Columbian. During the Indian Wars, the generals of the army were Major General Winfield Scott (Indian Removal; Mexican War), Major General George B. McClellan, Major General H. W. Halleck, General Ulysses S. Grant, General William T. Sherman, General Philip H. Sheridan, and Lieutenant General John McAllister Schofield, in addition to five subordinate major generals and sixteen brigadier generals and numerous colonels and lieutenant colonels. The U.S. adjutant general was the administrative officer of the army. The punitive expedition against the Navajo in 1863, known as the *Long Walk*, and the Black Hills Gold Rush of the 1870s are a few of the significant events fueling the United States' longest war—the Indian Wars of 1813 to 1898, with eruptions in 1973 with Wounded Knee II. The last official military campaign of the

Indian Wars occurred at the Leech Lake Reservation in northern Minnesota in October 1898.

Campaign medals were issued for the U.S. soldiers involved in the numerous Indian Wars. Indeed, those soldiers who operated the machine guns (Hotchkiss gun—a version of the hand-crank Gatling gun) that killed some three hundred unarmed Indian men, women, and children at Wounded Knee in December 1890 received the Congressional Medal of Honor—the nation's highest military honor. U.S. Army Private Oscar Burkard was the last to receive the Medal of Honor during the Indian Wars, doing so at the Leech Lake Reservation battle in 1898. It was not until 2010 that the U.S. government decided to change the markers at "Commutative Sites" that mark U.S.-Indian engagements involving unarmed Indians from a "battle" status to that of a "massacre" site. Included here is the November 1864 Sand Creek Massacre and the numerous deadly forced removals (*ethnic cleansing*) under the guns of the U.S. Army.[11]

During the Civil War, Confederate prisoners of war (POWs) were recruited to fight Indians in the west for the Union forces. Southern POWs were offered the opportunity to join the Union to fight in the western Indian wars with the promise that they would not be fighting fellow confederates. These *galvanized Yankees* had to swear allegiance to the Union and would receive a full pardon in exchange for their successful service with the U.S. Army. Freedmen, liberated former black slaves, were also recruited by the U.S. Army to fight in the Indian wars. They became known as *buffalo soldiers*, a name given them by the Indians because of their bravery and similarity between the hair and color of black soldiers. The buffalo soldiers, like the galvanized Yankees, were enlisted men, led by white northern officers. The buffalo soldiers fought in the Indian Wars and the Spanish American War, producing twenty-three Medal of Honor recipients for their valor. Pershing was one of the officers in charge of buffalo soldier units both during the Indian Wars and in the Spanish American War, hence his nickname, *Black Jack*. Interestingly, George Armstrong Custer, former brevet major general during the Civil War, was offered the higher rank of full colonel if he led a buffalo soldier unit. He declined; hence, his lower rank of lieutenant colonel.[12]

INDIAN POLICE AND POLICING INDIAN COUNTRY: MILITARY VERSUS CIVILIAN JURISDICTIONS

The practice of using Indian scouts usually involved employing traditional enemies such as Custer's use of Crow scouts in his battles with the Sioux and Cheyenne; or the use of same tribe Indians who were lured into service because they were "progressives" who wanted to be on the winning side, as illustrated by General Crook's Apache scouts. In some instances, Indian scouts also served as Indian police. At any rate, the Indian scout held more status and was better paid than his Indian police counterpart. Indian law enforcement, regardless if it was imposed by the army or civilians, relied on the unique judicial and administrative rules that governed Indian Country, a process that evolved rapidly from the earlier Trade and Intercourse Acts. In the early years, the War Department provided the enforcement arm in Indian Country, while the Indian agent, later upgraded to the title of commissioner of Indian affairs in 1832, determined which issues required adjudication. The regulation of non-Indians within federally protected Indian Country was first established by Congress in 1817 with the Federal Enclaves Act, also known as the General Crimes Act. The purpose of this act was to extend federal law into Indian Country, given that the federal government held exclusive jurisdiction in Indian Country.

At the same time, Indian tribes were struggling for legal parity during this era of diminished tribal authority and increased control and regulations placed upon them, a process which was clearly one-sided, with whites having a substantial legal advantage over Indian clients. A landmark case reflecting this dilemma was that of Standing Bear, who filed a writ of habeas corpus before the federal courts questioning his forced incarceration in Indian Territory (Oklahoma). His tribe, the Ponca, was removed from its traditional home in eastern Nebraska to make room for the forceful removal of the Santee (Dakota) Sioux following the uprising in Minnesota in the early 1860s, which led to the largest federally sanctioned execution in the United States with thirty-eight Sioux warriors hanged together on December 26, 1862.[13] Standing Bear and his followers left the horrid conditions of their new reservation in Oklahoma and headed home to Nebraska, now the home of the interned/removed Santee Sioux. The group was subsequently arrested by General Crook's forces, and it was at this time that Standing Bear presented his habeas corpus writ to the U.S. Circuit Court, District of Nebraska. In a landmark decision, Judge Elmer S. Dundy, on May 12, 1879, ruled in Standing Bear's favor, essentially granting American Indians the official status of *human beings* (*persons*), albeit not U.S. citizens. American Indians no longer had to be referred to as bucks, does, and fawns in official military reports, but rather as men, women, and children.[14]

The Federal Enclaves Act was subsequently replaced with the Assimilative Crimes Act of 1825, the Major Crimes Act of 1885, and Public Law 280 in 1953. The Assimilative Crimes Act stipulated that offenses in Indian Country, while still under federal jurisdiction, would now use state or territorial statutes and sentences as a guide for federal jurisdiction, mainly for offenses committed in Indian Country by non–Indians. Tribal customs and traditions remained the mainstay for intratribal matters. Thus, the local, state, or territorial laws where the reservation was located would be used by the federal government for those crimes not specified by federal code.[15] While the intent was for tribal justice to operate within Indian Country for crimes by Indians against Indians, the white Indian superintendent virtually held absolute authority in dealing with all issues within his authority. Most significantly, he had the resources of the army at his disposal as an enforcement agent. In the constant friction between the army and the Department of the Interior, Indian agents began creating their own reservation police forces. Thomas Lightfoot, the Indian agent for the Iowa, Sac, and Fox tribes in southeastern Nebraska, is credited with the movement to recruit Indians as police in Indian Country outside the Five Civilized Tribes, who continued to use their police and court systems once removed to Indian Territory, in 1869. Three years later, in 1872, the military special Indian commissioner for the Navajos organized a horse cavalry of 130 Navajos to guard the newly drawn up reservation, following the Navajo's return from incarceration at Fort Sumner (the *Long Walk*, 1863–1868). Meanwhile, the Cherokee Nation created the position of high sheriff in 1875.[16]

At about the same time, Indian Agent John Clum was experimenting with his own Indian police force on the San Carlos (Arizona) Reservation. Clum did this mainly as an attempt to wrest civilian control from the military in Indian Country, given that he subscribed to the cultural genocide policy spelled out in Grant's Quaker or Peace Policy where church groups were incorporated to teach the heathen Indians the superiority of Christianity. Although not entirely successful, agents Clum and Lightfoot were successful in establishing a parallel Indian police force, albeit poorly paid and trained, in Indian Country. The Apache police, as did many of their colleagues in other tribes, also served as scouts when operating with the army. Two years following the Cherokee initiative and those of Indian Agents Clum and Lightfoot, U.S. Indian Commissioner Ezra A. Hayt officially petitioned the U.S. Congress for authorization for more Indian police on reservations. Based on Commissioner Hayt's recommendations, the U.S. Congress, in 1879, authorized pay for 430 Indian privates, supervised by 50 white officers. Forty-three men served on the Indian police in Indian Territory (Oklahoma), a vast territory providing each police officer a 712-square-mile jurisdiction. Moreover, the Indian police had to work with the U.S. Marshals and other police in bringing law to this vast haven for outlaws. Indian police were greatly restricted by the U.S. Congress. Indian police actually acted under the direction of the white Indian agent administering his form of martial law, as against enforcing written federal, state, or territorial laws. Congress deliberately set the pay for Indian police far below that of others working for the government in Indian

Country. They were paid five dollars per month and had to provide their own horse, gun, and other equipment needed for the job. Indian teamsters and Indian scouts were earning three times that amount and with better benefits. As late as 1906, Indian police earned only twenty dollars per month. A further stigma was that Congress would only authorize the use of poorly maintained, used pistols, fearing that if they had rifles they could use these in a rebellion.[17]

Congress also forced them to wear gray uniforms like those of the defeated Confederate soldiers, instead of the Union blue worn by soldiers and even Indian scouts. Hagan noted that pistols that wouldn't fire, starvation wages, and shoddy uniforms plagued Indian police while, at the same time, forcing them to be janitors and handymen to the Indian agent. Clearly the Indian police were used to enforce and protect the administration of the white Indian agent in charge of the reservation. Agent John Clum's success was that he was able to consolidate the five Apache agencies in Arizona Territory into one large concentration at San Carlos, appeasing both the federal government, making it easier to hunt down "hostile" Apache, and the local white settlers, notably the "Tucson Ring," which benefitted from having the Apache being restricted to one area. Altruism or compassion for Apache culture never entered into the equation. Indeed, it was clear that the appointment of Indian police and Indian judges by Indian agents was a clear attempt to abrogate traditional tribal authority and traditions and to replace these with Euro-American ways.[18]

Some of the Indian police were also outlaws or accused of crimes. Bob Dalton, of the infamous Dalton gang, served as a U.S. Deputy Marshal and as chief of the Osage police. He was forced out of these positions when he and his family were exposed as bootleggers. He then used his talents in robbing banks and trains. On the other hand, police heroism was exemplified by Sam Sixkiller, son of Redbird Sixkiller, former high sheriff of the Cherokee Nation, a captain in the Union Agency Indian Police, and a U.S. Deputy Marshall, who was killed in the line of duty in the streets of Muskogee in 1886. Both Dalton and Sixkiller illustrate the turbulent situation in Indian Country where lawlessness prevailed and agent provocateurs agitated Indian unrest, setting the stage for another unique chapter in American jurisprudence, that of the *court of no appeal*.[19]

Indian Territory became a haven for outlaws following the Civil War, gaining the titles "Robbers Roost" and "the land of the six-shooter." In an attempt to bring some justice to the territory, a unique form of justice prevailed, one in which the U.S. district judge performed both the petit court and appellate court functions—hence, federal courts of no appeal. Judge Isaac Parker best illustrates this phenomenon. He was appointed to the U.S. Court for the Western District of Arkansas at Fort Smith with jurisdiction over all of Indian

Territory (Oklahoma). Judge Parker became known as the *hanging judge*, and this image eventually led to changes. In 1883, the U.S. Congress split up his district, assigning the western half of Indian Territory to the U.S. Judicial District of Kansas and the southern region to the Northern District of Texas. In 1889, Congress acted to abolish the circuit court powers of the district courts with all capital cases tried before a U.S. court, requiring review of an appellate court before judgment could be exercised. State law replaced territorial jurisprudence when Indian Territory became the state of Oklahoma in 1907. This still gave Judge Parker authority over the Five Civilized Tribes. He was appointed at age thirty-five and served in this capacity for twenty-one years (1875–1896), adjudicating 13,490 cases with 344 capital offenses of which 160 were sentenced to death.[20] Shirley described Parker's judicial reign as follows:

> The death penalty was prescribed more often and for more flagrant violations of law than anywhere on the American continent. That Judge Parker's administration was stern to the extreme is attested by the fact that he sentenced 160 men to die and hanged 79 of them. His court was the most remarkable tribunal in the annals of jurisprudence, the greatest distinctive criminal court in the world; none ever existed with jurisdiction over so great an area, and it was the only trial court in history from the decisions of which there was, for more than fourteen years, no right of appeal. . . . In cases of homicide, his tribunal functioned as a circuit court, and federal statutes made no provision for having his findings reviewed by the Supreme Court of the United States. To that extent his court was greater than the Supreme Court, for it possessed both original and final jurisdiction. His decisions were absolute and irrevocable.[21]

The U.S. Marshal represented the federal law enforcement presence in Indian Country since 1804 when Congress designated the southern Mississippi Valley the Territory of Orleans and provided it with a federal district court, along with a U.S. Marshal's office. President Thomas Jefferson appointed Francis J. L. D'Orgenay, a Creole, as marshal of the territory, making him the first "western" marshal. Among the duties of the western marshals was policing the vast territory obtained under the Louisiana Purchase, including all the Indian tribes located in this newly acquired Indian Country. While tribes addressed their own internal disputes, the 1834 Indian Intercourse Act extended the general laws of the United States into Indian Country, where Indian-white cases were now brought before the federal courts of Missouri and the Territory of Arkansas. Here, the federal marshal and his deputies, supported with the army, had the primary duty of enforcing federal laws, as well as acting as officers of the federal court. Judge Parker relied on the U.S. Marshal and his deputies to police his vast jurisdiction, as did other federal judges in Indian

Country. Sixty-five deputy marshals died during the twenty-year tenure of Judge Parker carrying out his law in Indian Territory. Of these noted lawmen was Marshal Crawley P. Dake's deputy, Virgil Earp, in Tombstone, who also presided over the Lincoln County War and the pursuit of Billie the Kid, and Marshal Zan L. Tidball, marshal of Arizona Territory during the Geronimo and San Carlos episodes.[22]

In 1883, the Courts of Indian Offenses were established under the influence of President Chester A. Arthur's Secretary of the Interior, Henry M. Teller. Teller approved a *code of Indian Offenses* designed to prohibit American Indian traditional ceremonial activities throughout Indian Country, notably traditional customs, dances, and plural marriages, that now could be prosecuted by the Courts of Indian Offenses. These courts also adjudicated minor offenses in Indian Country already defined by the Federal Enclaves and Assimilative Crimes Acts. The idea behind the Courts of Indian Offenses was to appoint "progressive" Indian judges, those dedicated to the promotion of Euro-American customs as against traditional "heathenish" practices. One of the most notable and colorful Indian judges was Quanah Parker, who was appointed in 1886 to the First Court of Indian Offenses for the Kiowa and Comanche. He was later dismissed for continuing to practice certain traditional practices.[23]

During this time, the Crow Dog incident was progressing through the federal courts. Preliminary to this case was the strong anti-Indian sentiment in the United States fueled by President Grant's clandestine actions against the Sioux, resulting in Custer's Last Stand at the Little Big Horn in 1776. The Crow Dog case was equally sensational in that it involved the killing of federally sponsored Sioux leader, Spotted Tail, by a former Indian police chief, Crow Dog. Both were Brule Sioux from the Rosebud Reservation in South Dakota just north of the Nebraska border. Given that the newly established Courts of Indian Offenses only dealt with minor cultural infractions and was not in effect at the time of the incident, the murder of Spotted Tail was left to be handled by tribal custom and protocol. Spotted Tail was the head chief of the Brule at the time of the treaties of the 1860s that established the Great Sioux Reservation and was favored by the U.S. government because he kept the Brule Sioux out of the 1876 uprising that led to Custer's defeat. Crow Dog was a traditional Sioux and respected warrior and leader of the Big Raven Band. He was a close associate of Crazy Horse and accompanied him when he surrendered in 1877. He was also a close associate of Sitting Bull.

Both Spotted Tail and Crow Dog were vying for leadership positions that the new Rosebud agency carved out of the once promised Great Sioux Reservation. The federal government favored Spotted Tail who they saw as a "progressive" Indian to Crow Dog who remained a "traditionalist." These ideological differences aside, the actual altercation leading to Spotted Tail's demise was most likely over a woman, Light-in-the-Lodge. Accordingly, Spotted Tail was seen as attempting to entice Light-in-the-Lodge away from her disabled elderly husband, and Crow Dog took it upon himself to right this wrong. On August 5, 1881, the forty-seven-year-old Crow Dog shot fifty-eight-year-old Spotted Tail as they approached each other on a road near the agency. Since this was seen as an intratribal matter, it was presumed to be exempt from federal or territorial jurisdiction under the existing Federal Enclaves/General Crimes Act regulating Indian Country. The matter was subsequently resolved in a traditional fashion between the respective clans representing both Spotted Tail and Crow Dog, with Crow Dog' clan compensating Spotted Tail's clan with a restitution of six hundred dollars, eight horses, and a blanket.

While this restored balance to the Brule Sioux, it did not resonate well with the federal Indian agents and the U.S. Army. Crow Dog was then arrested under the orders of Indian Agent John Cook. Crow Dog was brought to Fort Niobrara in Nebraska for trial with the blessings of the U.S. attorney general. At the federal trial, Crow Dog was portrayed as a bad Indian like his colleagues Crazy Horse and Sitting Bull, deserving to be executed for his crime. Given these sentiments from the prosecution, there was little doubt that the all-white male jury would find Crow Dog guilty of capital murder and sentence him to be executed by hanging by Judge G. C. Moody. In his appeal (remember Indians are now deemed "persons"), the First Judicial District Court of Dakotas upheld his sentence with G. C. Moody again presiding. The case then went to the U.S. Supreme Court (something that would not have happened in Judge Parker's jurisdiction). In its December 17, 1883, decision, *Ex parte Crow Dog* upheld Crow Dog's petition and had him released from incarceration. Essentially the U.S. Supreme Court agreed with Crow Dog's contention that there were no federal laws relevant to his case and that the district court did not have jurisdiction in an internal tribal case.[24]

The U.S. Congress responded to the *Crow Dog* decision by passing the *Major Crimes Act* in 1885. This represented a significant encroachment on tribal authority, providing overlapping jurisdiction with the Federal Enclaves Act by applying federal jurisdiction to any offender in Indian Country. U.S. Marshals could now arrest Indians and non-Indians alike for major offenses in Indian Country, subsequently bringing them before a federal court for adjudication. The original seven major crimes outlined in this law were murder, manslaughter, rape, assault with intent to kill, arson, burglary, and larceny. These soon became known as the seven *Index Crimes*. The Major Crimes Act was challenged in 1886 in *United States v. Kagama* but upheld by the U.S. Supreme Court. In March 1893, U.S. attorneys were provided original jurisdiction in representing all federal Indian wards of the United States.[25]

This policy clearly established the superior weight of the U.S. and white interest in Indian Country. An obvious problem with the law was that American Indians did not have equal weight before the courts, especially when cases were being adjudicated before a white judge and jury. It would be another thirty-nine years (1924) before American Indians were granted federal citizenship. Even then this did not guarantee equal legal status in local jurisdictions, notably those where American Indians did not enjoy state citizenship. This practice continued until the Eisenhower administration and the imposition of Public Law 280 unilaterally (without tribal consent or input), allocating certain states primary legal authority in Indian Country existing within their boundaries. Clearly, the imposition of white-dominated law enforcement in Indian Country set the stage for *allotment* and the end of Indian Territory and other land areas set aside specifically for American Indians through treaties [26]

J. Edgar Hoover, the former head of the FBI, used the Major Crimes Act to expand the authority of the FBI throughout the United States. The *Index Crimes* provided the basis for federal data collection, presented in the Department of Justice's annual *Uniform Crime Report: Crimes in the United States*, with FBI director Hoover taking credit as the author. Eventually, the seven major crimes were expanded to thirteen offenses with carnal knowledge of any female, not his wife not yet age sixteen (statutory rape); assault with the intent to commit rape; incest; assault with a dangerous weapon; assault resulting in serious bodily injury; and robbery—many of these mere refinements of the original seven Index Crimes. The Major Crimes Act allowed for the FBI to have jurisdiction in Indian Country, beginning with its origin in 1908. However, J. Edgar Hoover did little to publicize the presence of the FBI in Indian Country until it took on the American Indian Movement (AIM) in 1973 on the Pine Ridge Reservation in what became known as *Wounded Knee II*.[27]

Utley and Washburn summarized the post–Civil War *Indian problem*, noting the blatant government corruption and the hardships associated with forced reservation accommodation:

> Few government agencies lent themselves more readily to patronage politics and corruption than the Indian Bureau, and none achieved a worse reputation. Blanketing the nation, it afforded hundreds of government jobs in which the consequences of bad appointments fell chiefly on people who had little effective means of protest. . . . The bureau offered special opportunities for fraud. Annual appropriations of $7 million were customary. Most of this sum went for the purchase of food, clothing, and other goods for issue to the Indians. From factory to agency warehouse, corrupt alliances enriched government officials and suppliers and penalized the

Indians in both quantity and quality of issue. . . . The reservation system featured a concerted effort to destroy tribal organization and identity and emphasize the individual, to root out the beliefs and customs of the old life and substitute new ones from the white man's culture, and to carve up the reservations into individual homesteads, returning "surplus" lands to the public domain for white settlement. Coercion marked this program. The agent controlled rations and could cut off issue to the uncooperative. Indians working as police and judges backed his authority and sought to enforce a long list of "Indian offenses"—such . . . as feasts, dances, plural marriages, and the medical and religious practices of the medicine men.[28]

II

LAW AND ORDER IN THE
AMERICAS AND BEYOND, 1898–1946

· 5 ·

U.S. Colonial Expansionism in the Caribbean and Pacific

THE SPANISH AMERICAN WAR AND
SPANISH ACQUISITIONS IN THE CARIBBEAN

The *Monroe Doctrine*, while initially intended for policing the Americas, was expanded during the Spanish American War (1898) when the United States gained Spanish colonial possessions in the Pacific. The pretense for the war with Spain was an explosion on the USS *Maine* on February 15, 1898, that occurred in Havana, Cuba, resulting in the deaths of 260 sailors. Interestingly, the Indian War generals, notably Nelson A. Miles, and buffalo soldiers played a role in this short war that ended on December 10, 1898, with the Treaty of Paris. In addition to the acquisition of the Caribbean Island, Puerto Rico, and a foothold on Guantanamo Bay, Cuba, (GITMO) the United States also took command over the Spanish colonial holdings of Guam and the Philippines. This was considered the United States first foreign war, leading to the creation of the Veterans of Foreign Wars organization. The United States also held possession of Cuba for four years until its independence on May 20, 1902. Prior to its independence, the United States signed a treaty that provided the United States a ninety-nine-year lease on a navy base at GITMO. The 1901 Platt Amendment required U.S. approval for all foreign treaties made with Cuba. Fresh from its one-sided victory over Spain, the United States continued in its colonial acquisitions in the Pacific, including Hawaii (1898) and American Samoa (1899), as well as other islands such as the Carolina Islands and Wake Island, territories that played a significant role in the horrendous, colonial war with Japan (1941–1946). The Spanish-American War also catapulted Theodore Roosevelt into the limelight and presidency (1901–1909).

An extension of the Spanish-American War and a precursor to the Mexican Revolution were the aggressive actions of President Theodore Roosevelt, who fostered a paternalistic view of Latin America. In 1904, he proclaimed his Roosevelt Corollary, establishing the right of the United States to unilaterally intervene in the Caribbean and Central America in order to prevent foreign nations from interfering with America's interests in the region. This policy authorized the subsequent use of the United States Marine Corps (USMC) to act as a de facto international police force in protecting U.S. business interests in the Americas. These police actions resulted in U.S. interventions in Cuba, Nicaragua, Haiti, and the Dominican Republic before it was replaced with President Franklin D. Roosevelt's Good Neighbor policy in 1934.[1] Like the Indian Wars, policing the Monroe Doctrine south of the U.S. border during the late nineteenth and early twentieth centuries replenished the U.S. military with a host of new military leaders: General Smedley Butler and Lewis "Chesty" Puller for the USMC; and Army Generals Leonard Wood, John "Black Jack" Pershing, George Patton Jr., and Arthur and Douglas MacArthur.

PACIFIC ACQUISITIONS AND THE PHILIPPINE REBELLION

While winning the Spanish-American War was seen as a quick victory for the United States, acquisition of the Philippine Islands proved to be the opposite—a brutal sectarian war pitting America against both the Roman Catholic administration inherited from Spain and the Islamic population of Moroland (1899–19013). The United States had its earliest influence in Southeast Asia in the Philippines as part of the 1898 Treaty of Paris, making the Philippines its first foreign colonial outpost outside the American continent. The First Philippine War involved the United States and the Katipuneros, who declared Philippine independence on June 12, 1898.

The U.S. suppression of the revolutionary forces for independence continued until 1902. The Second Philippine War was fought in the Muslim south and was not resolved until 1913, when a civilian became the colonial governor. Deployed U.S. generals who had recently fought in the U.S. West used Indian war tactics for the destruction of entire villages (scorched-earth campaigns), the execution of surrendering prisoners, torture (including waterboarding), and internment (concentration camps) of civilians who were suspected of being sympathetic to the local revolutionaries. The U.S. forces had one of the most disproportionate enemy casualty rates recorded at the time, with fifteen Filipinos killed for every one wounded. The coverage of the atrocities in the world press, along with those associated with the British military in the Boer War in South Africa, led to the establishment of the

Hague Conventions of 1899 and 1907, which articulated the rules of international and military law and behavior, including the treatment of prisoners and civilians.

General Arthur MacArthur (U.S. Civil War, Indian Wars), his son, Douglas MacArthur (World War I, World War II, Korean conflict), Dwight D. Eisenhower (World II), and John J. Pershing (Spanish-American War, Punitive Expedition; World War I) all served in the Philippines during the U.S. colonial era. Arthur MacArthur served as military governor in 1900 along with his son Douglas, a second lieutenant who went on to become the field marshal of the Philippines. Dwight D. Eisenhower served as Douglas MacArthur's aide when Douglas served as field marshal, while John J. Pershing, commanding general of U.S. forces during World War I, served as the last military governor-general of Moro Province (1909–1913). During the First Philippine War, the United States forcefully confiscated property of the Roman Catholic Church, giving it to U.S. business interests. Even then, Catholicism thrived in the northern Philippines, while Islam continued to dominate the southern Islands, notably Mindanao.[2]

In his book, *The Savage Wars of Peace*, Max Boot noted:

> The Filipinos stubbornly resisted their new colonial masters, and though successive U.S. generals proclaimed victory at hand, American soldiers kept dying in ambushes, telegraph lines kept getting cut, and army convoys kept being attacked. Among the most stubborn of guerrilla commanders was General Vincente Lukban, scion of a rich family of mixed Chinese and Tagalog origin who directed resistance on Samar. Lukban's men had begun by executing all the Spanish clergy on the island and replacing them with native priests. Afterward they targeted not only Americans but also their collaborators, burying three *americanistas* alive, tying another to a tree and hacking him to bits. The Americans retaliated in kind. . . . It was not at all the kind of conflict that soldiers like. This dirty war offered no heroic charges, no brilliant maneuvers, no dazzling victories. Just the daily frustrations of battling an unseen foe in the dense, almost impassable jungle.[3]

UNITED STATES AND THE MEXICAN REVOLUTION: PRELUDE TO THE MODERN U.S. MILITARY

Manifest Destiny and U.S. Expansionism at Mexico's Expense

The genesis of contemporary animosities and anti-Hispanic sentiments in the United States has its origin in the early years of the republic when American citizens heeded Spanish-Mexico's call for settlers in its northern territories.

American settlers took advantage of the empresario land grants offered by the Spanish colonial government in Mexico. Moses Austin, formerly from Missouri, was granted the first empresario permit on January 17, 1821, allowing him to settle three hundred families in what is now Texas. Two major events in the United States precipitated this southern migration—the economic panic of 1819 and the increasing cost of U.S. public lands, especially for slaveholders. Empresario grantees became de facto lord or governor of their land grant, giving them considerable authority over their subgrantee settlers. Austin's land grant contract allowed 23,000 acres per one hundred settler families. These land grants were interspersed with other elements of the Spanish frontier community, which consisted of Roman Catholic missions, presidios (frontier garrisons), ranchos, farms, towns, and villages. The empresario grants in Coahuila and Tejas (what became Texas) continued following the establishment of the Republic of Mexico on September 27, 1821, with the largest grantees being Austin, Green de Witt, and Haden Edwards.[4]

Under the Imperial Colonization Law, immigrants (settlers) were compelled to be of the Roman Catholic faith or to convert to Catholicism in order to receive land within the empresario. Mexico held the deed to the settler's land for six years. Title transfer was contingent upon all conditions being met. These conditions were enacted by the Legislature of Coahuila and Texas on March 24, 1825, setting the maximum limit of a single empresario to eight hundred families. The conditions for settlement were:

- establish boundaries (survey) of the proposed colony;
- respect the legal titles already existing in the proposed colony;
- settle the required number of families within six years;
- settle Catholic families of good moral character;
- prohibit criminals;
- organize and command a national militia force (Texas Rangers);
- make all official and public communications in Spanish; and
- after April 6, 1830, an immigrant ban from adjoining countries, notably the United States.

One of the major factors leading to the Texas rebellion was the Republic of Mexico's 1821 antislavery law. This led to the first attempt at independence known as the Fredonian Rebellion in 1826. The Edwards brothers (Haden and Benjamin) were awarded empresarial grants in April 1825, entitling them to settle up to eight hundred families in the Nacogdoches area north of the Austin grant. Their authoritarian methods and hostility to local residents led to a federal investigation. In reaction, the Edwards brothers raised their own militia and declared the region independent of Mexico, to be known as the

Republic of Fredonia. Their short-lived rebellion and independence ended on January 31, 1827, with the remaining rebels fleeing back to the United States.

The Edwards brothers set the stage for the rest of the American immigrants with slaveholding leading to continued unrest and the eventual war of succession leading to the Republic of Texas, a country with strong links to the U.S. Southern slave states. *"Remember the Alamo"* was the war cry of Americans who abandoned the United States and swore allegiance to first Spain, then Mexico, in order to get large tracts of land, who then rebelled in defense of slavery. The Alamo is a shrine to deceit and slavery and not to high Christian values attributed to it today. Following Texas's independence, the republic struggled for recognition and acceptance for nine years, while all along begging for its annexation to the United States. Once Texas became part of the United States in 1845, slavery exploded, increasing from 30,000 in 1845 to 182,566 in 1860. Slavery was a critical issue at the time of the Mexican War (1846–1848). President Polk saw the war with Mexico as an opportunity to again greatly expand the United States, doing this under the mandate of both Manifest Destiny and the Monroe Doctrine. Polk's war with Mexico was not universally supported by the U.S. Congress, and the Mexican War spelled the demise of the Whig Party and the emergence of the Republican Party.[5]

The Texas Rangers' Ethnic War of Terror

The law enforcement agency historically associated with U.S.-Mexico border jurisdiction is the Texas Rangers. Long lauded as a heroic force for justice in myth and in the media, a closer examination paints a different picture. Contemporary analysis portrays the Texas Rangers as a cruel, extermination squad, ridding Texas of Hispanics, Mestizos, and American Indians. The Texas Rangers trace their origins to 1821 and the Austin empresario in Mexico, where ten men were hired as rangers with the mandate of protecting Anglo settlers from Indian raids. The rangers were the authorized militia stipulated in the empresario contract. During the Texas Revolution, the rangers were expanded into companies of fifty-six men, each under the control of a major. On October 17, 1835, the rangers became the republic's police force until November when the army, the rangers, and other militias fell under the command of the commander in chief. While placed under the authority of the new army, the Texas Rangers were an irregular force, and they were not involved in any of the major battles. Their duties during the revolution were to continue protecting the Anglo settlers from Indian attacks.[6]

What distinguished the Texas Rangers from both the regular military (army and navy) and other militias was its adoption of the Colt revolver, the first repeating firearm at the time. The Republic of Texas became the proving grounds for this innovative weapon. Samuel Colt of Hartford, Connecticut, patented his repeating handgun in 1836—the same year Texas declared its independence from Mexico. Texas was Colt's first customer, ordering 180, .36-caliber five-shot revolvers for its navy in 1839. Texas Rangers, on the other hand, had been ordering them individually since they first became available in 1837. Once President Sam Houston disbanded the Texas navy, the Paterson Colts were reassigned to the Texas Rangers. Consequently, with the advent of the Paterson Colt repeating single-action revolver, the Texas Rangers could fire as long as they could fan the hammer which rotated the cylinder. Texas Rangers often carried three or more revolvers with loaded extra cylinders, increasing their firepower and greatly enhancing their image as a deadly force. Following annexation, the Texas Rangers became the de facto Texas state police. And during the Mexican War, the Texas Rangers again proved the superiority of the Colt revolver, even providing practical adaptations leading to the six-shooter and a protective trigger guard. The Colt revolver went on to become the most popular sidearm of both sides of the Civil War—thanks to its endorsement by the Texas Rangers.[7]

Unfortunately, as is still evident today, the combination of racist white-elitism and superior firepower do not promote the tenet of *justice for all.* During the Mexican War, the Texas Rangers exhibited racist and ruthless atrocities branding them the title, *diablos Tejanos*—Texan devils. C. H. Harris noted, "From the Rangers' point of view, the war was a splendid opportunity to kill Mexicans and get paid for it."[8] These killings and abuses were rampant, prompting General Zachary Taylor to threaten to imprison an entire Ranger unit. Even then, the Texas Rangers used the Mexican War as license to continue with their blatant violations of international law, conducting cross-border raids well after the war's end, including the 1855 destruction of the Mexican town, Piedras Negras.[9]

The Texas Rangers reign of terror resurfaced in 1874 when old pro-confederate Democrats again took over the mantle of power in Texas. The Texas Rangers, the military, militias, and outlaws were now armed with a more advanced form of the "six-shooter"—one that used cartridges (bullets). The development of the self-contained (integrated) cartridge (bullet) further enhanced the firepower of repeating weapons, both rifles and pistols, and allowed for more rapid-firing, breech-loading, single-shot rifles such as the Sharps military carbine, widely used during the Indian Wars. Prior to the self-contained cartridge, both long guns (smooth bore or rifles) and handguns (including the revolver) required the additional step of activating the "cap-and-ball" sequence, whereby black powder had to be packed into each cylinder (muzzle loading) along with the installation of a firing cap at the hammer. The early cartridges had the powder held together in a cardboard bullet that was either rim- or center-fired by a firing pin that ignited the percussion cap. The French were the first to invent the cartridge, which soon evolved from a cardboard to a metallic shell (shotgun shells still use the cardboard format). Indeed, the .22 caliber percussion cap soon became a bullet in itself, with the .22 long rifle one of the most popular calibers today. The advent of the bullet led to new adaptations to the revolver, notably the Colt single action army revolver, introduced in 1873. The civilian model of this .45 caliber "six-shooter" was commonly known as the *Peacemaker*. It was used by both the military during the Indian War and by law enforcement, notably U.S. Marshals and county sheriffs, as well as being popular with outlaws that roamed the West during the post–Civil War era up until the First World War.

For the rest of the nineteenth century, the Texas Rangers served as the private police for the governor of Texas and Anglo ranchers. The Texas Rangers had carte blanche when it came to maintaining Anglo financial interests in the area, via their Special Forces and Frontier Battalion. Interestingly, "special forces" still connote military and police units that operate with a license to kill outside the restrictions of either military or civil justice. Clearly, the Texas Rangers were to Mexicans, Mestizos, and American Indians what the Ku Klux Klan was to blacks, until they were brought under the authority of the Texas Department of Public Service in 1935. Then, the Texas Rangers could no longer be used merely as the private police force for the governor of Texas. From 1935 on, they were accountable to the general statutes applicable to all law enforcement agencies within the state.[10]

UNITED STATES AND MEXICO:
THE EMERGING BORDERLANDS

An important chapter in United States-Mexico relations occurred during the latter part of the nineteenth century and early twentieth century. During this time the United States and Mexico witnessed an era of cooperation during the reign of Porfirio Diaz, a period from 1872 to 1911 known as *The Porfiriato*. Diaz, a general under President Juarez, the first indigenous Mexican leader, during the rebellion against the European-installed dictator, Archduke Maximilian, made a name for himself as leader of the May 5, 1862, defeat of Napoleon III's troops at Puebla. This became a major event in Mexican history and folklore, celebrated to the present as *Cinco de Mayo*. Diaz was also involved in the final defeat and execution of Maximilian in 1867. Diaz rose to the presidency following Juarez's death, confirmed as president in 1877.

Diaz soon became one of the United States' favorite despots, maintaining the Monroe Doctrine and keeping European and other outside interests out of Mexico, while at the same time providing an environment favorable to U.S. business and political interest. Specifically, President Diaz opened up Mexican resources (copper, oil, and the like) and markets for U.S. capitalist endeavors. During the Porfiriato era, Mexico had the semblance of political stability and economic growth. The national debt was paid and the treasury had some 70 million dollars cash reserves at the end of his tenure in 1911. But this prosperity for big business and the upper classes came at a price, one that eventually led to the revolution of 1910. The indigenous Indians and poor lower-class Mestizos suffered under the classist and racist policies of the Porfiriato era. Ironically, it was these same practices that endeared Diaz to U.S. political and business interests.

Ironically, a newly emerging middle class surfaced during the Porfiriato era, comprised of clerks, teachers, small businessmen, and legal and clinical/health practitioners. While creating a buffer between the elite cientificos and the large peon/peasant class, the middle class, by virtue of its limited influence, also felt marginalized by the Diaz government. The prosperity of the Diaz regime did little to increase the quality of life for the rank-and-file Mexican workers and their families. Even in U.S.-operated enterprises, Mexican workers earned less than workers from the United States who were employed at the same facility. American miners were paid five dollars for a ten-hour day at the Mexican mine while Mexican workers were paid one-dollar-fifty for the same work. The double-wage system led to strikes in mines, and the bloody suppression of the Mexican workers only fueled discontent. Borrowing techniques from the Texas Rangers, the Mexican strikers were brutally suppressed by government goon squads called *rurales*. Diaz even allowed U.S. businesses to bring in their own strike breakers. U.S. police and vigilante militias were employed in Cananea mining strike of 1906 under the pretense of protecting U.S. lives and property:

The first flashpoint was the mining town of Cananea in Sonora, which was, in effect, a U.S. company town belonging to the Cananea Consolidated Copper Company. A protest over wage differentials between the 6,000 Mexican employees and their 600 U.S. counterparts led to a riot in which company guards fired on the workforce. The excessive use of force was compounded by the permission granted to the company by the governor of Sonora, Rafeal Izabal, to allow 260 Arizona rangers to cross the border to restore order, in what was widely criticized at the time as an open violation of Mexican sovereignty.[11]

The ensuing two-day battle left more than twenty Mexican minors and six company men dead. A year later, strikes at Mexico's textile mills were also brutally suppressed by troops and rurales, resulting in striking workers being killed and five union leaders executed. These actions merely served to solidify the solidarity of the workers, including female workers. Textile strikes in Puebla, Tlaxcala, and Veracruz were met with harsh treatment by the government and business owners. Hence, law and order during the Diaz era came at a high price. Civil liberties and rights were suppressed for the majority of Mexicans, especially those of Indian descent. This double-standard of justice followed public sentiments in the United States—that indigenous and poor lower-class people of color were biologically, racially, and morally inferior and, therefore, not eligible for judicial standards offered the privileged elites.[12]

Following three decades of abuse, Mexicans revolted over the exploitations of Mestizos and Indian peasants as well as the restrictions placed upon the new emerging middle class. The Maderista Revolt against the Diaz regime was launched on November 10, 1910, by Francisco Madero, a member of the privileged elite. Madero ran against Diaz in the 1910 elections, resulting in his arrest. He escaped from jail and fled to the United States. On November 10, 1910, Madero and his forces crossed into Mexico from the United States at Piedras Negras in the state of Coahuila, initiating the Mexican Revolution. Two popular revolutionary leaders quickly emerged, igniting popular support for the overthrow of Diaz—Emiliano (Emilio) Zapata, an indigenous Mexican, and Francisco "Pancho" Villa (Doroteo Arango), a Mestizo. In May 1911, Madero's forces took Ciudad Juarez across from El Paso, Texas, leading to the Treaty of Juarez where Diaz agreed to resign and leave the country to live in exile in France. The end of the Porfiriato era did little to quell the divisions within Mexican society. Madero succeeded Diaz as president—only for him and his vice president, Pino Suarez, to be assassinated in a coup d'etat led by General Victoriano Huerta in 1913. Huerta, in turn, was forced into exile in 1914, resulting in the revolution split between the forces of Generals Carranza and Obregon (Constitutionalists) versus the Conventionists and the generals of the popular forces—Emilio Zapata and Pancho Villa. The Constitutionalists represented a strong Mexican federal government free of U.S. controls, while the Conventionists also fought for an autonomous country, but with a redistribution of the land in the hands of the wealthy elite and support for the aboriginal communal village (Pueblo) system. Zapata was assassinated under orders of General Pablo Gonzalez while Pancho Villa's forces raised havoc in northern Mexico, finally giving his support to President-elect Adolfo deal Huerta in 1920.[13]

WILSON'S CRITIQUE

A consequence of the Mexican Revolution was the migration of hundreds of thousands of Mexicans to the United States. It is estimated that nearly 900,000 immigrants crossed the border between 1910 and 1920. Fearful of border conditions during the Revolution, President William Howard Taft ended the U.S. long-held nonintervention policy with the Diaz regime, instead creating a Maneuver Division of (black) buffalo soldiers to patrol the U.S. side of the border, beginning in March 1911. These soldiers were stationed in San Antonio, Texas, as a readiness force to counter any cross-border attacks. Taft's successor, President Woodrow Wilson, took an even more active military approach toward border security and Mexican politics with his paternalistic *Wilsonism Critique*. Wilson's intent was to side with the Constitutionalists because he felt they would best protect U.S. oil, mining, and manufacturing interests in Mexico. When all parties in the Revolution objected to Wilson's plan, the United States reacted by using gunboat diplomacy with military intervention into Mexico in April 1914, occupying Veracruz until November, again raising the U.S. flag over Mexico. The U.S. Marine Corps seven-month occupation resulted in four hundred Mexican casualties compared to four U.S. deaths. President Wilson also supported General Pancho Villa in the early stages of the Mexican Revolution.

General Villa's January 1914 attack on Ojinaga forced Huerta's forces to cross over into the United States and surrender to the army instead of chancing their fate with Villa's army. Now the United States was responsible for the care of some 5,000 Mexican combatants, as well as 1,000 women, 500 children, and 3,000 horses and mules. Huerta's forces were initially held at Fort Bliss in El Paso, Texas, and later transferred to Fort Wingate, New Mexico, near the Navajo Reservation. The victory of Ojinaga gave Villa's forces control of northern Mexico, including the Mexican-U.S. border. Both General Hugh L. Scott and Secretary of State William Jennings Bryant became confidants and strong supporters of General Villa. With northern Mexico secure, President Wilson felt safe in sending marines to Veracruz as a message to Germany to cease interfering in Mexico by lending support to Huerta's forces.[14]

It was General Villa's break with Carranza that eventually led to this falling out with the United States. Now Villa's forces were fighting the Carranzitas under General Alvaro Obregon who had U.S. support. The United States first alienated Villa in April 1915 in the battle of Matamoros when the United States allowed the Carranzitas to cross the border into the protection of Brownsville, Texas, while at the same time stopping Villa's forces at the border. Here, Brigadier General "Black Jack" Pershing and his buffalo soldiers played a major role in selectively securing the U.S.-Mexico border. President Wilson's recognition of Carranza over Villa was probably an effort to end the internal strife within Mexico, which many in the United States felt was being fueled by Germany in its effort to draw the U.S. military into the Mexican Revolution, thereby keeping them out of the ongoing European war (1914–1918). Evidence of German motives came later with the Zimmerman Communiqué of May 3, 1916. Most likely Germany saw General Villa's

March 9, 1916, raid on the U.S. Army base in Columbus, New Mexico, as the likely catalyst for full U.S. intervention into the Mexican Revolution. The resulting Punitive Expedition actually had the opposite effect, mobilizing the National Guard for the first time and transforming the U.S. military from the nineteenth-century horse tactics to a mechanized force in the form of the highly successful Rainbow Division led by Brigadier General Douglas MacArthur under the overall leadership of the Army Chief of Staff General "Black Jack" Pershing. Harsh reactions to the *Plan de San Diego* by the United States, notably the actions of Texas Rangers, also aggravated the situation, contributing to General Villa's cross-border attack on a U.S. military base.[15]

PLAN DE SAN DIEGO

U.S. intervention and interference in the Mexican Revolution helped precipitate the *Plan de San Diego*, an ill-fated manifesto initiated January 16, 1915, by a small radical element of Mexican revolutionaries calling for a bloody revolt by both Mexicans and Mexican Americans in order to regain territory lost to the United States since 1845 with the annexation of Texas. The plan was ill-fated in that it did not gain support from either the major groups involved in the Mexican Revolution—Constitutionalists or the Coventionists—although there is some evidence that followers of General Carranza were tacitly involved. Those involved made cross-border raids during its year-long existence, resulting in twenty-one U.S. deaths. Also contributing to the animus of the time was President Wilson's strong endorsement of the widely disseminated propaganda film, *The Birth of a Nation*, in 1915. This movie justified the brutal suppression of blacks by the Ku Klux Klan, with the KKK portrayed as the protectors of Aryan white supremacy, further widening the divide between American whites and people of color with the depiction of blacks, American Indians, Mexicans, Catholics, and Jews as being lesser humans. Accordingly, a vicious race war emerged along the Rio Grande Valley in south Texas, resulting in the murder of more than three hundred Mexicans or Mexican Americans, many summarily executed by the Texas Rangers.[16]

The brutality of the Texas Rangers is depicted in Benjamin Heber Johnson's book, *Revolution in Texas*:

> Tejanos (Texas Hispanics) paid a high price for the newfound unity of Anglo south Texans. . . . Those suspected of joining or supporting the raiders constituted the most obvious of targets, as they had from the uprising's beginning. Ethnic Mexican suspects were lynched after nearly every major raid in 1915. Shortly after the attack on the Norias ranch house, for example, unknown assailants killed three Tejanos . . . presumably for

suspicion of aiding or participating in the attack. The Texas Rangers who had arrived after the fight might have been responsible. In any event, the Rangers' actions encouraged such measures: the next morning, they posed with their lassos around the three corpses, and the picture soon circulated as a postcard.[17]

U.S. soldiers, who were not permitted by military law to execute their prisoners, often turned Mexican or Tejanos suspects over to local sheriffs or the Texas Rangers, knowing that they would execute them without a trial. In a battle on September 28, 1915, Texas Rangers battled with raiders near Ebenoza, in Hidalgo County, taking more than a dozen prisoners who they summarily hanged, leaving the bodies to rot with empty beer bottles stuck in their mouths. Relatives did not dare to take the bodies down for burial, fearing that they could be targeted for death themselves by the local sheriff or the Texas Rangers. Many felt that the death count of three hundred was low with a local paper, *Regeneracion*, placing the count closer to 1,500. U.S. Army Scout Virgil Lott noted that hundreds of Mexicans were killed and unaccounted for because their bodies were concealed in the thick underbrush and many deaths were unreported.[18]

The Texas Rangers' reign of terror in south Texas generated a pervasive fear, resulting in many Mexican-Americans, those who lived in the region for generations prior to U.S. acquisition of Texas, fleeing across the border to Mexico never to return, much to the glee of the large Anglo landowners. Indeed, Robert Kleberg, manager of the King Ranch, called for martial law in south Texas, with Mexicans and Tejanos rounded up and placed into concentration camps. Kleberg further suggested: "When a certain man [who] is discovered to have taken part in a bandits' raid is captured or killed in such a raid, his brothers, half-brothers, and brothers-in-law are assumed to be guilty and are immediately arrested or killed."[19] It should be noted that the King Ranch's 1.25 million acres were stolen from Mexicans and Tejanos following the 1848 Treaty of Guadalupe Hidalgo, a process legitimized by Anglo judges and courts. Many of the former owners were then placed into servitude as sharecroppers on their own land. Toward this end, the Texas Rangers acted as the King Ranch's private police force.[20] The remaining Tejanos organized themselves, giving rise to Mexican American political influence under the League of United Latin American Citizens (LULSC).

PANCHO VILLA'S ATTACK ON THE UNITED STATES

The massacre of Mexicans and Mexican Americans (Tejanos) by the Texas Rangers and local Anglo sheriffs in south Texas and across the border into northern Mexico had a negative impact on the warring parties involved in the

Mexican Revolution. The harsh treatment of Hispanics following the ill-fated Plan de San Diego soured General Villa, the leading general in northern Mexico, leading to his own cross-border raids into the United States. The most notable of these raids being the 1916 raid on the U.S. Army base at Columbus, New Mexico. General Villa, long alienated from the Carranza faction, was also upset over President Wilson's formal recognition of Carranza as the legitimate leader of Mexico. Villa felt that this arrangement was a return to the old Diaz era.

Two months prior to the raid, on January 11, 1916, Villa's troops stopped a train at Santa Ysable, Chihuahua, Mexico, executing seventeen Texas mining engineers who were invited by President Carranza to reopen the Cusihuiriachic mines in Mexico. In retaliation, U.S. vigilantes killed more than one hundred Mexican Americans in the United States. On March 9, 1916, General Villa and 485 troops made an early morning raid on the 13th U.S. Cavalry at Camp Furlong on the outskirts of Columbus, New Mexico, former Mexican territory until the 1853 Gadsden Purchase. The raid had a dramatic effect on U.S.-Mexican relations because of its audacity and not so much on its effectiveness. U.S. casualties consisted of only ten military and eight civilians killed. The aftermath of the raid had far more devastating consequences for Mexicans and Mexican Americans. James Hurst, in his book on the Villista prisoners, indicates that abuses occurred immediately following the raid, with U.S. soldiers indiscriminately killing anyone who looked Mexican during the so-called hot pursuit led by Major Frank Tompkins's forces. President Wilson's reaction was one of intervention into Mexico under the authority inherent in the Monroe Doctrine.[21]

President Wilson unilaterally deployed some 12,000 army troops under the command of Brigadier General John J. (Black Jack) Pershing in an eleven-month Punitive Expedition. He federalized two state army National Guard units for this deployment—New Mexico and Massachusetts. This represented a new era of policing in America given that the Posse Comitatus Act restricted federal use of the National Guard to Acts of Insurrection. These two National Guard units remained on the U.S. side of the border during the Punitive Expedition, providing a supportive function. However, this use of the National Guard greatly aided in the rapid expansion of the U.S. Army for deployment during the First World War via the Defense Act of 1916. This also put an end to volunteer regiments, like the Rough Riders during the Spanish American War, which were often poorly trained and equipped and holding allegiance only to their politically appointed leaders.[22]

Criticism of Wilson's intervention into Mexico, coupled with the U.S. entry into the First World War, led to the abrupt end of the Punitive Expedition. The U.S. reaction to the New Mexico raid elevated General Villa to that of a national hero, along with his martyred counterpart Emiliano Zapata, forcing the Carranza administration to include many of the Conventionists planks into the 1917 Mexican Constitution such as compulsory, secular, free public primary education (six grades) and for land reform, effectively ending the large landholdings by both Mexicans and foreign interests. The new Constitution also restored the *ejido* communal land system enacted under President Juarez in 1856, an eight-hour workday, and laws prohibiting child labor. The United States, under President Coolidge (1923–1929), finally ended its attempts to interfere with Mexican elections, agreeing to recognize the duly elected Mexican administrations regardless how distasteful to U.S. business interest—thus ending the border wars of the early twentieth century.[23]

PUNITIVE EXPEDITION'S AFTERMATH: CRUEL AND UNUSUAL RETRIBUTION

While the Punitive Expedition brought considerable hardships to Mexicans along both sides of the *Borderlands*, it did not accomplish its intended mission—the capture of General Pancho Villa. Instead, the retaliatory invasion into Mexico raised havoc among the rural, poor Mexicans residing in northern Mexico. Pershing's forces also clashed with Carranza's government forces in the town of Carrizal, resulting in the deaths of dozens of Mexicans, more than the U.S. casualties from the Columbus raid. Anticipating another full-fledged war with Mexico, the U.S. Congress passed the National Defense Act in June 1916, authorizing doubling the size of the U.S. Army and authorizing the federalization of the National Guard. Following passage of the act, President Wilson authorized the federal activation of some 75,000 National Guardsmen to be stationed along the U.S.-Mexico border.

Mexico showed considerable restraint during these trying times by not abusing U.S. POWs despite the harsh treatment afforded the Mexican soldiers captured in the Columbus raid. Seven Mexican soldiers were captured during the Columbus raid and were tried in civilian courts, resulting in the death penalty by hanging. Racial sentiments played a major role here—much like it did in south Texas during the Plan de San Diego retaliation by the Texas Rangers and local sheriff's departments. Anti-Mexican sentiments ran high among Anglo-Americans in New Mexico, in the southern part bordering Mexico, which was part of Mexico until 1853, especially in Deming, just north of Columbus. The captured Mexican prisoners were not treated as soldiers, following the Geneva Convention; instead, they were labeled *bandits*, excluding them from military justice. Another nineteen soldiers were captured by General Pershing's troops in Mexico and were also charged with murder and tried in U.S. civilian courts. Six Mexican soldiers were executed (hanged) in June 1916 while six of the seven soldiers captured in Columbus eventually received full, complete, and unconditional pardons from the governor of New

Mexico in November 1920. His decision was influenced by the 1907 Hague Convention regarding the laws and customs of war on land. These rules were adopted in response to the brutal treatment of the Boer (Dutch) by the British in South Africa during the Boar War (1899–1902) and the atrocities attributed to U.S. troops in the Philippines in the aftermath of the Spanish-American War. Despite the governor's pardon, these same prisoners were then arrested by Luna County, where Deming is the county seat, and again charged with murder. They were easily convicted and sentenced to prison terms in violation of the U.S. constitutionals guarantee against double jeopardy.[24]

This disdain for justice was just a continuation of abuses extending back to the war with Mexico when U.S. occupation forces arrested Mexicans and Indians for rebelling against their occupation of northern New Mexico, which was still a part of Mexico. James Crutchfield addressed this injustice in his book on the New Mexican and Indian insurrection of 1847 when non-Anglo combatants were accused of treason against America while fighting on their own land. Tried by Anglo occupiers in April 1847, seventeen locals were hanged on April 9 and 10 and May 7. Crutchfield noted the U.S. Army's presence at the execution:

> The American army took no chances. In one hanging incident . . . soldiers positioned themselves on the roof of the jail and aimed the mountain howitzer that had been used in the battle at Taos Pueblo at the gallows. A soldier stood erect over the fuse with a lighted match in his hand. Two hundred and thirty American soldiers marched down the street in front of the jail in a show of force. The sheriff and his assistant placed the nooses around the prisoner's necks as officials balanced the men off a board that stretched across a wagon drawn by two mules.[25]

Questions were raised over the sentencing of Mexican nationals and indigenous Indians for treason while in defense of their own land during a war incited by the United States for the deliberate purpose of westward expansion. President Polk had to admit that perhaps conviction for treason against the United States was not the appropriate sentence. This belated admission came forth prior to a ruling by the U.S. Supreme Court in *Fleming v. Page* that also resulted from U.S. haste to claim war-occupations as U.S. territory. *Fleming v. Page* addressed U.S. occupation of Tampico in the Mexican State of Tamaulipas during the Mexican War. Although decided in 1850, the incident extended to the 1847 occupation of Tampico and the imposition of U.S. laws by the military commander relevant to port activities. The high court ruled that U.S. laws had no bearings on the activities of the port of Tampico in that it was a foreign port and that occupation did not signify U.S. ownership. The U.S. Supreme Court noted that acquisition of territory does not allow the United States to subjugate the enemy's country. This can only be done via treaty. While the Mexican State of Tamaulipas did not become part of the United States following the 1848 Treaty of Guadalupe-Hidalgo, portions of New Mexico did. Even then, the 1848 treaty specified the Spanish-Mexican recognition of the autonomy of the Pueblo Indian tribe's land grants, including that of the Taos Pueblo implicated in the 1847 uprising.[26] Clearly, this decision came too late for those executed defending their homeland.

Reinforcing WASP White Supremacy

Eugenics and Prohibition

EUGENICS AND WHITE SUPREMACY—
A SAD TWENTIETH-CENTURY LEGACY

The Puritan's quest for white supremacy continued into the twentieth century now shrouded in secular terminology; calling itself the American Eugenics Movement. This movement gained favor at the turn of the twentieth century, coinciding with the massive non-Protestant migration of southern and eastern Europeans and the massive migration north for freedmen. The American Eugenics Movement was hatched in the "White Elitist Colleges and Universities" (WECUs, aka Ivy League and affiliates) and promoted by both leading academics and business leaders. Academics followed the racist tenets of Woodrow Wilson, who saw people of color as inferior to whites, hence secondary citizens whose best lot in life was that of tenant fieldworkers or servants to whites such as train porters. Indeed, academia played a significant role in ensuring the "separate but equal" social system of the time—a social phenomenon that transcended the Jim Crow South. By creating stratified educational facilities, a social-class and racial-caste system was institutionalized, hence creating a self-fulfilling prophecy that justified not only white supremacy but also racial segregation and allowing for further laws and for social engineering like eugenics and sterilization.

The 1862 Morrill Act established the land-grant state university system in the United States. These colleges and universities were designed to augment the WECUs by providing agricultural and mechanical instruction needed for America during the post–Civil War era as it transformed itself from substance farming to an industrial and manufacturing society. The earlier Protestant-based elitist facilities made a clear distinction between their austere elitist position vis-à-vis these newly created state colleges and universities. Essentially, the state universities were designed mainly for whites who had ability but not the inherited social class required for the WECUs. Both the Ivy League and emerging state university systems were segregated by gender. This new educational stratification defined the class structure within racial categories (caste system). Clearly, blacks, American Indians, Hispanics, and Asians had parallel, but independent, class structures just like Anglos.

While Texas established its black college at Prairie View on the same day it created Texas A&M University at College Station in 1876, other black state universities were authorized under the second Morrill Act in 1890, leading to a network of facilities of higher education known as *Historical Black Colleges and Universities* (HBCUs). As a result of the second Morrill Act, seventeen Southern states established separate black agricultural and mechanical colleges and universities. Ironically, this effort to improve the quality of black higher education was an outgrowth of Jim Crow segregation, which the United States Supreme Court validated in its 1896 *Plessy v. Ferguson* decision. Here, the nativism and populist movements joined forces in their effort to curtail black integration into the majority American society. W. E. B. Du Bois, the leading black social critic of this period, warned that Jim Crow segregation was being legitimized at all levels of society and that the segregated education system was the major vehicle for enforcing black ignorance as well as keeping blacks in their place as sharecroppers and low-level factory workers. Franklin Frazier, on the other hand, described the black social stratification system in his work, *Black Bourgeois.*[1]

The *American Heritage Dictionary* defines *eugenics* as the study of hereditary improvement of the human race by controlled selective breeding. The term itself stems back to the late nineteenth century with the British psychologist Sir Francis Galton, cousin of Charles Darwin, who coined the term and proposed the science of eugenics in order to produce a highly gifted race. Galton's theory of *social Darwinism* and the creation of a superior race were widely supported in the United States during the early twentieth century.[2] Indeed, the concept of white supremacy in the United States dates back to its early history with the long-held concept of Manifest Destiny—that belief that white males were predestined by God to be superior to all others. Nazi Germany later followed the United States in supporting the social engineering of a superior Aryan race. Clearly eugenics and racism are closely associated, providing a seemingly objective rationale for social discrimination along lines of race, class, caste, and even gender. It fostered such practices as apartheid, ethnic cleansing, and genocide (a concept coined in 1947 following the Nazi war trials).

Blacks, American Indians, Asians, and other nonwhites, and even non-Protestant whites, as well as those mentally deficient, were quickly labeled as being *genetically defective* and needed to be cleansed from the U.S. population.

In Nazi-influenced Europe, the classes of human defectives included Jews, Gypsies (Roma), nonwhites, and even whites not considered the genetic equivalent of northern and western European Caucasians. The Nazi atrocities were widely publicized, due largely to the extremes taken in the *final solution*. What is less known is America's well-kept secret of sterilization, institutionalization, and execution of those deemed genetically inferior to the dominant white society. The white elite in U.S. society found a champion for their cause at Stanford University with psychologist Lewis M. Terman and his revision of the original 1908 French Binet-Simon IQ test.[3]

Lewis Terman was influenced by his mentor Francis Galton, who was considered to be the founder of scientific psychology and set the stage for the use of psychological tests to implement the dictates of social Darwinism. Eugenics, implemented partly through involuntary sterilization, was seen as the means for achieving successful social Darwinism in the United States. The goal of eugenics was the improvement of the human race through the elimination of what were considered to be defective gene pools. It was Terman who provided the seemingly objective measure of determining who was unfit. Terman was confident that his version of the IQ test would accurately weed out the genetically deficient members of American society, what he termed the serious deviant. His solution included plans for eliminating these genetic inferiors through institutionalization and sterilization. Terman proposed his 1916 IQ test, the *Stanford Binet*, as a scientific tool for determining those in society that needed to be controlled and eventually taken out of the gene pool. What was not factored into this test was the racial and class bias of his sample—the upper-middle-class white faculty and families at Stanford University.[4]

By 1926, twenty-three states had enacted compulsory sterilization laws, and this practice was condoned by the U.S. Supreme Court in 1927 in its decision, *Buck v. Bell*, based mainly on Terman's contention:

> It is safe to predict that in the near future intelligence tests will bring tens of thousands of these high-grade defectives under the surveillance and protection of society. This will ultimately result in curtailing the reproduction of feeble-mindedness and in the elimination of an enormous amount of crime, pauperism, and industrial inefficiency. . . . Not all criminals are feeble-minded, but all feeble-minded are at least potential criminals. That every feeble-minded woman is a potential prostitute would hardly be disputed by anyone. . . . Considering the tremendous cost of vice and crime . . . it is evident that psychological testing has found here one of its richest applications.[5]

Of course, this assessment did not take into account the poor educational opportunities afforded blacks and other minorities in U.S. society under de jure and de facto segregation, hence further fueling existing discriminatory practices that not only produced substandard education but a biased measurement of someone's true intelligence. Also, the stigma associated with being genetically inferior led to harsh solutions for those falling into this category, even if their only *societal offense* was procreation. It is estimated that over 60,000 individuals, mainly African American and American Indian females, were involuntarily sterilized in thirty-five states at both the state and federal levels (Indian Country is federally administered) until this practice was challenged during the Civil Rights era of the 1960s when it was disclosed that those most likely to be subjected to this practice were poor minorities. While California recorded the most cases (20,000), North Carolina continued this practice until 1974. While the practice of compulsory sterilization began to wane in the late 1960s and early 1970s, the practice of ethnic and genetic cleansing continued in U.S. society through other avenues, most notably incarceration and the death penalty.[6] Barnes and Teeters noted that sterilization had its roots within the criminal justice system, with the first operation being performed in 1899 at the Jeffersonville Indiana Reformatory.[7] The horrors of Nazi eugenics during World War II played a role in its demise in the United States.

Nonetheless, the eugenics movement in the United States clearly contributed to the general stereotype of racial inferiority, a status often based on flawed testing, and the need to control these "inferior" human beings. The controversy over the stigma associated with psychological testing came to a head in 1972, as sterilization was being discredited. This controversy came to a head in California, the state that led the country in forced sterilizations. The issue involved the use of standardized tests to label students within the California public schools as being mentally deficient, a stigma that followed them throughout their lives. It is interesting that Terman and his Stanford–Binet test played a significant role in this controversy. The legal case, *Larry P. v. Riles*, began in 1972 about the same time that forced sterilization was coming to an end and school integration was being forcefully implemented throughout the United States. Part of the problem with this unfounded stereotype was that it fostered the association between racial inferiority, mental deficiency, and the potential for violence. This stereotype continued to plague American society into the twenty-first century, leading to the *Black Lives Matter* outcry, which was that these "inferior" people of color also had a greater potential for violence.

In *Larry P. v. Riles*, a class of black California elementary school children challenged the use of standardized IQ tests for labeling children as *educable mentally retarded* (EMR) and subsequently placing them in special education classes. This case was filed primarily on the ground that this process resulted in placement of a disproportionate number of black and other minority children in these classes. Petitioners contended that this was in violation of Title IV of the 1964 Civil Rights Act, the 1973 Rehabilitation Act, and the 1975 Education for All Handicapped Children Act. They argued that the stigma associated with a special education curriculum placed blacks at a disadvantage in the job market once they left school. Since the main criterion for placement is the score generated in the IQ tests, the validity of the standardization on which these instruments are based, was questioned—especially their sensitivity to cultural differences within the United States.[8]

LEGISLATING MORALITY

The secularization of white supremacy in the latter part of the nineteenth century and early twentieth century followed the new science of Darwin evolution, notably human evolution known as social Darwinism. Terman was in good company in promoting this revised definition of *Divine Providence* and white (WASP) supremacy. Joining Stanford University were the Carnegie Institution, Rockefeller Foundation, Harriman Rails, Kellogg, Harvard University, and other Ivy League schools. Members of the privileged white elite then embarked on attempts at proving their views on social Darwinism by exploring "primitive" atavistic societies notably in European and American colonies such as Africa, the Pacific islands, and Alaska, as well as Indian reservations. These endeavors had the support of the Smithsonian Institute, the National Geographic Society, and the U.S. Bureau of Ethnography. Toward this end, ethnographers, sociologists, anthropologist, and others went about documenting what they viewed as primitive, aboriginal societies as snapshots of earlier evolutionary stages of mankind.

Indian Country provided a convenient laboratory now that all tribes were confined to government-controlled reservations. Alaska, on the other hand, provided a raw view of aboriginals for the social Darwinists. Western European and Protestant white America became the metric from which these "primitive societies" were to be measured, creating a new pseudo-scientific process known as *ethnocentrism*. These inquiries during the 1890s up until World War II led to the wholesale theft of aboriginal artifacts in the belief that these primitive societies were soon doomed to extinction, hence the extensive collections at the Smithsonian and major European museums. According to Robert Campbell, in his study of Alaska's Tlingits, the ethnocentric racialism metric was the degree of deviance from the WASP norm:

> Hierarchies of race as understood on the frontier of the nation-state translated easily into hierarchies of class differences elsewhere. . . . "Savage

Indians," the "Black Irish," Jewish "White Negros," and other whose class status marked them as well, the prostitutes, whiskey traders, menial laborers—all were fixed as beyond the pale. Along with prostitutes and homosexuals, working-class trade-unionists and anarchists, Tlingits represented a threat to civilized norms, clear evidence of the degraded effects of a "race" given over to their primitive idolatries and desires. Bourgeois whiteness, with its sexual self-control and social rules, had been normalized as the defining American characteristic.[9]

In addition to John Muir, Campbell lists Herbert Spencer, Sigmund Freud, James Frazer, and Thorstein Veblen as social Darwinists of the time. A popular view of the native Alaskan was that they would soon be gone due to their inherent inferiority. He quotes a popular view of the Tlingits held by the white elite traveler to Alaska at the time:

> What are we going to do with these miserable natives? They are a bad lot. Indians are not good for much anyhow. They are lazy, dirty, and shiftless. We shall have to get rid of them some way. But we need not trouble ourselves about it; only let them alone, and they will get rid of themselves. Whiskey will do the business better than fighting. We have only to let the whiskey come in freely, and in this way we shall civilize them off from the face of the early. It is only carrying out the law of the survival of the fittest, which is the great law of nature. The Indian must go, as other feeble races have gone before him. It is the will of the Almighty.[10]

Enforcing the Monroe Doctrine: WWI, the Great Migration, and Policing Urban Ghettoes

Massive input of eastern and southern European migrants, as well as freedmen, migrated to northern industrial centers during and following the First World War, greatly challenging the role not only of the privileged white elite but leading to conflict between competing racial and ethnic groups. Georg Simmel stated that threats to any group leads to a greater degree of social cohesion: "out-group hostility leads to in-group cohesion." This is true especially when competing for the same resources. Barnes and Teeters, on the other hand, noted that the American dream is based largely on *the Acquisitive* Urge—the principle that we have a right to these resources, regardless who controls them at any given time. This belief, according to Barnes and Teeters, fosters illicit behaviors such as organized crime, racketeering, political graft and corruption, and white-collar crimes: "A large share of the settlers who came to these shores lived in the hope that great wealth could be made in this land of opportunity. Some were dedicated to hard work, but many believed fortunes could be obtained by short-cut measures."[11]

Competition among workers often led to violence. Taft and Ross, in the 1969 *Eisenhower Report*, claimed that the United States had the bloodiest and most violent labor history of any industrial nation in the world—often between ethnic and racial groups. The army was often deployed for labor disputes prior to the First World War. During the period between the First World War and the Great Depression, federalized National Guard units were called in to intervene in hostile labor disputes in Colorado, New Mexico, Utah, West Virginia, Pennsylvania, Tennessee, Wyoming, Oklahoma, Kansas, and Washington. Laws replaced riots during and following F. D. Roosevelt's administration, including the Wagner Act and the Taft-Hartley and Landrum-Griffin Acts.[12]

While labor violence had an end in mind, race riots were predicated by hatred. Jim Crow segregation and second-class citizenship were the norm following Reconstruction up until the end of World War II. Blacks became emboldened following the First World War under the leadership of W. E. B. Du Bois and the National Association for the Advancement of Colored People (NAACP) and its philosophy of self-defense:

The agitation of the recently founded NAACP, whose membership doubled in 1918–1919, the propaganda of fighting a war to make the world safe for democracy, and especially the great Negro migration to the Northern cities which Southern peasants and workers viewed as a promised land, all created new hopes for the fulfillment of age-old dreams, while Negro soldiers who had served in France returned with new expectations. But the Negro's new hopes collided with increasing white hostility. Northern Negroes assigned to southern army camps met indignities unknown at home. They rioted in Houston and came so close to rioting in Spartanburg, South Carolina, that the army hastily shipped them overseas. In the northern cities like East St. Louis and Chicago, Negroes found not a promised land, but overcrowded ghettos and hostile white workers who feared Negro competition for their jobs. The Ku Klux Klan was revived beginning in 1915, and grew rapidly in the North and South after the war ended. . . . Negros of the World War I era resisted white insults and attacks only as long as they had hopes of being successful in the resistance. . . . During World War I and its aftermath, the modern form of the race riot developed in Northern and border cities where the Negro was attempting to alter his position of subordination. These outbreaks had two predisposing elements. First, relatively large numbers of new migrants—both Negro and white—were living in segregated enclaves in urban centers under conditions in which older patterns of accommodation were not effective. The riots were linked to a phase in the growth and transformation of American cities. Second, the police and law enforcement agencies had a limited capacity for dealing with the outbreak of mass violence and often conspired with the rioters against the Negro population. . . . Frequently the police were very deficient in their duties and occasionally assist the white rioters. In any case they were not prepared for such outbreaks. The state militia or federal troops were used repeatedly and generally displayed a higher level of professional standards. Without overlooking the casualties that were caused by the police themselves, the fundamental anatomy of these riots was a communal clash between Negros and Whites.[13]

The Great Depression, Prohibition, and Gangsters

The combination of the economic devastation of the Great Depression and Prohibition led to the gangster era and the emergence of the Federal Bureau of Investigation and the seeds of the War on Drugs. Draft dodgers during the First World War combined with the fear of communist infiltration into American labor unions created challenges for the U.S. government, notably its newly minted Bureau of Investigation in 1908. The Bolshevik revolution and emerging communist state in Russia sent fears throughout capitalist countries, notably in the United States. The Industrial Workers of the World (IWW) was seen as being strongly anti-capitalism, hence, anti-American. A struggling Bureau of Investigation under the U.S. Attorney General's Office could hardly handle the actions of the IWW and the massive draft resistance movement at the time. This vacuum was quickly filled by the creation of a special capitalist vigilante groups, the *American Protective League* (APL). The APL, ostensibly a nongovernmental group (NGO), would work hand-in-hand with the Bureau of Investigation (forerunner of the Federal Bureau of Investigation, created in 1935) in rounding up labor leaders and draft dodgers during the war years and immediately thereafter. The APL was created in March 1917 by a Chicago advertising executive, A. M. Griggs. It was not an official government entity and had no power of arrest. It was independently funded from capitalist groups whose members carried their own badges that stated: "American Protective League, Secret Service Division."[14]

The Bureau of Investigation's ranks of a few hundred men paled in comparison to the APL's membership of hundreds of thousand operatives. J. Edgar Hoover joined the Bureau of Investigation in the midst of these challenging times, policing both the May 1917 Selective Service Act and the May 1918 Sedition Act. Hoover was put charge of the enemy alien registration section. In an effort to address this national problem, a combined task force was created in August 1917, composed of local law enforcement, APL operatives, National Guardsmen, and the Bureau of Investigation. On September 3, a three-day raid was conducted in a multicity, multistate dragnet for draft dodgers and aliens, resulting in some 50,000 arrests. This action also led to the first criticism of the FBI from the mass media, as well as the U.S. Congress:

On the Senate floor, Senator Hiram Johnson of California told his colleagues "to humiliate 40,000 citizens, to shove them along with bayonets, to subject them to prison and summary military force, merely because they are 'suspects,' is a spectacle never before presented in the Republic [for whites, at any rate]. . . . The weight of opinion was against the manner in which the slacker raids had been handled and President Wilson asked . . . for a report [which not forthcoming due to the end of the War on November 11, 1918."[15]

A major outcome of the raid was the realization within the Department of Justice that vigilantism had no place in legitimate law enforcement. The APL was officially disbanded on February 1, 1919, with many members now joining the emergent Ku Klux Klan. A further stigma for these vigilante groups was the 1917 lynching of Frank Little in Butte, Montana, a member of the IWW Executive Committee. The lynching occurred despite the presence of federal troops called in by the governor to control IWW strikers. While the U.S. Department of Justice, under Attorney General Gregory, felt that the IWW should be curtailed, it did not want the negative attention drawn by the actions of the APL such as the lynching of Frank Little. Consequently, federal troops continued to be deployed as strike breakers throughout the country, including Montana.[16] Hoover continued to progress within the Bureau of Investigation, becoming assistant director in 1921 and director three years later. His initial rise within the U.S. Department of Justice is linked to aliens and labor unions, with new attention shown by his staunch anti-Communism—a principle he pursued even if it required extralegal measures. His star rose further during Attorney General Palmer's "red raids." But it was the hunt for desperados during the Prohibition and Depression era, along with the advent of the radio and movie newsreels, that propelled him and the FBI to national status.

Prohibition existed in Indian Country long before the Eighteenth Amendment to the U.S. Constitution in 1919. Prohibition was an element of federal laws governing the interaction of whites with Indian tribes, a standard that began in 1808 under President Thomas Jefferson in his instructions to the governors of states and territories. Federal jurisdiction was expanded in Indian Country with the Federal Enclaves Act (General Crimes Act of 1817), which established exclusive federal jurisdiction superseding state or territorial jurisdictions. The Federal Enclaves Act authorized punishment for all crimes, including bootlegging, committed by non-Indians in Indian Country, as well as crimes by Indians against whites. The Indian Intercourse Act of July 9, 1832, specifically prohibited the distribution of alcohol to Indians anywhere in the United States, in or off tribal lands. This was part of the authority vested in the newly created U.S. Commissioner of Indian Affairs:

> Be it enacted. . . . That the President shall appoint, by and with the advice and consent of the Senate, a commissioner of Indian affairs, who shall under the direction of the Secretary of War, and agreeably to such regulations as the

President may, from time to time, prescribe, have the direction and management of all Indian affairs, and of all matters arising out of Indian relations, and shall receive a salary of three thousand dollars per annum . . . Section 4. And be it further enacted, That no ardent spirits shall be hereafter introduced, under any pretense, into Indian country.[17]

This policy was not effectively enforced, as was reported by Reuben Snake Jr. during testimony before 1976 Congressional Task Force Eleven: Alcohol and Drug Abuse:

The reservation, although encased by specific boundaries, was still so vast and thinly populated that bootleggers and smugglers of liquor and other articles were never effectively controlled by the available enforcement officers and therefore left to flourish. Prohibition for Indians was to continue past the repeal of the 18th Amendment in 1933 even though they were granted full citizenship in 1924. The bootlegger and smuggler continued to peddle their intoxicating wares at great expense to the Indian people, both financially and legally. It is from this prohibition era in Indian history that both the patterns of drinking and causative factors for that drinking can be seen emerging. Gulp drinking and rapid ingestion of alcohol, as particular drinking patterns of the American Indian, are said to evolve strongly from this era. The very illegality of the drink "may have in fact increased its appeal, especially for the adolescent and young adults."[18]

Criminologists Barnes and Teeters viewed Prohibition as the greatest social upheaval in U.S. history:

Here for the first time a law was passed by a bare majority that was regarded by many as a rank encroachment on the freedom of a minority composed of many millions. The provision of illicit liquor for this minority furnished a perfect testing ground for the ideas and techniques of organized criminals. "Bootlegging" became a remunerative criminal activity that was especially difficult to control by ethnical inhibitions or the force of public opinion, since violation of the Volstead Act was regarded in many quarters as respectable, smart, and even indispensable in the service of national need. For every "bootlegger" who supplied liquor, there were dozens of "respectable" law-abiding citizens who condoned the flouting of the law by serving as customers. This breakdown of ethical and legal norms was conjoined with the economic and political plunder of the Harding era, and in turn, with remarkably widespread corruption in municipal affairs.[19]

Along similar lines, some scholars viewed Prohibition as an attempt by the WASP elitist faction to attempt to *legislate morality* by legalizing their values as being superior to non-Protestants, regardless of race or class. At any rate, the combination of Prohibition and the Great Depression was an interesting one for law enforcement, notably J. Edgar Hoover and the FBI.

The Great Depression led to continued social unrest and conflict between the corporate elite and the working class. This era also represented a shift in federal policy away from laissez-faire support of big businesses and toward improving working conditions. The Dust Bowl migration from Oklahoma to California and the creation of federal relief for the unemployed, such as the Civilian Conservation Corps (CCC) and the Works Project Administration (WPA), forced the U.S. government to rethink its policies of unabashed support for big business and other capitalist endeavors. The National Labor Relations Act (Wagner Act) of 1935 represented the turning point, with federal protection for the right of workers to organize and engage in collective bargaining. The Social Security Act and Public Contracts Act (Walsh–Healey Act) followed, providing labor standards and setting minimum wages and overtime pay, as well as child labor and safety provisions. These standards help smooth the transition from the Depression era to the war production period during the Second World War. President Franklin D. Roosevelt strengthened these acts in 1943 via executive order by creating the Committee on Fair Employment Practices, while the War Labor Dispute Act (Smith–Connally Act) of 1943 authorized federal plant seizures if industry did not comply.[20]

With strike breaking on the wane, federal law enforcement turned its attention to the gangsters that emerged during Prohibition and the desperados who robbed banks during the Depression—both elements were widely publicized by the emerging media (newsprint and radio) at the time. Other factors distinguishing this period from the previous outlaw era were the advent of the automobile and high-powered, rapid-firing weapons. Ford Motor Company's 1932 Model A, with its powerful V-8 engine, set the stage for fast, high-powered automobiles that became the envy of both criminals and law enforcement, adding the element of speed and rapid interstate chases and escapes. At the same time, the six-shooter revolver, lever-action rifle, and horse were made obsolete with the advent of new military weapons developed for the U.S. military during the insurgency in the Philippines and the First World War.

The semiautomatic, single-action .45 caliber M1911, seven-shot pistol was created in 1911 during the Philippine-American War, replacing the six-shot revolver that served the U.S. military through four wars (World Wars I and II; Korea; and Vietnam) with continued use even today. It fires a shorter ACP (Automatic Colt Pistol) cartridge made specifically for slide action weapons. The .45 caliber cartridge is also used in submachine guns like the Thompson and its various adaptations. The M1911 semiautomatic pistol was unique in that it was gas-operated so that the slide extracted the spent round and cocked the hammer on the back stroke while chambering another round from the magazine on its return. The M1911 was single-action in that the initial round needed to be manually fed, which, in turn, cocked the hammer. It replaced the double-action .38 caliber military revolver that proved ineffective against the Moros during the Philippine resurrection early in the twentieth century.

The M1918 Browning Automatic Rifle (BAR) was designed in 1917, and while it saw limited action during the First World War, it remained the light machine gun for both the army and the marine corps up through the Vietnam War where it was replaced by the M60 machine gun. The BAR used the powerful 30-06 caliber bullet and came with 20-round magazines and a bi-pod for prone firing. The M1928A1 Thompson submachine gun (Tommy Gun) was also developed at the end of the First World War (1921) and chambered the .45 ACP round that the military 1911-model .45 pistol used. It came with a variety of magazines, holding from thirty to one hundred rounds. It was used during World War II, Korea, and Vietnam. It was widely used by law enforcement agencies in both the United States and Israel and by U.S. gangsters and the Irish Republican Army (IRA) during the 1969–1998 conflict known as *The Troubles*.

In comparison, the BAR was accurate up to five hundred yards, with open sites making it a versatile military weapon, and was issued as the automatic weapon among USMC squads. The Thompson, on the other hand, had a limited effective range, like its .45 pistol, of about fifty to sixty yards. Indeed, these two weapons were often stolen from National Guard armories and used by criminals like Pretty Boy Floyd, the Barrow Gang, the Barker-Karpis Gang, the Baby Face Nelson Gang, the Dillinger Gang, and Bonnie and Clyde during the Depression era. This use of deadly force by these gangs armed with Thompsons and BARs provided J. Edgar Hoover the incentive he needed to petition the U.S. Congress to finally arm the FBI, which up to that time remained unarmed and had to rely on either local law enforcement agencies or the U.S. Marshals for backup.

The resulting high death rate associated with these weapons led to passage in 1934 of the National Firearm Act (NFA). The NFA covered machine guns, like the notorious Thompson, and sawed-off shotguns (short-barreled firearms). The categories covered by the NFA were a) machine guns: automatic weapons that fire a "burst of fire"; b) short-barreled rifles (SBRs): weapon with a barrel less than sixteen inches or overall length under twenty-six inches, including modified manufactured weapons; c) short-barreled shotguns (SBSs): similar to the SBRs but with a smoothbore barrel less than eighteen inches or a minimum overall length of twenty-six inches; d) silencers: portable devices designed to muffle or disguise the report of a portable firearm; and e) destructive devices (DDs): grenades, bombs, poison-gas weapons, explosive missiles; and large bore (over one-half inch) weapons other than a legitimate shotgun. A sixth category includes specialty concealed weapons. Collectively, these are categorized as AOWs (Any Other Weapon). The NFA did not ban these weapons but instead imposed a hefty transfer tax on them, often more expensive than the weapons themselves. Then, as today, Second Amendment rights violations were raised, leading to lawsuits, which led to the U.S. Supreme Court's *Miller v. United States.* In this case, defendant Miller was arrested for possession of an unregistered short double-barreled shotgun and for interstate transportation of such. In 1938 the federal district court for the Western District of Arkansas ruled that Miller's arrest was an unconstitutional violation of his Second Amendment right. The U.S. Supreme Court overturned this decision in 1939 in *Miller v. United States,* stating that the weapon in question was not a viable weapon likely to be used by a legitimate militia as implied in the Second Amendment: "A well regulated Militia, being necessary to the security of a free State, the right of the people to keep and bear Arms, shall not be infringed."[21]

The Great Depression affected postwar Europe as much as it did the United States. The United States played a significant role in the economic crisis. The rapid downturn in the once vibrant U.S. economy was the standard in the postwar years leading up to the Great Depression. Troubles began when the United States reduced the flow of capital abroad and added prohibitive tariffs, shutting out European goods. The worldwide economic crisis dominated the 1930s until the start of the Second World War in Europe in 1939. Indeed, the U.S. insistence on continued German reparation payments during this crisis is seen as a contributing factor in the rise of Hitler and his Nazi Party. For the nine-year period of 1930–1938, the U.S. unemployment rate averaged 18.3 percent, compared to 19.8 percent for Germany and 11.8 percent for Great Britain.[22] Interestingly, both Germany and the United States used the Depression to mobilize and militarize its young men—Germany with its Aryan youth groups and the United States with the Civilian Conservation Corps (CCC).

The CCC was a major element of Franklin D. Roosevelt's *New Deal* programs and was known officially as the *Emergency Conservation Work Act* (ECW) and was in effect from April 5, 1933, until June 30, 1942. This was a corporative venture between the U.S. Departments of Labor, Agriculture, Interior, and the War Department. The latter was responsible for the training programs and camp regiment with U.S. Army Reserve Officers in charge of the military-style camps. This level of regimentation was such that failure to comply with the conditions of enrollment could result in a "Dishonorable Discharge." General Douglas MacArthur was in charge of the military component of the CCC program given his role as army chief of staff, a role he held until Roosevelt assigned him U.S. Far East Commander at the start of the Second World War in 1941. The CCC program was open to unmarried, unemployed males between the ages of eighteen and twenty-eight who were U.S. citizens. Southern and western states demanded that the CCC be segregated, like the military itself at the time. Like with the buffalo soldiers, minority camps (blacks, Hispanics, American Indians) were run by white army officers.

Overall, more than 3 million men, including whites, military veterans, and minorities, worked in 4,500 camps located in every state and Alaska, Hawaii, Puerto Rico, and the Virgin Islands. More than two hundred thousand army personnel (captains, lieutenants) ran these facilities. These men planted trees, fought fires, built parks, developed public campgrounds, and built roads. The CCC worked on the growing National Park System (established in 1916) as well as in 482 state parks. The CCC also provided relief for many WWI veterans, including those who participated in the ill-fated Bonus Army encampment in Washington, DC, in 1932. These specialized CCC veterans' camps were integrated. CCC veterans needed to be certified by the Veterans Administration. These camps did not have an age limit for enrollment, and the veterans could be married. When America entered the Second World War, it now had a substantial paramilitary force to draw on either through enlistment or the draft. Here, the CCC provided a similar purpose as the federalization of the National Guard during the Mexican Revolution did for military readiness during U.S. involvement in the First World War.[23]

The end of Prohibition in 1933 with the Twenty-First Amendment to the U.S. Constitution helped Americans cope during the Great Depression; if not through self-medication, it also spelled the end of the raging gangster wars over bootlegging illicit liquor. This did not deter J. Edgar Hoover and his plans on gaining national attention as a top law enforcement officer. His actions were pure Madison Avenue self-promotion, but very effective in that shortly following the killing of John Dillinger by his agents in 1934, Hoover not only got top billings as a federal law enforcement agency but the agency got a name change, in 1935, as well—the Federal Bureau of Investigation, known worldwide as the FBI. His self-promotion efforts also allowed him to arm his agents, hence the widely promoted picture of him with a Thompson sub-machine gun. But Hoover's actions were not without its critics, notably other law enforcement agencies, and it labeled him and the FBI with illegal practices and procedures, tarnishing the Bureau's image, a stigma that continues to the present. J. Edgar Hoover and the FBI's abuses of power and blatant racism and discrimination also were noted as a contributing factor toward the history of violence in America. This was also noted in Bryan Burrough's 2004 book, *Public Enemies: America's Greatest Crime Wave and the Birth of the FBI, 1933–34*:

Today, going on four decades after his death in 1972, it's difficult to re-member a time when Hoover was not the monolithic figure whose secret files cowed American presidents, who underwrote Senator Joseph Mc-Carthy's star chamber, who hounded national figures as varied as Martin Luther King, Jr., Alger Hiss, and the Rosenbergs. For four decades Hoover dominated American law enforcement as no person before or since, single-handedly creating the country's first national police force. . . . Before Hoover, American law enforcement was a decentralized polyglot of county sheriffs and urban police departments too often crippled by corruption. By and large, it was Hoover who brought the level of efficiency, profes-sionalism, and centralized control the nation knows to this day. But his accomplishments will forever be sullied by the abuses of power—rampant illegal wiretapping, break-ins, and harassment of civil rights groups—of his later years.[24]

In his book, Burrough traces the emergence of the FBI's prominence to the Great Crime Wave of 1933–1934 when bank robbers like the St. Paul Yeggs, Pretty Boy Floyd, the Barrow Gang, the Barker-Karpis Gang, the Baby Face Nelson Gang, and the Dillinger Gang became heroes among the working-class populace struggling to survive during the Great Depression. Interestingly, Hoover did not gain prominence by fighting organized crime during this time. The FBI was the protector of the banking industry, which was viewed negatively by many during the Great Depression, thus enhanc-ing the profiles of these gangs. Hoover's need for acknowledgment became paramount, even at the expense of his men. Denenberg detailed how Hoover minimized the accomplishments of FBI Agent Melvin Purvis in the assassina-tion of "Public Enemy No. 1," John Dillinger, in 1934. Purvis's role in getting Dillinger led to him being labeled, "the man who got Dillinger." Purvis went on to dispatch the new "Public Enemy No. 1," "Pretty Boy" Floyd, again stealing the limelight from J. Edgar Hoover. Hoover did not want anyone else being lauded within the FBI, insisting that only he would be identified as "Mr. FBI," a title he manipulated until his death in 1972:

Hoover had become adept at using publicity to popularize himself and the bureau. *He* was Mr. FBI. Unlike the other nameless and faceless agencies in the federal government, the FBI was symbolized by one man—J. Edgar Hoover. And Hoover wanted to keep it that way. So Hoover decided to get rid of Mel Purvis. Unable to fire him because of his immense popular-ity, he decided to harass him till he resigned.[25]

Burrough documents Hoover's encouragement of the use of extralegal techniques such as physical and psychological torture, known as "the Third Degree." In court depositions, Hoover's men were accused of using what

J. Edgar termed, "vigorous physical interviews." These techniques included beatings, sleep deprivation, starvation, threats of death, and the like.[26] Pulitzer Prize–winning author Robert Unger went further, strongly suggesting that J. Edgar Hoover framed the wrong people in the 1933 "Union Station Massacre," including "Pretty Boy" Floyd and Adam Richetti, which led to both men's execution. Many in law enforcement knew of Hoover's techniques of falsification or manipulation of evidence—"Hoovered up the evidence." Gathering data from the FBI's own files, using the Freedom of Information Act (FOIA), Unger noted:

> History has taught us about FBI excesses, about break-ins and wiretaps and intimidation and deceit and cover up. Yet the most ardent of the Bureau's supporters cling to the belief that the bad came at the end, in Hoover's dotage, after he lost the shine of youthful honesty and devotion. . . . Hoover's own file screams otherwise. The FBI didn't go bad; it was born bad, right there in the blood of Union Station. The file doesn't speak of a proud birth. It describes original sin.[27]

On the other hand, Hoover needs to be credited with establishing an educated police force not racially and gender biased. He created a homogenous white, male, college-educated police force where personal appearance was paramount to the FBI's and Hoover's image. He selected men mainly from the southern (cowboys) and western (Mormon) states.

With the end of Prohibition and the Great Depression, Hoover and the FBI shifted their focus on yet another minority-based activity—that of the prohibition of substances other than alcohol like narcotics and marijuana, especially drugs used by people of color, notably blacks and Hispanics—doing so in concert with his ally, Harry Anslinger, director of the newly created (1930) Federal Bureau of Narcotics (FBN). Despite their eagerness to pursue a new War on Drugs, the problem with narcotics began well before their involvement in government agencies. Actually, the Opium Wars of 1839–1842 laid the foundations for the current drug wars in the United States. China banned the opium trade in 1799, but Western countries, notably Britain, continued to export opium, resulting in China confiscating and destroying a year's supply of the British East Indian Company's trade opium in the 1830s. Using this act as a pretense for expanding their influence in China, Great Britain declared war on China in 1839 with the Treaty of Nanking (1842), ceding Hong Kong to England for a 150-year lease as well as granting British merchants full rights at major Chinese ports.

The United States joined this charade two years later as a signee to the 1844 Treaty of Wanghai, gaining access to Chinese ports. These trade rights were expanded in 1858 with the Treaty of Tientsin, which now extended these rights to France and Russia as well. United States gunboat diplomacy in China included the opium trade and cheap Chinese laborers, especially for the transcontinental railroad system. In 1900, the United States joined the other Western colonial powers in putting down the Boxer Rebellion when China attempted to purge foreign capitalist interests. Here, the United States again used the U.S. Marine Corps as its international police force. And while opium was a common ingredient in patent medicines at the time, the drug was also used to specifically discriminate against the same Chinese immigrants brought here as a source of cheap labor.

The long history of racial discrimination against Asians in the United States began in San Francisco in 1875, eventually leading to passage of the Harrison Narcotics Tax Act of 1914. But it was Harry J. Anslinger, along with J. Edgar Hoover, who set the stage for class and race discrimination relevant to the current *War on Drugs*. Federal enforcement began with the Eighteenth Amendment to the U.S. Constitution in 1919 and the creation of the Prohibition Unit under the Bureau of Internal Revenue, which became the U.S. Bureau of Prohibition in 1927. Two years later, Anslinger became an assistant commissioner in the U.S. Bureau of Prohibition. He then became the commissioner of the newly created FBN in 1930. When alcohol prohibition was abolished with *Repeal* in 1933, the FBN, under Anslinger's direction, turned to other drugs that needed policing. Toward this end, Anslinger turned his efforts toward marijuana. Like Hoover, he used the emerging mass media at the time to promote his cause, doing so despite opposition by both the American Bar Association and the American Medical Association and scientific research that did not support his claims of a strong association between marijuana use and dangerous mental illness. Serving through five administrations, from Hoover to J. F. Kennedy, Anslinger was perhaps the single most significant purveyor of the dangerousness of marijuana and its link to minorities, contributing to the "dangerous minority drug fiend"—an image of minorities shared by J. Edgar Hoover and his FBI.

An ulterior motive, other than keeping the FBN under his control for more than thirty years (1930–1962), was promoting the interests of capitalists and industrialists who wanted to replace hemp with synthetic fibers like nylons. The *reefer madness* movement, leading to passage of the 1937 Marijuana Transfer Tax Act, was seen as part of a hemp conspiracy involving William Randolph Hearst, Andrew Mellon (Anslinger's father-in-law), and the du Pont family. With the advent of the decorticator machine, hemp was seen as a more economical alternative to paper pulp used in the newspaper industry. Hearst felt his large timber holdings threatened while Mellon, the richest person in the United States at the time and secretary of the U.S. Treasury, had a strong interest in the DuPont industries, the makers of the new synthetic nylon fiber. These capitalists felt that for nylon to succeed, it had to replace hemp. This capitalist propaganda effort then linked racial fears with hemp use (marijuana). Hearst played a major role in promoting this unwarranted fear through his newspapers, a process known as *yellow journalism*. Anslinger added to this fearmongering through radio announcement and publication of his "Gore Files"—stories linking marijuana use, notably by blacks and Hispanics, and resulting violence and mental illness. He continued to promote this myth up until the end of his tenure, repeating his race–drug use–violence theme.[28]

J. Edgar Hoover, in turn, convinced U.S. lawmakers that American society had an inherent bad core of "mad dog" criminals, comprised of lower-class whites and all classes of blacks, Hispanics, and American Indians—any group of color. Hoover is the person most responsible for "dead-end penology" and the creation of prisons, like Alcatraz, that were primarily for punitive retribution with no pretense of rehabilitation. Barnes and Teeters provides a compilation of his speeches:

> Criminals are not just criminals. They are: "Scum from the boiling-pot of the underworld," "public rats," "lowest dregs of society," "scuttling rats in the ship of politics," "vermin in human form," "the slimy crew who feed upon crimes," "desperadoes," "vermin spewed out of prison cells to continue their slaughter," "the octopus of the underworld." These "post graduates of outlawry" and "professors of crime" thrive "in the great fog of crime," and the "swamp and morasses of suffering" amidst the "appalling scourge of perjury" and the "oleaginous conniving of venal politicians," aided and abetted by "sentimental yammerheads," "moronic adults" of "asinine behavior," "maudlin sentiment," and "inherent criminal worship." Away with these "moocow sentimentalities" with their "mealy mouthings" and their "whining pleas for sympathy"; these "hoity-toity professors."[29]

Those who challenged Hoover and Anslinger were denigrated as "cream-puff criminologists." One such criminologist was Frank Tannenbaum, who warned against the dramatization of evil, a process leading to a self-fulfilling prophecy—whereby targeting and labeling a particular group (minorities) as being beyond redemption, placing them outside the socially acceptable boundaries of society, you deliberately intensify the problem you set out to eliminate. Clearly, both J. Edgar Hoover and Harry Anslinger understood this principle and used it to maintain a racial divide within American society—one that their respective organizations, the FBI and FBN, could profit from. In retrospect, J. Edgar Hoover can be credited with fostering the movement toward increased incarceration for drug users as well as the creation of the "supermax prisons," two phenomena stigmatizing the United States in the twenty-first century.

THE U.S. MARINES AS MONROE DOCTRINE POLICE

Defending American capitalism extended beyond the boundaries of the United States during the early years of the twentieth century, leading up to and including the Second World War. The "gunboat diplomacy" of the mid-nineteenth century continued with renewed purpose under President Theodore Roosevelt (1901–1909) under the *Roosevelt Corollary to the Monroe Doctrine*. Ironically, he was also known as "trust buster" in that his administration was equally successful in breaking up the large business monopolies at the time via the anti-trust Sherman Act. Paradoxically, T. Roosevelt was seen as being both "for" and "anti" big business. And while history seems to favor his domestic successes, the use of the U.S. Marines as hemispheric police remains hidden from most historical accounts. The *Historical Encyclopedia of the United States Marine Corps* articulates the effect of the Roosevelt Corollary:

> The pattern of interference in the domestic affairs of Caribbean and Central American states continued during the first quarter of the 20th century. It became an official policy of the United States after the announcement of the Roosevelt Corollary to the Monroe Doctrine whose intention was to interfere directly when the corrupt and inefficient governments might lead to European interference. The Marine Corps became the primary agent or this policy, which was continued by Roosevelt's successors. In the first of these actions, marine units were sent to Panama in 1903 to protect the new government there while the canal was being built. Another very troubled area was Santo Domingo. Marines were dispatched there in 1904, and some stayed for three years. Further disturbances there in 1916 brought the marines back, and they remained until 1920. The neighboring state of Haiti was even more challenging. A marine detachment was landed in December 1914 to protect the government from rebel forces. By mid-1915 over 2,000 marines were deployed. . . . Only after order was restored were they withdrawn in 1909. The most troublesome area was Nicaragua. In 1909 a regiment of marines arrived to support the government. . . . The last units were not withdrawn until 1933.[30]

More on the enforcement of the Monroe Doctrine at this time is presented in another marine document, *The Compact History of the United States Marine Corps*, in chapter 9, The "Banana Wars":

> For the first thirty years of the twentieth century, with the interruption of a World War, most of the Marine Corps spent most of its time in Latin America and the Caribbean. The victory over Spain had ushered in an era of "Yankee Imperialism," and the spirit of Manifest Destiny, long dormant,

was once more abroad in the land. The phrase that had served as a rational-ization for the conquest of Texas and California, now served as an excuse for a "large policy" in the Caribbean. The intervention of the United States in Panama in 1903 constituted one of the less savory incidents in our history. It also caused our motives to be suspect throughout Latin America for several decades to come. . . . It took a considerable amount of "intervention" for the preservation of Cuban independence. Between 1906 and 1917 Marines were required to step into Cuban domestic affairs on eight different occa-sions. Notably among these were those with the Army of Cuban Pacifica-tion, during the Negro Rebellion and the Sugar Intervention. . . . As part of the Army of Cuban Pacification in 1906, a brigade under the multi-names Colonel Waller garrisoned no less than 24 stations throughout the island. During the Negro Rebellion of 1912, a provisional regiment was assigned to troublesome Oriente Province. Their mission consisted primarily of main-taining law and order in the towns throughout the province, and guarding mining property, sugar plantations and railroads against the frequent raids of the insurgents. The Cuban government specifically requested Marine guards for each of their railroad trains in the area. For four months Marines rode on every train that moved. . . .

Since we would not permit European powers to intervene in the West-ern Hemisphere, it was up to us to intervene in their behalf. In effect, this was the policy laid down by Theodore Roosevelt during his administration and implemented by Woodrow Wilson when the situation demanded. It was this so-called "dollar diplomacy" concept that underlay our operations in those two Caribbean nations, Haiti and the Dominican Republic. At the time these two countries were undoubtedly the two worst trouble spots in the Western Hemisphere.[31]

During the Haitian campaign, marine noncommissioned officers (cor-porals and sergeants) were awarded commission ranks in the Haitian national police (*Gendarmerie d'Haiti*), commanding local police in enforcing the laws in the country. Lewis B. "Chesty" Puller served as a captain in the Haitian police while a USMC sergeant, while Smedley Butler, a major in the USMC, was in charge of the Haitian police, holding the rank of major general, four grades higher than his U.S. commission. Butler later rose to the rank of major general, the highest rank within the USMC at the time. He began his career as a second lieutenant during the Spanish-American War, served in the Philip-pines and China (Boxer Rebellion) prior to a long stint in the Caribbean and Central America (Panama, Nicaragua, Haiti, Mexico) where he earned two Medals of Honor (the only U.S. Marine to do so). He became the youngest brigadier general (age thirty-seven) during his service in World War I, and was later promoted to major general. In 1931, he was the senior general in the USMC and expected to be appointed as commandant but he was deemed too controversial and was by-passed by Congress. He retired in 1931 after thirty-three years of service.[32]

General Butler played a domestic police role when he was loaned to Philadelphia from the USMC to serve as director of public safety from 1924–1925 in order to enforce federal Prohibition. But Butler's discontent with being denied the role of USMC commandant led to his publication, *War Is a Racket*, a monograph based largely on his 1931 address to the American Legion:

> War is a racket. Our stake in that racket has never been greater in all out peace-time history. It may seem odd for me a military man, to adopt such a comparison. Truthfulness compels me to. I spent 33 years and 4 months in active service as a member of our country's most agile military force—the Marine Corps. I served in all commissioned ranks from Second Lieutenant to Major General. And during that period I spent most of my time being a high-class muscle man for business, for Wall Street and for bankers. In short, I was a racketeer for capitalism. . . . Thus, I helped make Mexico and especially Tampico, safe for American oil interests in 1914. I helped make Haiti and Cuba a decent place for the National City Bank boys to collect revenues in. I helped in the raping of half a dozen Central American republics for the benefit of Wall Street. The record of racketeering is long. I helped purify Nicaragua for the international banking house of Brown Brothers in 1901–12. I brought light to the Dominican Republic for American sugar interests in 1916. I helped make Honduras "right" for American Fruit companies in 1903. In China in 1927 I helped see to it that Standard Oil went its way unmolested. During those years, I had, as the boys in the back room would say, a swell racket. I was awarded with honors, medals, promotions. Looking back on it, I felt I might have given Al Capone a few hints. The best he could do was to operate his rackets in three city districts. We Marines operated on three continents. . . . We don't want any more wars, but a man is a damn fool to think there won't be any more of them. . . . There is no use talking about abolishing war; that's damn foolishness. Take the guns away from men and they will fight just the same. . . . No pacifists or Communists are going to govern this country. If they try it there will be seven million men like you to rise up and strangle them. Pacifist? Hell, I'm a pacifist, but I always have a club behind my back.[33]

Domestic tranquility on the home front was challenged during the Great Depression, leading to the army's intervention in the 1932 Bonus Expeditionary Force (BEF), a group of some twenty-five thousand World War I veterans and their families who set up makeshift camps in Washington, DC, demanding a promised bonus for their military service. MacArthur was chief of staff (the forerunner of the current Joint Chiefs of Staff) with a greatly diminished military (ranked sixteenth in the postwar era), but who shared both J. Edgar Hoover's and General Butler's anti-Communism, anti-pacifist sentiments. MacArthur, certain that the Bonus Army comprised of Communists and pacifist sympathizers who were attempting to pass as veterans, attempted to convince President Herbert Hoover that the camp must be dismantled. Hoover's orders not to engage was ignored by MacArthur who ordered his military personnel, including Majors Dwight D. Eisenhower and George Patton Jr. to assist the DC police in destroying the camp and evicting the veterans. Major General Courtney Whitney, a strong supporter of MacArthur's actions, fueled the public paranoia by stating that the camp was infested with criminals charged with rape, robbery, blackmail, and assault and that a secret document was captured detailing a Communist plan to hold public trials and hanging of high government officials in front of the Capital with General MacArthur leading the list.

No such list was found. Also dismissed was the falsehood that the BEF consisted of nonveteran radicals. A Veterans Administration survey later showed that 94 percent of the BEF were, in fact, veterans, with 20 percent representing disabled American veterans. MacArthur, ignoring the president's order, led the attack:

> Then he led his men across, and the tents, shacks, lean-tos, and packing crates which had sheltered the bonus marchers and their families were put to the torch. Two babies were dead of tear gas and a seven-year old boy trying to rescue his pet rabbit had been bayoneted through the leg. Since, the President [Hoover] was MacArthur's commander in chief, the General had been flagrantly insubordinate. But before Hoover could act, MacArthur outmaneuvered him. Law-and-order Republicans, he knew, would approve his show of strength. Therefore, he called a midnight press conference, disclaimed responsibility, and praised Hoover for shouldering it.[34]

MacArthur, Butler, J. Edgar Hoover, and Anslinger all fueled the anti-Communist, anti-pacifist furor that, for the most part, was directed toward minorities. Concerned over international influences and anarchism during the Great Depression, a favorable trend toward fascism in the United States emerged. The apparent success of fascism in Italy, Germany, and Spain led to a movement by big business in the United States to introduce its own form of fascism. The fear of Communism led to a right-wing swing by the captains of U.S. capitalists. Drawing on the former ranks of both the American Protection League and the American Legion (the largest veteran's organization), the American Liberty League (ALL) was established specifically to challenge President F. D. Roosevelt's New Deal initiatives.

Here, the leaders of the ALL (heads of DuPont, Goodyear, Bethlehem Steel, Standard Oil, Ford Motor Company, J. P. Morgan banks, Wall Street bankers, and the like) planned a quiet revolution, one headed by retired USMC

General Smedley Butler. ALL founder, Irene du Pont and her stakeholders, felt that Butler, son of a U.S. congressman and one of the most respected military figures in the United States, was the person who could muster support not only from the active military but from the two largest veteran organizations, the Veterans of Foreign Wars (VFW) and the American Legion, to lead this revolt. In their plan to overthrow President Roosevelt, General Butler was to muster an army of 500,000 veterans to stand against the 132,000 standing army under General MacArthur, if needed, and march on Washington, DC, with the pretense of protecting President Roosevelt from plotters. Subsequently, Roosevelt would be forced to resign and the American Liberty League would install a "Secretary of General Welfare" and a fascist regime fashioned after that in Italy. The ALL's first action would be to restore the gold standard. To their chagrin, General Butler not only refused to participate in this coup, he reported it to both President Roosevelt and the U.S. Congress.

Surely, President Roosevelt, as commander in chief, could have ordered General MacArthur, in his capacity as army chief of staff, to mobilize the millions of young men trained by his officers in the CCC. It would not have been too difficult to exchange shovels for 30-06 Springfield rifles, augmenting his standing 132,000 active duty personnel. But President Roosevelt and the U.S. Congress were magnanimous, essentially forgiving the privileged elite of American society (the du Ponts, Grayson Murphy, Henry Ford, John D. Rockefeller, John and Allen Dulles, and so on) for this misadventure, resulting in a sanitized 1934 report from the McCormack-Dickstein Committee, the special committee that investigated propaganda activities. Indeed, the report left out the names of the prominent business and political leaders and no action was taken against the plotters.[35]

Entry into the Second World War (WWII) not only changed the fortunes of the mutinous business privileged elite, it allowed for a redirection of collective frustration in America to again be directed toward a nonwhite group—Japanese Americans. World War II was the epic colonial and ideological war of recorded history, pitting Japanese colonial interest in the Pacific and Southeast Asia against United States and European colonies (aka protectorates), while ideological wars raged in Europe over the colonial spoils of Africa, South Asia, and the Middle East, in addition to holdings in Southeast Asia. America was not alone in targeting minority groups as the holocaust attests. Nonetheless, the removal of targeted populations has a long American tradition that certainly influenced other forced removals during WWII given New England's colonial involvement in the Acadian Expulsion and the deadly extermination and/or forced removal of American Indian tribes during the nineteenth century.

Just a few months following the Japanese attack on Pearl Harbor in the U.S. territory of Hawaii, President Franklin D. Roosevelt signed Executive

Order 9066, on February 19, 1942, authorizing the War Department to remove all persons of Japanese descent from designated military areas (e.g., the
West Coast):

> From March through May, all Japanese Americans, including persons with
> as little as one-sixteenth Japanese blood and foster children brought up in
> Caucasian families, were told to wind up their affairs in a week to 10 days
> and show up at an appointed time with bed rolls and no more baggage
> than they could carry. The Army moved the ethnic Japanese to assembly
> centers in converted livestock stalls and stadiums throughout the West. A
> bare room furnished only with cots, blankets and mattresses and separated
> from others by a thin partition made up a family apartment. . . . There they
> will live in centers encircled by barbed wire and watch towers. Guards are
> instructed to shoot anyone who tries to leave. All of this is taking place
> despite the fact that there have been no criminal charges.[36]

The ten concentration camps were located at Poston and Gila Bend,
Arizona; Jerome and Rohwer, Arkansas; Minidoka, Idaho; Tule Lake and
Manzana, California; Topaz, Utah; Granada, Colorado; and Heart Mountain,
Wyoming. Over 100,000 people of Japanese descent were removed (relocated) and incarcerated in these concentration camps while in Hawaii where
Japanese made up over one-third of the population, only a little over 1,000
were interned. Public fear and negative stereotyping of the "Jap" contributed
greatly to the fears generated on the west coast, a stigma that was not prevalent
in Hawaii where Asians, Polynesians, and Anglos had long coexisted and inter-
bred. Nonetheless, Hawaii and surrounding U.S. territories and the Aleutian
Islands of Alaska territory were placed under martial law for the war's duration. In 1944, the U.S. Supreme Court validated this gross violation of habeas
corpus if not the selective use of martial law on a targeted civilian populace.[37]

• 7 •

Post–World War II
Challenges to Law Enforcement

Many changes occurred following the epic Second World War (WWII), including the media with the advent of television and increased forms of mass communication allowing for greater access to news and events not only within the United States, but worldwide. Mutual protection concerns led to the creation of the United Nations (UN) and the North Atlantic Treaty Organization (NATO). War tribunals led to international standards of justice and protection for both civilian and military personnel, including the addition of "war crimes" (genocide and crimes against humanity) as well as standards for military behavior, including a prohibition against torture (Geneva Convention). The vast scope of WWII forged interactions between unlikely peoples, including areas long sheltered from outsiders. Moreover, although officially segregated, U.S. military personnel (GIs) were often exposed to people from different religions, geographical regions, races, and ethnicities. GIs brought these experiences back home with them, with many no longer satisfied with the prewar status quo of either de jure or de facto segregation and discrimination. Ethnic whites (Irish, Italian, French Canadian, Portuguese) and racial minorities distinguished themselves during the war and no longer wanted to return to the old status quo. Moreover, they had their own heroes to look up to—General Benjamin O. Davis, Sr., the Tuskegee Airmen, Hispanic guardsmen at Bataan, Ira Hayes, the Navajo Code Talkers, Daniel K. Inouye and the Nisei 443 Regimental Combat Team, Rene Gagnon, and so on. Many of these returning GIs made inroads into local government, within their ghettos, parishes, reservations, and barrios—those areas outside the Jim Crow South that seemed impregnable eighty years following passage of the Fourteenth Amendment to the U.S. Constitution that guaranteed "equal rights" for all. Returning ethnic and racial GIs were eager to finally challenge the WASP concept of *the divine rights of whites* and their stranglehold on U.S. society.

MILITARY SERVICE AND ITS IMPACT ON MINORITY GI ACTIVISM AND MOVEMENTS TOWARD DESEGREGATION

President Truman officially desegregated the U.S. military services in 1948 via an executive order (July 26): "It is the declared policy of the President that there shall be equality of treatment and opportunity for all persons in the Armed Services without regard to race, color, or national origin."[1] Truman's action played a significant role in the United Nation's *police action* aka the Korean War (1950–1953), making this the first officially integrated U.S. combat force, again with blacks, Hispanics, American Indians, and Asians represented either through enlistment or the draft. Returning black GIs were emboldened by President Truman's actions, notably the GI Bill—although diminished for blacks, it still provided an avenue for higher education for returning veterans through the existing black colleges and universities (HBCUs). But Jim Crow laws in the South and de facto segregation elsewhere led to a more militant resistance among returning GIs of color. W. E. B. Du Bois, leader of the National Association for the Advancement of Colored People (NAACP), was quick to point out the discrepancies between the infusion of money and resources toward Europe and Asia, including the enemy nations and resources for black Americans.[2] The Nation of Islam, on the other hand, provided another alternative to Jim Crow segregation, that of black-instigated racial segregation. It began in 1930 in Detroit, Michigan, and continues to exist today. It claims to be the originator of the black pride movement, and spurred on variants like the Black Panthers during the 1960s.

Du Bois and A. Philip Randolph agitated for better social and working conditions for black Americans, paving the way for both the forces challenging segregation leading up to the 1954 *Brown v. Board of Education* Supreme Court decision and the ensuing Civil Rights Acts of the 1960s. A. Philip Randolph was actually the father of the civil rights movement, holding prayer pilgrimages in the 1950s and leading the 1963 March on Washington. He is the mentor of Martin Luther King Jr., who later became the most visible and recognizable leader of the civil rights movement. But not everyone was content with the passive, nonviolent approach to change within black communities, especially when the white political and law enforcement leaders in the South viciously attacked blacks exercising their right to peaceful demonstrations, leading to the creation of more assertive black movements.

American Indian veterans also became more involved in tribal affairs within Indian Country. Indian veterans of the First World War (WWI) were granted federal citizenship in 1919, a status conferred on all enrolled Indians in the United States on June 2, 1924—more than fifty years after freedmen were granted citizenship under the Fifteenth Amendment to the U.S. Constitution in 1870. Federally recognized tribes (Indian Country) were now under close federal supervision under the provisions of the Indian Reorganization Act (IRA—Wheeler-Howard Act of 1934), allowing for limited political autonomy by tribal leaders. Military veterans, long recognized as tribal elders, filled many of these positions via tribal elections. Toward this end, tribal members felt the need to organize in order to promote their own interests given that it was obvious that the federal government was often delinquent in its trust responsibilities. Veterans were leery of whites representing their interests, like the Association on American Indian Affairs (AAIA) created following WWI in 1922, and instead forged a stronger organization, the National Association on Indian Affairs in 1933 during the IRA era, which later became the National Congress of American Indians (NCAI) in 1944, its all-Indian membership enhanced by returning WWII veterans. These veterans felt that they could manage their own affairs without patronizing white leadership. The IRA led to an increased involvement of the Bureau of Indian Affairs (BIA), including tribal policing using tribal members, mostly returning military veterans. Even then the BIA police had limited jurisdiction, restricting it to enforcing misdemeanors and tribal ordinances, while the FBI and U.S. Marshals retained original jurisdiction for felonies (Major Crime/Index Crimes). Matters became more challenging during the Eisenhower administration, further complicating policing American Indians both on and off reservations, issues that came to a head during the 1970s on the Pine Ridge Reservation in what is known as *Wounded Knee II*.

BROWN V. BOARD OF EDUCATION AND THE ROAD TO DESEGREGATION AND JIM CROW RESISTANCE

Efforts were underway to put teeth into the Fourteenth Amendment, which has remained basically ineffective with various laws designed to disenfranchise minorities in the United States. The civil rights movement had its greatest impetus in challenging the WASP domination and the continued myth of *Divine White Supremacy*, doing so with the *Brown v. Board of Education* case. The case began because a Topeka, Kansas, black third-grader, Linda Brown, had to walk past a conveniently located white school to attend her all-black school located across a dangerous railroad switchyard. With the help of the NAACP, Linda's father filed for an injunction in 1951. At the hearing before the U.S. District Court, District of Kansas, on June 25 and 26, 1951, the charge was that segregated schools promoted institutionalized racism, whereby blacks were manifested as being inferior to whites. Citing *Plessy v. Ferguson*, the U.S. District Court ruled in favor of the Board of Education. Brown and the NAACP appealed to the U.S. Supreme Court, which agreed to hear the Kansas case along with a similar challenge from South Carolina, Virginia, and Delaware. The Supreme Court heard the case on December 9, 1952, but was unable to reach a decision. The reargument was heard a year later with focus on the Fourteenth Amendment of 1868—the amendment regarding civil rights: "No State shall make or enforce any law which shall abridge the privileges or immunities of citizens of the United States: nor shall any State deprive any person of life, liberty, or property, without due process of law; nor deny to any person within its jurisdiction the equal protection of the laws."[3] The landmark unanimous decision was reached on May 17, 1954, striking down the "separate but equal" concept supported by *Plessy v. Ferguson*—thus requiring the desegregation of schools in the United States.

Black psychologists, Kenneth and Mamie Clark, and lawyer, Thurgood Marshall were instrumental in swaying the white Supreme Court justices. Kenneth B. Clark was Columbia University's first black PhD recipient and was on the faculty of City College of New York at the time of the *Brown* decision. In their classic study, Kenneth and Mamie Clark devised their famous *doll test*, whereby they presented young children with four identical dolls (black male, white male, black female, white female) asking them to indicate which doll was "best," which was "nice," which was "bad," and which one they would prefer to play with. Regardless of race, a statistically significant number of the children rejected the black dolls in preference to the white dolls. This was the study presented to the U.S. Supreme Court, proving scientifically that segregation had/has the intent, latent or manifest, to foster and maintain a racial self-fulfilling prophecy of racial inferiority and white supremacy—the foundations of institutionalized racism in the United States—contrary to the Fourteenth Amendment to the United States Constitution.

Dr. Kenneth B. Clark went on to become president of the American Psychological Association and one of the most noted psychologists in the country. Thurgood Marshall, on the other hand, was the leading NAACP attorney presenting the Brown case before the U.S. Supreme Court. He served as legal director of the NAACP from 1940 until 1961 and, along with his mentor, Charles Hamilton, was the first African American to win cases before the U.S. Supreme Court. President John F. Kennedy appointed Marshall to the Federal Courts of Appeals for the Second Circuit in 1961. Marshall served as the solicitor general under President Lyndon B. Johnson from 1965 to 1967, at which time he was appointed to the U.S. Supreme Court—the first black to sit on the high court. He retired in 1991.

Mexican Americans suffered under the same Jim Crow segregation as did black Americans, but without protection of law since their segregation was of a de facto nature due to their "other white" status, a label given them by the WASP leaders. Nonetheless, both Hispanics and blacks were affected by the U.S. Supreme Court *Brown* decision. The emerging political activism among Mexican Americans following WWII had the unintended consequence of intensifying anti-Mexican sentiments in the United States, especially in white communities in the border states, notably Texas, California, and Arizona. The creation of the League of Latin American Citizens (LULAC) in 1929 following the harsh reaction to the Plan de San Diego provided a sense of cultural and political clout for "white" middle-class Mexican Americans (Criollos heritage), and this process was rejuvenated with the return of Hispanic GIs during both WWII and the Korean conflict. No longer satisfied with the existing Jim Crow apartheid system operating in the United States, returning GIs, charged by their patriotism and worldly experience, abandoned the Jim Crow status quo for one that was ethnic-sensitive. This new ethnic-pride focus extended to the working class, long ignored by LULAC, including documented and undocumented Mexicans living in the United States. Like other minorities, returning Mexican American veterans found the same discriminatory practices existing as when they left, despite participating in the epic World War.

What the Mexican American GIs did get was access to the GI education bill. Now more Mexican American GIs were armed with college degrees, better preparing them for the civil rights battles ahead. Concerned about social and educational equality for all Hispanics, the returning GIs in Los Angles formed the Council of Mexican American Affairs (CMAA) in 1954, making the 1950s the decade of rapid political awareness among Hispanics and setting the stage for collective activism to follow in the 1960s. A major factor in the Hispanic movement was the establishment of the *American GI Forum* (AGIF) comprised of returning Mexican American veterans. One of their initial complaints was the segregation of congressionally approved veteran's organizations—the Veterans of Foreign Wars (VFW) and the American Legion. When allowed to join these organizations, they had to establish separate ethnic-specific posts. The denial of federal benefits was another crucial issue, including the right to be buried in local cemeteries along with white veterans.

Regarding education, Mexican Americans suffered under the same Jim Crow segregation as black Americans, but without the protection of law since their segregation was of a de facto nature due to their *other white* status. Both Hispanics and blacks were affected by the Supreme Court decision in *Brown v.*

Board of Education. Part of the problem with the added layer of discrimination of Hispanics was the effort of LULAC to gain inroads to being Americanized, even if they had to appease the white dominant society by accepting "second-class" status. Shortly following LULAC's establishment in 1929, the 1930 *Del Reo ISD v. Salvatierra* court decision emerged, labeling Mexican Americans as the "other white race." This status was initially welcomed by LULAC in that it legally separated them from the African American population.

Hispanic GIs were not pleased with this distinction, and educational inadequacies became a major issue with the creation of the AGIF in 1948. A major focal point for the Mexican American educational reform movement was San Antonio, Texas, home of the Alamo and Texas white supremacy, and the Hispanic reactionary group the Pan-American Progressive Association. Together these Hispanic organizations led a challenge to end segregation in public schools, as spelled out in the 1930 *Del Rio ISD* standard. Similarly, another case was working its way through the California courts. At this time, it was estimated that 27 percent of those of Mexican heritage in Texas had no schooling at all and that the separate schools for Spanish-surname children had minimal facilities with poor curriculum restricted to domestic and vocational training.[4]

This challenge gained momentum in March 1945 when a number of Mexican American families filed suit in U.S. District Court in Los Angles (*Mendez v. Westminster School District*), complaining that thousands of children of Mexican ancestry were segregated into inferior schools within Orange County, another conservative white bastion. The district court ruled in favor of the plaintiffs, rendering its decision on February 18, 1946. The school district, in turn, appealed the decision to the Ninth Circuit Court in San Francisco, which ultimately upheld the lower-court decision. Yet this decision did not settle the "separate-but-equal" issue addressed in the 1896 *Plessy v. Ferguson* case, mainly due to the "other white" status conferred on Hispanics in the *Del Rio ISD* decision. The NAACP, represented by Thurgood Marshall and Robert L. Carter, joined *Mendez v. Westminster* as amicus curiae ("friends of the Court"). This was before they argued the *Brown v. Board of Education* case before the U.S. Supreme Court.[5]

Neither the *Delgado* nor *Brown* case immediately resolved the de facto segregation issue in Texas public schools. Again, the major issue was the argument that Mexicans were not legally considered to be a "colored" minority and as "other whites" they did not benefit from the de jure ruling decided in the 1954 *Brown v. Board of Education* U.S. Supreme Court case. The rationale offered for the separate, and grossly unequal, education offered Hispanics in Texas school was the "language" barrier. Following the *Brown* decision, Texas districts transferred black students into the inferior Mexican schools under the pretense that they were now in compliance with the U.S. Supreme Court decision. This charade was hotly contested by both blacks and Hispanics. The issue of desegregation of Texas school was finally resolved in 1957 with the *Herminca Hernandez et al. v. Driscoll Consolidated ISD* case. The next battle for Hispanics was the recognition of Mexican Americans of mixed-blood, aka Chicanos and Mestizos.[6]

THE EISENHOWER ADMINISTRATION: ENHANCED STATE POLICING; THE ROOTS OF SOCIAL UNREST

Dwight D. Eisenhower was yet another military general to occupy the White House (1953–1961). As a five-star general, his tenure in the army included graduating from West Point and serving under other famous generals, including John (Black Jack) Pershing (general-of-the armies, a status only shared with George Washington) and Douglas MacArthur (another five-star general). And while he famously warned about the "military-industrial complex," he, like Donald Trump, stacked his cabinet with rich, conservative, businessmen, including the Dulles brothers of the *American Liberty League* notoriety. His first-term cabinet was termed, "eight millionaires and a plumber."[7] Of course President Trump's cabinet consists of some billionaires (of which some of Eisenhower's men would be in today's currency). Postwar prosperity was challenged during Eisenhower's administrations by the heated "Cold War" and the fear of Communist intrusion into the Americas, as well as fears from domestic uprisings—a period shrouded in *McCarthyism* paranoia. Added to this was J. Edgar Hoover's FBI secret wars against perceived threats from minorities and student leftists, actions fueled by the 1954 attack on Congress by Puerto Rican extremists, and the trial and execution of Julius and Ethel Rosenberg as spies who gave the Soviet's nuclear secrets. His administration set the stage for destabilization in the Middle East (Iran), Africa (Congo), Latin America (Guatemala), and Southeast Asia (Indonesia, Vietnam). Domestically, some of the most dramatic changes during his administration affected American Indians when he and his Republican Congress attempted to undo the long-needed changes made by his two predecessors in Indian Country.

CIVIL RIGHTS DURING THE EISENHOWER ERA

The *Brown v. Board of Education* U.S. Supreme Court decision occurred on his watch, as did the initial resistance from the Deep South. President

Eisenhower's decisions were often difficult for him personally given that his sentiments were with the Jim Crow South, having been born and raised in Denton, Texas (it is doubtful that if President Truman had not integrated the military—that Eisenhower would have done so during his tenure). But to his credit, in 1957–1958, President Eisenhower sent U.S. federal troops to Little Rock, Arkansas, to protect black students attending previously white-only schools. Given the political nature of the National Guard, especially in Southern states, Presidents Eisenhower, Kennedy, and Johnson had to override state governor's authority (Arkansas, Mississippi, Alabama) when clearly using the National Guard for their political agendas. When the National Guard could not be trusted to enforce federal law, Eisenhower sent in the regular army to do so. In the desegregation of Central High School in Little Rock, Arkansas, Governor Orval Faubus ordered the National Guard to prevent blacks from attending the previously all-white high school. President Eisenhower, in turn, overruled the governor by federally activating the Arkansas National Guard, ordering it instead to protect black students attempting to matriculate at the Central High School. As an added measure, Eisenhower brought in a component of the 101 Airborne Army division as well as U.S. Marshals to enforce the federal desegregation order. Here, President Eisenhower used an exception to the Posse Comitatus Act of 1878 by using the Enforcement Acts that allowed the U.S. president to call up military forces when state authorities are either unable or unwilling to suppress violence that is in opposition to the constitutional rights of citizens. It is a step away from martial law in that it does not otherwise deny Bill-of-Right guarantees such as habeas corpus.

Other key civil rights catalysts occurred on Eisenhower's watch, including the much publicized 1955 murder of Emmett Till, a black fourteen-year-old teenager from Chicago, while visiting relatives in Mississippi. The refusal of the federal government, notably the FBI, to get involved in this case, and the reaction to this inaction, was certainly a precursor to subsequent involvements such as that two years later in Little Rock, Arkansas. Part of the problem was the influence J. Edgar Hoover held over the Department of Justice, where his blatant racist views prevailed, although now posed as fighting the surge of domestic communism. On December 1, 1955, Rosa Parks made history in Montgomery, Alabama, by refusing to cede her front-row seat (blacks were relegated to the "back of the bus" in the Jim Crow South) to a white man. The bus stopped, and Miss Parks was arrested. In retrospect, it appears that Miss Parks's civil disobedience was actually staged by the NAACP, where she worked as secretary of the local chapter. Nonetheless, given the mass media coverage of the event, it ignited a 381-day boycott that gained national attention and propelled a young civil rights minister, Martin Luther King Jr., and his newly established (1957) Southern Christian Leadership Conference

(SCLC) to the forefront of the emerging civil rights struggle. The nonviolent, but economically devastating, boycott resulted in a federal appeal of Miss Parks's conviction (fined ten dollars) in 1956, the first federal appeal of a state conviction based primarily on the 1954 U.S. Supreme Court *Brown v. Board of Education* ruling. This case effectively ended bus segregation throughout the United States. It also propelled three young black civil right activists to the forefront of the ensuing struggle: Fred D. Gray, Martin Luther King Jr., and Ralph Abernathy.

The Rosa Parks incident and its NAACP and, later, SCLC, advocates greatly irritated J. Edgar Hoover, setting the stage for FBI surveillance and dirty tricks, and Hoover's seemingly pathological hatred of Martin Luther King Jr.:

> J. Edgar Hoover believed that the civil rights movement was being influenced secretly by the communists, that agents of the Soviet Union were using the civil rights movement to try to destroy the United States government. Hoover believed that the civil rights movement was neither spontaneous nor genuine, so in 1958, the FBI began watching Dr. King. Three years later, Hoover decided that watching wasn't enough. The bureau began an investigation.[8]

And Hoover's fears continued through the remainder of Eisenhower's administration with the "sit-in" begun by black college students on February 1, 1960, integrating the Woolworth lunch counter in Greensboro, North Carolina, home to the white-women's University of North Carolina and the HBCU North Carolina A&T College, where Jesse Jackson attended and the noted black sociologist Joe Himes taught. What irritated Hoover most was the passive, nonviolent nature of the emerging civil rights movement, despite continued savagery directed toward blacks promoting racial equality.

THE SEEDS OF LATIN AMERICAN UNREST AND ITS UNINTENDED CONSEQUENCES

While it could be argued that the FBI and federal law enforcement were only paying token attention to domestic civil unrest, the notorious Dulles brothers were heavily involved in clandestine matters, including undermining anticolonial governments emerging from the devastation of WWII. Once inaugurated, Eisenhower, in an unprecedented act, made John Foster Dulles, U.S. secretary of state and his brother, Allen Dulles, head of the Central Intelligence Agency (CIA). Together they played havoc with the existing world order, causing chaos that continues to the present. In this sense, Eisenhower was as easily led as his famous four-star predecessor, Ulysses S. Grant, and as reckless as his twenty-first-century successor, Donald Trump, with these actions taken under the guise of "promoting capitalism" and American interest at any cost.

The seeds for U.S. involvement in Vietnam began on February 23, 1955, when President Eisenhower authorized sending "military advisors" to aid the South Vietnamese government. This followed the president's January 28 declaration of U.S. defense of the Formosan Islands, notably, Quemoy and Matsu, small islands situated between Taiwan and mainland China. Both of these "police actions" were seen as stemming the encroachment of Communist China, a challenge to capitalist democracy, which Eisenhower coined, *The Domino Effect*. The potential for involvement in the region, including Indonesia, was established with the creation of the *Southeast Asia Treaty Organization* (SEATO) in 1954. To further distinguish U.S. "free market" democracy as a Christian mandate, the clear antithesis of "godless" Communism, President Eisenhower, on June 14, 1954, signed a congressional resolution that altered the *Pledge of Allegiance* to add "under God" to the phrase "one nation indivisible" to "one nation, under God, indivisible." Hence, clearly abandoning the idea of a secular society free of religious interference (like France, Mexico, and so on), one which protects personal religious choices (including the choice to be agnostic or atheist); instead setting the stage once again for a renewal of the proponents of Manifest Destiny and its inherent components of divine rights, capitalism, and white supremacy, with a clear preference for Protestant sects and the privileged aristocratic elite.

With Allen Dulles in charge of the CIA, the Eisenhower administration began its clandestine operations in Latin America, pitting of Indians and Mestizo peasants against the elite and favoring continued U.S. business investments and the exploitation of local resources and labor—all this being done under the illusion of protecting the hemisphere from coming under Communist domination. Put within the Cold War perspective of the post-WWII era, two contravening ideologies "Communism" (China, Soviet Union) and "Free-Market Democracies" (United States, Western Europe) were competing for "Third World" alliances. At one end of the continuum is the United States and its form of a capitalist theocracy while at the other pole lies the godless socialism of Red China and the Soviet Union. Even then, the fear of the "domino effect" is not a viable threat given that Marshal Tito established a communist republic outside of the Soviet realm. But it was these nonaligned nations that suddenly emerged once freed from their colonial yokes that the United States and its communist nemesis were competing for; under the real threat of an all-out nuclear war.

Indeed, these competing ideologies led to the greatest proliferation of "weapons of mass destruction" in recorded history. With Europe devastated by

WWII, the United States took on the mantel of "protector" of the *free world*. President Eisenhower and the Dulles brothers were not so much concerned with preserving "democracy" in Third World nations, notably those within the Americas, as much as they were bent on preventing an infusion of communist influences like that which occurred in Cuba in 1959. Toward this end the goal often involved destroying socialist-leaning democracies and replacing them with brutal dictatorships as long as they were loyal to the United States. These clandestine operations often involved assassinations carried out by both competing ideological groups. These operations needed to be kept from the public given that each group labeled themselves as the "good guys" and the other group as the "bad guys." Even when disclosed by the media, these events met with denial at the highest levels of government that is until the Trump administration. In a February 5, 2017, interview on Fox News, Bill O'Reilly called Russian President Putin "a killer," and in defense of Putin, President Trump countered that the United States has a lot of [state-sponsored] killers [as well].

Following the tradition of previous administration invoking the Monroe Doctrine, the United States ruthlessly intervened in South and Central American affairs with deadly consequences beginning with Eisenhower (1953–1961) and continuing with President Ronald Reagan (1984–1989). The CIA, USA's *secret police*, was instrumental in training U.S. allies in the arts of torture, assassination, and terror. During the period 1952–1990, it is estimated that CIA-sponsored death squads killed hundreds of thousands in Latin America, greatly contributing to the current unrest in these countries in the twenty-first century. The 1954 Guatemalan coup clearly illustrates this phenomenon. Guatemalan leader, General Jorge Ubico, a U.S.-sponsored dictator since 1930, one who gave large landholdings to American United Fruit Company (UFCO) as well as allowing for U.S. military bases, was overthrown in 1944 during the country's first democratic elections. A number of events led to the U.S.-sponsored coup ten years later: the first president, Juan Jose Arevalo, established a minimum wage to the dismay of UFCO, which had long exploited its local workforce; while the second elected president, Jacobo Arbenz, made further social reforms, including granting small landholdings to peasants (mostly Mayan Indians and Mestizos), hence breaking up the large landholdings of UFCO. This was too much for American capitalist's interests, and plans began under President Truman to undermine these democratically elected presidents by labeling them "communists." Direct action began when the Dulles brothers instigated the coup of 1954. A U.S.-sponsored paramilitary coup (Operation PBHISTORY) overthrew Arbenz and installed a military dictator, Colonel Carlos Castillo Armas, the first of the U.S. puppet dictators. This process was discontinued in 1996 because of media cries of genocide against the Mayan population.[9]

CIA-sponsored interventions continued throughout Latin America, in Honduras, Panama, Bolivia, Columbia, Paraguay, Uruguay, Brazil, Costa Rica, El Salvador, Nicaragua, the Dominican Republic, and Haiti, where death squads targeted mostly indigenous peasant populations and their traditional communal lifestyle. Much of this was hidden from the U.S. and world public until the Iran-Contra debacle under President Ronald Reagan. The U.S. Army School of the Americas (SOA), established in 1946 and headquartered in Panama until expelled in 1984, was the CIA's headquarters for Latin American interventions. It was relocated to Fort Benning, Georgia, in 1984. It was here that the CIA and U.S. Army manuals detailing torture techniques originated. They, in turn, were used to train their Latin American counterparts, notably in El Salvador, Guatemala, Ecuador, and Peru, in these techniques. The manuals address coercive interrogation techniques that are likely to psychologically disorient their prisoners: early morning arrests; blindfolded, stripped naked, held incommunicado, sleep deprivation; toilet deprivation—all done in special windowless, soundproof, dark interrogation rooms. Waterboarding and other physical tortures were taught as well, in addition to giving sanctions to special techniques such as "disappearances," such as being thrown from helicopters.[10]

ATTACKS ON INDIANS AND MESTIZOS NOT LIMITED TO LATIN AMERICA

The controversy over Mexican workers in the United States became heated in the 1950s with the conservative, anti-Communist McCarthyism movement. A major target of McCarthyism was racial and ethnic minorities who were associated with being un-American by Senator Joseph McCarthy, J. Edgar Hoover, and Harry Anslinger. This phenomenon led to the heated bracero debate of 1951, which eventually fostered *Operation Wetback*, as well as the subsequent backlash that emerged during the turbulent 1960s when anti-immigrant sentiments abounded, spelling the eventual end of the joint U.S.-Mexico bracero farmhand program. Despite these anti-immigrant sentiments, Congress, with pressure from U.S. agribusiness, passed Public Law 78 on July 12, 1951, establishing the first effort at legislating the Mexican guest workers program, an effort that guided the guest farmworkers agreement for the next thirteen years.

In the end, over four and a half million Mexican workers were involved in the exchange of labor program sanctioned through the official Bracero Agreement. Ironically, the Bracero Program also contributed to a rush of undocumented Mexican workers into the United States. It is estimated that while a little over 200,000 guest Mexican workers were contracted for 1953, nearly 900,000 others also entered the U.S. workforce, mostly recruited to work in Texas where businesses willfully skirted the Bracero Agreement in order to pay these workers less than that stated in the U.S.-Mexico agreement. However, social and political events in the United States during the 1950s and early 1960s spelled the end of the Bracero Agreement. Increased mechanization in harvesting agricultural products, like cotton, led to a reduced need for the guest workers, legal or illegal. The fact that the guest workers program existed from 1951 until the end of 1964 was due mainly to the efforts of the Mexican government. The end of Public Law 78 did not, however, stem the flow of undocumented Mexican workers, now entering the United States to work in any venue where cheap labor was needed.[11] The cry to expel illegal Mexican workers had support not only from anti-Mexican white groups, but from Mexican Americans themselves. The 1950s was the decade of rapid political awareness among Mexican Americans, notably returning Hispanic GIs who formed the CMAA in 1954. These Mexican Americans initially supported Operation Wetback until it led to an out-of-control mass reaction toward all those of Mexican descent, including U.S. citizens and those here legally.

Although short-lived, Operation Wetback was significant in that it established the U.S. Border Patrol as a viable law enforcement agency and a legal process for adjudicating undocumented Mexicans entering the United States. Operation Wetback emerged during the conservatism of the Eisenhower administration as a reaction to complaints from Texas, Arizona, and California officials concerning an unsubstantiated stereotype of Mexican workers as being potential criminals, a label encouraged by J. Edgar Hoover and Harry Anslinger. President Eisenhower put Army General Joseph M. (Jumping Joe) Swing in charge of Operation Wetback. Swing was recently retired as commander of the Sixth Army and was a classmate of Eisenhower at West Point. He also participated in the Punitive Expedition into Mexico in 1916. In his new role, General Swing was appointed commissioner of immigration in 1954 and placed in charge of Operation Wetback, where he could conduct military-type operations against illegal Mexican immigrants without fear of an international backlash. He was in effect the de facto military head of the U.S. Border Patrol and was instrumental in transferring agents who were reluctant to follow his orders to the U.S.-Canada border.

General Swing hired two other army generals, Frank Partridge and Edwin Howard, as consultants to his border operation. Under his plan, the U.S. Border Patrol was consolidated into four districts, with the southwest region designated as that along the U.S.-Mexico border. General Swing's border patrol operation established mobile task forces, rapid response teams, and other military-style tactics, including airlifts, buslifts, trainlifts, and boatlifts for the purpose of transporting captured illegal Mexicans (Mojados) back to Mexico, away from the border frontier where they could easily return to the United States. The use of tracking dogs was also implemented by the border patrol, setting the stage for the system still employed today in law enforcement. While short-lived and expensive, Operation Wetback set the stage for future border patrol enforcement endeavors. General Swing significantly changed the border patrol while soliciting cooperation with the Mexican government in the control of illegal immigrant workers. In its two-month life, the border patrol is purported to have deported over a million illegal Mexican workers, mostly from California and Texas. The negative stigma associated with the widely publicized program had a detrimental effect on all people of Mexican heritage, especially those of Indian or mixed-blood (Mestizos). Accordingly, many U.S. citizens of Mexican descent were confronted and forced to prove their citizenship. Those who could not were summarily arrested and immediately deported without due process to habeas corpus protection. Apparently, President Eisenhower, the U.S. attorney general, and the FBI were not opposed to the public and media attention paid to Operation Wetback being played out within the highly charged anti-minority McCarthyism movement of the time.[12]

The Eisenhower administration also had dire plans for Indian Country, attempting to end U.S. treaty obligations and reverse the progress made during the F. D. Roosevelt administration. In 1953, the newly elected president reappointed Dillon Myer, the former head of the Japanese-American Relocation Centers, to be the BIA commissioner. Myer was noted for his dictatorial methods, which were equated with that of General Scott during the forced removal of the Cherokees in 1838 (*Trail of Tears*) and those of Colonel Kit Carson in the deadly forced removal of the Navajos in 1864 (*Long Walk*). *Termination* was introduced into law as House Concurrent Resolution 108 in conjunction with Public Law 280. These laws were based on the actions taken by the State of New York that adopted similar laws for the tribes under their administration (nonfederalized at the time). The initiative of the new Eisenhower administration and his Republican Congress for the termination of Indian Country began in August 1953 with passage of two complementary congressional acts: House Concurrent Resolution 108, which ended federal responsibility among designated specific tribes, and Public Law 280, which replaced federal civil and criminal jurisdiction over Indian Country with that of the state in which the federal reservation was located. Initially the states and tribes were:

California: All Indian Country within the state;
Minnesota: All Indian Country within the state, except the Red Lake Reservation;

Nebraska: All Indian Country within the state;

Oregon: All Indian Country within the state, except Warm Springs Reservation; and

Wisconsin: All Indian Country within the state, except Menominee Reservation.

The Menominee Reservation was later added in 1954 and Alaska was added when it became a state in 1959. Accordingly, Public Law 280 affected Indians in sixteen states: Alaska (except Metlakatla Indians); California; Minnesota (except Red Lake Reservation); Nebraska (except Omaha Reservation); Oregon (except Warm Springs Reservation); Wisconsin (mandatory states); and Arizona, Florida, Idaho, Iowa, Montana, Nevada, North Dakota, South Dakota, Utah, and Washington (option states). The mandatory states held full state jurisdiction on the federal reservations (Indian Country), while optional states had more conditions placed on them. In theory, state and tribal authority was supposed to be concurrent, both the federal enclave laws and the major crimes were taken from federal authority (FBI and U.S. attorney) and wholly supplanted by the states, hence giving the states the authority to enforce their regular criminal and civil laws inside Indian Country. A major problem that led to a double standard of justice was the caveat that these states were not allowed to tax tribal governments for the services they were authorized to provide under the federal turnover. Later, in 1968, tribes were finally given the opportunity to opt out of PL 280, while states also had the option to engage the retrocession clause. Termination was done unilaterally without tribal consent. Indeed, no tribe agreed to termination although some 190 tribes were affected, including 1,362,155 acres in Indian Country, and 11,466 tribal members, resulting in the shrinkage of federal Indian trust lands by 3.2 percent. Excess lands generated by termination were appraised and sold by the U.S. government to a non-Indian bidder, often involving collusion, and the proceeds were then assigned to the tribe minus the processing fees determined by the secretary of the interior. Public Law 280 added insult to injury by forcing these terminated tribes to come under state control. All exemptions from state taxing authority ended with termination, and, at the same time, all special federal programs to tribes were discontinued, placing the tribal members at the mercy of the white-dominated political and law enforcement apparatus, essentially ending tribal sovereignty.[13]

Relocation was a companion program designed to empty what was left of Indian Country, a form of blatant *cultural genocide*. The relocation initiative, like termination, was picked up by Myer's successor, Commissioner of Indian Affairs Glenn Emmons. The majority of the first wave came from the Great Plains tribes, followed by tribes from the southwestern region—the tribes that were involved in the Indian Wars of the 1860s–1890s. Returning Indian veterans from WWII were specially targeted for fear that they would cause a disruption once they returned to their home tribes. By 1954, relocation offices existed in Denver, Salt Lake City, Los Angeles, San Francisco, Oakland, San Jose, St. Louis, Dallas, Cleveland, Oklahoma City, and Tulsa. BIA figures indicate that by the end of 1954, over 6,000 American Indians had been resettled in these urban settings. Between 1952 and 1955, some 3,000 reservation Indians, mostly from southwestern tribes, were relocated to Chicago alone. But without adequate education and training, most of the jobs that were available ended up being low-paying seasonal jobs, setting up a self-filling prophecy of endless poverty among this new class of *urban Indians*.[14]

An assessment of termination from the American Indian perspective was expressed by the leaders of American Indian Historical Society:

> Religious groups and white-controlled humanitarian organizations generally embodied the worst of the growing paternalism toward the Natives. Finally, the federal government, jockeying precariously between policies of assimilation and the growing recognition that the tribes simply would not disappear together with their unique cultures, originate what has become known as the "Relocation Program." Indians were induced to go to the cities for training in the arts of the technological world. There they were dumped into housing that in most cases was ghetto-based, into jobs that were dead end, and training that failed to lead to professions and occupations. The litany of that period provides the crassest example of government ignorance of the Indian situation. The "Indian Problem" did not go away. It worsened. The policies of the Eisenhower administration, which espoused the termination of federal-Indian relationships, were shown to be a failure, a gross injustice added to a history of injustice. . . . Tribes found that termination brought deeper poverty, hopelessness, despair, thrusting the Indian into the darkest regions between two worlds, that of the Native American and that of the Euroamerican.[15]

Another view on termination/relocation was provided by the U.S. Congressional American Indian Policy Review Commission:

> After World War II, Indian perceptions of reservations and cities began to change. The war showed many Indians a world they had never seen and seldom heard of. There were opportunities for achievement in the military service which they had never found on reservations. They proved themselves capable of using those opportunities and returned home with confident hopes that they could make their reservations better places to live. This hope soon turned to despair as they tackled the obstacles which impeded reservation development. . . . At the same time, the Federal policy of assimilation manifested itself in a new way. A theory that reservations

were overpopulated gained credence. . . . Rather than pursuing a way to make Indian homelands financially secure places to live, the Federal government chose to follow a simpler approach, relocation of Indians away from the reservations. . . . The Federal government not only failed to provide needed services to the Indians it relocated, but actually refused to provide these services. The Federal relocation program was to be initiated by the BIA but was left to be implemented by local, state and county assistance programs, or churches or humanitarian organizations. The only thing that was shrugged off at the reservation boundaries, it turned out, was Federal responsibility.[16]

The combined policies of termination and relocation posed additional challenges to policing American Indians, now extending the long arm of the law to include state police, county sheriffs, and local police agencies, many of whom fostered strong anti-Indian sentiments. While the BIA police and FBI held primary jurisdiction in the remaining Indian Country, the status of relocated Indians returning to Indian Country, if only to visit relatives, added another complication regarding who had jurisdiction over these individuals. A major difference from the nineteenth century was the omission of the U.S. military in policing Indian Country—that is until the turbulent 1960s and 1970s. The policies of termination, relocation, and Public Law 280, during the 1950s and 1960s, served to strip a number of tribes of their criminal justice authority and set the stage for another era of congressional inaction relevant to both criminal and social justice for American Indians. Public Law 280 represented a last-ditch effort in the twentieth century to enforce cultural genocide in Indian Country.

The Eisenhower administration laid the foundation for the *militarization of law enforcement* as we know it today. He used both the federalized National Guard and army in enforcing domestic civil rights laws, taking the power away from Southern governors determined to use the National Guard as their own special militia enforcing Jim Crow standards. Now the job of resisting desegregation forced defiant governors to rely mainly on county sheriffs, local police, and the Ku Klux Klan to enforce the status quo. President Eisenhower was also responsible for militarizing the federal border patrol by placing General Swing in charge during Operation Wetback. Moreover, the CIA under Allen Dulles became the United States' "secret police," matching the Soviet Union's KGB in sponsored "death squads" among the military and paramilitary forces of Latin American dictators. Here, the CIA was sponsoring methods clearly outlawed by the U.S. Constitution, the UN, and the Geneva Convention, practices that continued up to the Reagan administration and reintroduced by President George W. Bush in the "Gulf Wars." The president and the Congress further complicated policing American Indians via their ignoble *final so-*

lution to the long-standing *Indian Problem*—termination and relocation. Here, the hope was to marginalize American Indians by destroying any remnant of their language and traditional culture by placing them under the control of often hateful state and county white politicians and law enforcement agencies, while at the same time forcing their youth off the reservation into impoverished urban ghettos where it was hoped that they would become indistinguishable from other "peoples of color"—blacks, Mexicans, Asians. Thus, the anti-minority rhetoric of WASP politicians and top law enforcement officials during this time clearly fanned the flames of divisiveness and discontent that erupted in mass disobedience in the 1960s and 1970s.

PROTESTS OF DISCONTENT: ANTIWAR STUDENT PROTESTS, CIVIL RIGHTS PROTESTS, RIOTS, AND CHAOS

Rosa Parks's challenge of bus segregation fostered the *Freedom Riders* in 1961, passing the civil rights controversy into the lap of newly elected Democratic President John F. Kennedy (JFK) and his brother, Robert Kennedy, the newly appointed attorney general. James Farmer of the Congress of Racial Equality (CORE) planned these events, along with members of the Student Nonviolent Coordinating Committee (SNCC), with the intent of engaging white college students into the civil rights movement, a factor in the larger anti-Vietnam, antidraft movement that exploded following the acceleration of the Vietnam War in 1965. The Freedom Riders were challenging Jim Crow segregation via the desegregation orders issued by the Interstate Commerce Commission. When the Freedom Riders were viciously attacked and their buses burned in Alabama, Attorney General Robert Kennedy sent in some six hundred U.S. Marshals to restore order and to counter the Alabama governor's martial law order, which he intended on enforcing by the deployment of the state National Guard. Similar actions occurred in Mississippi, where twenty-seven Freedom Riders were arrested.

In 1962, President Kennedy federalized the Mississippi National Guard in order to prevent white violence directed toward black student, native of Mississippi, and U.S. Air Force veteran James Meredith in attempts to keep him from matriculating into the University of Mississippi. In the ensuing riots, two people were killed and twenty-eight U.S. Marshals wounded. Conspicuously absent were the FBI and its all-white force. Then 1963 saw further intensification of Southern resistance to desegregation protest, resulting in the Reverend Martin Luther King Jr.'s arrest in April in Alabama. Then, on June 12 Medgar

Evers, a black NAACP field aide, was assassinated. The white suspect was subsequently acquitted twice by local white juries. President Kennedy had to again federalize a state National Guard in order to enforce a desegregation order, this time at the University of Alabama. Here, Governor George Wallace physically blocked black students from entering the University of Alabama in Tuscaloosa, and again a Southern governor was denied the use of the state's National Guard as a militia for segregation.

Another critical event leading to passage of the U.S. civil rights laws was the September 15 bombing of the black Sixteenth Street Baptist Church in Birmingham, Alabama, resulting in the deaths of four black children and injuring seventeen others attending Sunday school. Indeed, the culmination of these nonviolent black protests, and most likely the incentive for the Sixteenth Street bombing, was the Reverend Martin Luther King Jr.'s August 28 massive "I Have a Dream" rally in Washington, DC. The Kennedy administration ended with the assassination of the president on November 22, 1963, in Dallas, Texas.[17] President Kennedy most likely would have pursued civil rights and desegregation if not confronted with critical international issues such as the 1961 Bay of Pigs fiasco and the 1962 Cuban Crises, placing the United States and the Soviet Union on the brinks of a devastating nuclear war. Additional foreign conflicts added the Dominican Republic to the Latin American hotspots, while crises in Algeria and the Congo placed the ever-present U.S. Sixth Fleet on constant alert, and a further buildup in Southeast Asia, conditions that also plagued Kennedy's successor, Lyndon B. Johnson.

The Vietnam War added fuel to the civil rights movement at a time when events were being shown in real time via television and the evening news programs. Stephanson saw Vietnam involvement as yet another chapter in America's policy of Manifest Destiny. Accordingly, Henry Kissinger's *Realpolitik*, driven politics, was a reinforcement of the United States' divine anointment as leader of the "free world," whose duty it was to vigorously prosecute the cold war wherever this may take us, like Southeast Asia: With this philosophy came the policies of "regime change" and "world policemen."[18] And while President Lyndon B. Johnson eventually took the blame (it cost him his reelection campaign in 1968) by escalating the Vietnam War, he is also credited in getting the civil rights laws passed in a divided Congress.

The landmark Civil Rights Act, passed by the Congress, was signed by President Lyndon B. Johnson on July 3, 1964. This bill prohibits racial discrimination in public accommodations, employment, unions, and all federally funded programs and projects. The law passed despite a filibuster by Southern senators, setting the stage for the Southern white's last hurrah and the slow demise of the Confederacy, a process that lasted until the twenty-first century—with state legislatures finally removing the Confederate flag from their capitals and other state institutions. The Civil Rights Act was preceded by the January 1964 ratification of the Twenty-Fourth Amendment to the U.S. Constitution. The Twenty-Fourth Amendment prohibited the use of a poll tax, or any other device, used to prevent citizens from their constitutional right to vote in federal elections for president, vice-president, senators, or representatives. The poll tax was the primary Jim Crow de facto law used to disenfranchise impoverished peoples of color from voting. In 1965, the Congress legislated the Twenty-Fourth Amendment with passage of the Voting Rights Act, again due mainly to President Johnson's extensive lobbying of his former colleagues in the Congress. President Johnson signed the Voting Rights Act on August 6, 1965.

The seemingly schizophrenic atmosphere in Washington, DC, and the country at the time (passage of the Civil Rights and Voting Rights Acts, passage of Medicare and programs of Johnson's Great Society designed to end poverty, and Dr. King receiving the Nobel Peace Prize) were often overshadowed by the rapidly accelerating U.S. involvement in Vietnam and neighboring countries. The confluence of these issues resulted in massive civil disobedience. While many blacks were glad for these efforts at desegregation, this sentiment was not fully shared by those long suffering in ghetto poverty, leading to riots in New York City in the summer of 1964; the murder of three civil rights workers (James Chaney, Andrew Goodman, and Michael Schwerner), in Philadelphia, Mississippi, in August 1964; the Free Speech movement at the University of California at Berkeley in the fall of 1964; Malcolm X's assassination (February 21, 1965); the police brutality during the "March to Montgomery" (March 1965); race riots in Watts, Los Angeles (August, 1965), Atlanta and Chicago (September 1966), and Detroit (July 1967); and the spontaneous riots throughout the country following the murder of the Reverend Martin Luther King Jr. on April 4, 1968. College and university students joined in the mass antiwar protest movement, including the "March on the Pentagon" (October 1967); campus takeovers in 1968; the infamous riot at the 1968 Democratic Party Convention in Chicago; the coordinated antiwar protest in Washington, DC, and across the nation in the fall of 1969, concluding with the Kent State University and Jackson State University protests resulting in unarmed students killed by National Guard soldiers (May 4, 1970); and the Attica (New York) Prison riot (September 1971). These were the events that divided American society during this era, setting the stage for the "law and order" society that challenged the equal protection of all citizens, notably minorities, from biased policing.[19]

President Lyndon B. Johnson federalized the Alabama National Guard in an attempt to protect peaceful protestors in Selma and to prevent the brutal beating of protestors by state police and sheriff deputies in an earlier march. Later, in 1968, Johnson federalized National Guard units in Michigan, Illinois, and the federal district (DC) to assist local police in patrolling streets and prevent rioting following the assassination of Reverend Martin Luther King Jr. Federalized National Guard units, while under federal and not state control, did not always keep the peace as intended—instead often adding to the chaos, resulting in death and injury to protestors, even peaceful ones such as the deaths inflicted at Kent State University and Jackson State University in 1970. Despite J. Edgar Hoover's Communist conspiracy and Communist infiltrators and agitators among minorities and colleges and universities, none were found in the detailed government investigation of the riots and unrest of the 1960s and 1970s.

The comprehensive *Eisenhower Report* on the history of violence in America noted the lack of an organized conspiracy surrounding the era of unrest:

> The President's Advisory Commission on Civil Disorders (Kerner Commission) sponsored a variety of social research studies that focused mainly on the attitudes of the public and the rioters. . . . From all sources, one conclusion emerges, namely the absence of organized conspiracy in commodity riots. However, the absence of organized conspiracy does not mean the absence of a pattern of events. Thus, Jules J. Wanderer's analysis of 75 riots during the period from 1965–67 demonstrates the pattern of events in these outbursts. By means of the Guttman scale techniques, he demonstrated the consistent cumulation of a very similar configuration of violence from low to high intensity. The difference from one outburst to another involved the extent to which each one proceeded through the various stages of increased and intensified collective behavior. . . . The new type of rioting is most likely to be set off by an incident involving the police in the ghetto where some actual or believed violation of accepted police practice has taken place. The very first phase is generally nasty and brutish: the police are stoned, crowds collect, and tension mounts. The second stage is reached with the breaking of windows. Local social control breaks down and the population recognizes that a temporary opportunity for looting is available. The atmosphere changes quickly and this is when positive enthusiasm is released. But all too briefly. If the crowds are not dispersed and order restored, the third state of the riot is the transformation wrought by arson, firebombs, and sniper fire and the countermeasures then by police and uniformed soldiers.
>
> [Regarding the role of the National Guard] There is some evidence that one index to National Guard effectiveness is the extent of integration of units. Because of its fraternal spirit, most National Guard units have been able to resist Federal directives and Negros accounted for less than 2 percent of its personnel in 1967. In those cases where integration took place, it meant that the units were seen as more legitimate by the local population.

Moreover, units that were forced to integrate were more likely to be concerned with problems of conflict in the unit and developed an officer corps concerned with these issues. For example, units in Detroit and Newark were not integrated while Chicago-based units that were employed during the summer disturbances of 1965 were integrated and had Negro officers.

In contrast to the criminal interpretation [of the race riots], the alternative formulation of the commodity riots as a form of political insurrection appears equally inadequate, if by insurrection is meant an armed social movement with an explicit set of goals. The very absence of evidence of prior planning—either rightist or leftist—would weaken such an interpretation. In 23 disorders studied by the Kerner Commission, none were "caused by, nor were they the consequence of any plan or conspiracy." But more important, it is striking that during the riots of 1964 to 1967, there was a remarkable absence of visible leadership—either existing or emergent—that sought to press for collective demands. It is, of course, clear that the leadership and support of the civil rights movement were not centrally involved in the riots. The emphasis of the civil-rights leaders on issues such as school integration, access to public accommodation, and voting rights were less directly relevant to the immediate lives of slum dwellers, who were mainly concerned with the welfare system and the immediate employment opportunities. The impact of the riots of 1967 on the civil-rights movement was drastic in that it made the movement's demands more militant. But clearly the leaders of the civil-rights movement were not activists in these outbursts. If anything, they occurred because of the inability of the civil-rights movement to accomplish sufficient social change in the slums, although the movement made a decisive contribution in intensifying aspirations and group consciousness.[20]

Student campus protests, on the other hand, appeared to reflect political action. Considerable damage was done on campus throughout the country during "sit ins." Antiwar and civil rights groups coordinated their efforts in August in Chicago, where they planned a youth festival. These groups included the mostly white, middle-class National Mobilization Committee to End the War in Vietnam; the Youth International Party (Yippies); the Students for a Democratic Society (SDS); and the Black Panthers. The youth event coincided with the 1968 Democratic National Convention, where Mayor Daley called out both the police and the National Guard, some 23,000 in all, to provoke and attack the 10,000 unarmed protesters. The entry in the *American Century* provides a worldview of the 1968 Chicago police riot:

[Chicago, August 29, 1968] A splintered Democratic Party nominated Hubert Humphrey as its presidential candidate on the first ballot tonight. . . . The convention was haunted by the ghost of the slain Robert Kennedy; a move to draft his younger brother, Ted nearly split the party, and the platform committee refused to embrace opponents of the Vietnam War. All week Chicago was badly divided, and nowhere were the divisions more visible than in the blood-spattered streets near the convention Amphitheater. Ten thousand young people came to Chicago to protest the war, but flower power was no match for police power. "Kill 'em, kill 'em," the police shouted as they charged. "Pigs, pigs, oink, oink," the demonstrators screamed back. One witness heard an officer yell, "We'll kill all you bastards," as he clubbed a protester. And as news cameras rolled and clubs flew, the protesters chanted, "The whole world's watching! The whole world's watching!" Some 700 demonstrators were hurt and 650 arrested. Police reported 80 of their men injured. Critics said the cops acted like Nazis, but Mayor Richard Daley backed the 20,000 police, National Guard and soldiers. . . . Inside the convention hall, nervous security guards caught up in the violent scene scuffled with and clubbed some delegates and newsmen. Walter Cronkite, the normally reserved CBS anchorman, called the guards "thugs."[21]

The Justice Department, under President Richard Nixon, showed no mercy toward the student protestors, charging the "leaders" with conspiracy and incitement to riot. These leaders, Abbie Hoffman, Tom Hayden, David Dellinger, Rennie Davis, John Froines, Jerry Rubin, Lee Weiner, and Bobby Seale, became known as the "Chicago Eight." They were tried in February 1970 by Federal District Judge Julius Hoffman, whose biases became readily known in the televised trials. A separate trial was set for Black Panther leader, Bobby Seal, who was bound and gagged by the judge during his trail. The now "Chicago Seven" were found not guilty of conspiring to incite a riot, while five defendants, Davis, Dellinger, Hayden, Hoffman, and Rubin, were convicted of crossing state lines with intent to cause a riot. Judge Hoffman (no relation to Abbie) handed down maximum five-year sentences. Judge Hoffman added to these sentences for contempt. The convictions were ultimately reversed on appeal with the U.S. government declining to retry any of the defendants, if not for the massive worldwide backlash to what many perceived as a Soviet-type reaction to public protests.[22]

J. Edgar Hoover, Mayor Richard Daley, governors Ronald Reagan of California (1967–1975) and Nelson Rockefeller of New York (1959–1973), and President Richard M. Nixon (1969–1974) represented the "law and order" political hierarchy that fueled both the mass protests and the overreach by law enforcement and the military (National Guard) during this era. Nine months following the 1968 Chicago police riot, on May 4, 1970, Ohio National Guardsmen fired high-powered (30-06 caliber) rounds into antiwar protesters at Kent State University and eleven days later at Jackson State College (now University) on May 15, 1970, some seventy-five police, led by the Mississippi Highway Patrol, fired a volley of shotgun buckshot at student antiwar protesters. These were part of 451 campus protest that erupted in May as a reaction to the illegal "Martial-Law" actions of Nixon's Attorney General John Mitchell's roundup of protesters in a May 3, 1970, mass protest at a Washington, DC, rally, holding them without due process. At Kent State University, Ohio National Guardsmen killed four and wounded ten, while at Jackson State Mississippi State local police killed two students and wounded twelve. The last major event capping this harsh reaction to public dissent was the Attica Prison riot in New York in September 1971. This riot, like antiwar and civil rights protests, could have been resolved more peacefully if not for Governor Rockefeller's intransient "law and order" stance, one with clear racial biases. The circumstances surrounding this debacle are articulated in *The Official Report of the New York State Special Commission on Attica*:

> Forty-three citizens of New York State died at Attica Correctional Facility between September 9 and 13, 1971. Thirty-nine of that number were killed and more than 80 others were wounded by gunfire during the 15 minutes it took the State Police to retake the prison on September 13. With the exception of Indian massacres in the late 19th century, the State Police assault which ended the four-day prison uprising was the bloodiest one-day encounter between Americans since the Civil War. . . . At Attica there was no meaningful program of education for those who wished to learn and no rehabilitation program for those who were willing to rejoin society as constructive citizens. Idleness was the principal occupation. Most correctional officers were not equipped by training to communicate with their inmates charges, and did not consider it their duty to understand or to resolve inmate problems. It is scarcely surprising that the original uprising developed almost spontaneously out of small misunderstandings only indirectly related to the major grievances that smoldered below the surface. . . . The assault itself was not carefully planned to minimize the loss of life; the choice of weapons and ammunition was based upon ready availability, not upon the logic of the specific situation; no safeguards were established to protect against excessive use of force by those who were authorized to fire; no effective control was imposed to prevent firing by those who were not supposed to participate; no adequate arrangements were made for medical care of the severe casualties that should have been anticipated; and no responsible system was established to prevent vengeful reprisals against inmates after the retaking. Whatever explanation might be advanced for official failure to deal effectively with an emergency of crisis proportions, no excuse can justify the failure of the American public to demand a better system of criminal justice, from arrest, trial, and sentencing to ultimate release from confinement.[23]

The race factor was not adequately addressed in the Attica report, notably that the overcrowded prison held mostly urban inmates, 54 percent who were black and 9 percent Puerto Rican. White inmates were the minority (37 percent) while the 383 correctional officers were predominately white, most residing in rural upstate New York. Racial prejudices were another contributing factor in the riot. The catalyst, however, was the suspicious death of Black Panther member George Jackson two weeks earlier at San Quentin State Prison in California. Another factor was the growing influence of black Muslims within prisons throughout the county. This contributed to the Prisoners' Rights Movement where inmates were protesting living conditions and the lack of educational and rehabilitation services. Governor Rockefeller, while refusing to meet with the inmates, ordered that the prison be taken by force if the inmates did not surrender. Leading the assault force was A. C. O'Hara, a retired U.S. army general and former head of the New York National Guard. His assault unit consisted of New York State Police, National Guardsmen, and former prison guards volunteering for the "turkey shoot." On Monday, September 13, 1971, tear gas was lobbed into the prison yard, followed by a two-minute volley by shotguns fired blindly into the yard, resulting in thirty-three inmates and nine officers killed, all at the hands of General O'Hara's assault force. It was later found that one correctional officer was killed by inmates prior to the assault, as were four inmates (vigilante killings). The remaining inmates were stripped and paraded in the yard following the assault. Harsh retribution by guards continued until the Attica report became public. Clearly, Attica was a major factor in the civil unrest at this time.[24]

Attica attested to the increased division within the civil rights movement that now had the followers of the late Reverend Martin Luther King Jr.'s passive nonviolent component and the followers of the Nation of Islam and its leaders, Elijah Muhammad, Malcolm X, Louis Farrakhan, and Muhammad Ali. The former wanted to become fully integrated into American society while the latter sought out their own race-specific communities free of Jim Crow restrictions. This division within the ranks of African Americans, especially the successes attributed to the socialist-leaning Black Panthers Party, fed into J. Edgar Hoover's racist paranoia. Two factors greatly bothered J. Edgar Hoover, the socialistic nature of the Black Panther Party and its insistence on "open carry" of firearms as part of their community watch system that was used to monitor the police within their communities. The Black Panther Party began in October 1966 in Oakland, California, a massive urban ghetto just across the bay from San Francisco. Their community programs such as the Free Breakfast for Children Program, school tutoring, and health clinics were soon adopted throughout other impoverished black ghettos so that in two years, Black Panther Party officers and programs were located in sixty-eight communities.

But J. Edgar Hoover was not going to let this continue, and he engaged the FBI in clandestine illegal and extralegal offenses targeting the Black Panthers under his COINTELPRO offensive. Using agent provocateurs, Hoover was able to discredit and harass the Black Panther Party into extinction by 1982. Denenberg described the rationale for COINTELPRO:

> Hoover considered all black power groups extreme, so extreme tactics were called for. Hoover decided to implement COINTELPRO. COINTEL-PRO was the code name for *Counter Intelligence Program*. Counterintelligence meant that action would be taken to weaken these organizations. Convinced that these groups were out to harm the nation, Hoover set out to destroy them. The tactics that characterized COINTELPRO were the most extreme in the bureau's history. The use of these tactics marked a radical and major change in FBI methods. . . . FBI agents in the field were directed to take steps that would cause members of black radical groups to become fearful, mistrustful of one another, and confused. Agents were directed to exploit *all* avenues that might accomplish this and to recommend ideas. Organization leaders were arrested repeatedly for minor, and sometimes made-up, charges. The arrests were meant to drain the organization's personal and financial resources and hinder its ability to act. One COINTELPRO tactic had the odd-sounding code name "bad jacketing," and referred to a key individual becoming the subject of an FBI campaign to create suspicions about him or her within the organization. Once an individual was targeted for "bad jacketing," rumors were spread and evidence was made up. Sometimes there were attempts to convince other members that the targeted individual was an FBI informer. COINTELPRO tactics were used against all of the black power groups active in the late 1960s and early 1970s. In all, there were 360 separate operations. But the most unrestrained use of these tactics was aimed at the Black Panther party.[25]

J. Edgar Hoover's COINTELPRO-BLACK HATE initiative began while Martin Luther King Jr. was still alive, attacking his as well as other nonviolent black protest groups like SNCC, CORE, and the Nation of Islam, in addition to the Black Panther Party. But once Reverend King was assassinated, J. Edgar Hoover was determined to prevent the rise of another Black messiah. The core of this effort was to deny the rise of another respectable black leader, and in order to do this, he had to create a scenario whereby the public image of blacks met his hateful impression of the group. But Hoover did not stop there; once in place, the clearly extralegal, often outright criminal, COINTELPRO tactics were directed against all left-leaning groups regardless of racial affiliation. Interestingly, the CIA was a partner in these secret police activities, calling their program Operation CHAOS, again directing "dirty tricks" toward black protests, including those of Martin Luther King Jr.[26]

J. Edgar Hoover often enlisted the use of local police forces in assisting and carrying out blatantly illegal activities such as break-ins, planting incriminating objects within their homes, vandalism of individual and group property, assaults, beatings, and assassinations. This was in addition to using FBI informants within the Ku Klux Klan to carry out violence against black protestors, including murder.[27] The case that clearly illustrated the extent of these race-based illegal activities was the assassination of Fred Hampton, national spokesman for the Black Panther Party, in December 1969:

> In 1969, the FBI was investigating all 42 chapters and 1,200 members of the Black Panther party for possible violations of the law. But the Panthers were now talking less about violence and more about helping the community in other ways. They were organizing tenant strikes, daycare centers, and health clinics. One of their most popular activities was the free breakfast for children program. The FBI made repeated attempts to disrupt and destroy these programs. There were a number of shoot-outs between the police and the Panthers. . . . One of these cases involved the FBI's COINTELPRO tactics as they were used against Fred Hampton and the Illinois chapter of the Black Panthers. The FBI's "Racial Matters Squad" had compiled 4,000 pages of information on Hampton, the nationally known chairman of the Illinois Black Panthers. The [FBI planted] informer gave the bureau a floor plan of Hampton's apartment. The FBI worked closely with the Chicago police in planning their December 4, 1969, raid. At 4:30 A.M., fourteen Chicago policemen, supposedly looking for weapons, raided Hampton's apartment. They were armed with 27 guns, including 5 shotguns and a submachine gun. The police claimed they raided the house only after being fired on. But evidence shows that the Panthers fired only one shot, while the police fired between 83 and 99 shots. Forty-two were fired at Hampton's bed. He died in the raid.[28]

Blacks and other protest groups at the time were quite aware of the FBI's clandestine war being waged against them, one where their Bill of Rights (the first ten Amendments to the U.S. Constitution) were being circumvented. It was as if the FBI, CIA, and their surrogate local law enforcement agencies had declared martial law on groups bent on exercising their basic rights to free speech and assembly. Being killed certainly put an end to one's habeas corpus rights. Yet another ally in this clandestine war against minorities and student protestors was General Lewis B. Hershey, director of the Selective Service System. He was an enlisted man with the Indiana National Guard when his unit served along the Mexican border during the Mexican Revolution and later served with the American Expeditionary Force during WWI. He then joined the regular army, serving as the executive officer of the Selective Service System in 1941, and soon became the director, serving in this capacity until February 1970, spanning three wars—WWII, Korea, and Vietnam.

It was during his tenure during the Vietnam War that he used the draft as a form of punishment for those opposed to the war. As a reaction to campus demonstrations against military recruiting, he issued Local Board Memorandum No. 85, aka the Hershey Directive, whereby anyone "violating" their draft card was immediately reclassified as "available for service." The Hershey Directive was appealed to the Third Circuit Court of Appeals, which ruled in January 1970 that the director of the Selective Service System did not have the statutory authority to unilaterally reclassify [punish] those he felt were abusing their draft cards. All delinquent reclassifications were held invalid because the Hershey Directive voided due process, in addition to his lack of statutory authority to issue such an order in the first place. Nonetheless, President Richard Nixon rewarded Hershey by promoting him to full (four-star) general, allowing him to retire at this rank in 1973.[29]

Collectively, the FBI, CIA, and the Selective Service System aided J. Edgar Hoover in creating his self-fulfilling prophecy of the violent, Communist agitators bent on destroying America. The Hoover prophecy manifested itself in the emergence of extreme groups like the Weather Underground Organization (WUO) and the Black Liberation Army (BLA). Like in Europe at this time, radical white left-wing groups consisted not of impoverished disenfranchised minorities of color, but rather drew their ranks from the affluent upper-middle and upper classes. These were privileged white youth attending "good" colleges and universities. The *Weathermen* were part of the Revolutionary Youth Movement faction of the SDS. The Weathermen were the most radical component of the SDS, actually engaging in attacks on government buildings and banks and justifying these actions as antiwar protests. They also attacked government buildings in Washington, DC, including the Capital (March 1, 1971), Pentagon (May 19, 1972), and the Department of State (January 29, 1973), causing little damage, but gaining considerable attention to their opposition to the Vietnam War. The greatest damage was the March 6, 1970, premature explosion at the Weatherman's Greenwich Village safe house that killed three of the bomb makers—devices intended for a social event at Fort Dix. WUO leaders avoided prosecution due to illegal wiretapping by the FBI's COINTELPRO operations, and the SDS lost much of its campus support following the end of the Vietnam War in 1975.[30]

Black radicalism, unlike the radical actions of privileged white students, could be seen as a direct result of the government's efforts to destroy black protest groups, beginning with Martin Luther King Jr. The devastation wrought upon the Black Panther Party by the FBI contributed to the emergence of the BLA. The BLA was a radical, armed group determined to actively confront what they perceived as the oppression and tyranny of the U.S. government toward black Americans. Black Panther Eldridge Cleaver was a leader of the

BLA, which often targeted law enforcement officers in retaliation for the assassination of Fred Hampton, resulting in a dozen police deaths. The BLA's criminal acts included the 1972 hijacking of a Delta plane for one million dollars ransom and then diverting it to Algeria. One of their last violent criminal acts was the 1981 Brinks truck robbery in Nanuet, New York, of 1.6 million dollars, which also resulted in the death of a Brinks guard and two police officers. This incident was done in conjunction with assistance from former WUC members now part of the "May 19 Communist Organization." Again, the subsequent trials of BLA members opened up the government and law enforcement files and continued COINTELPRO tactics, including confessions gleaned from torture and evidence gained through extralegal and illegal methods. Hoover's plan for dismissing blacks as an inferior human subtype inadvertently led to the rise of a new black leader—that of Muhammad Ali. Hoover's death on May 2, 1972, at age seventy-seven, most likely prohibited him from realizing the extent of the public outrage over his secret wars on race and class in America. Nonetheless, President Richard M. Nixon appreciated Hoover's militant policing of America's "public enemies" and provided him with a state funeral with military honors.[31]

BRONZE POWER PROTEST AND CESAR CHAVEZ'S FARMWORKERS

During the turbulent civil rights and antiwar era of the 1960s and 1970s, Cesar Chavez became a prominent figure of the Brown-Power Mexican American movement. The Brown Power movement was designed to empower the Mestizo population, mixed-blooded Mexicans—those long ostracized by the middle-class "other white" Hispanics who claimed to be of "pure" Spanish heritage. The intragroup race and class division within Hispanics was borne out with Operation Wetback, when the "other white" Mexican Americans were eager to have their "lesser" brown Hispanics ceremoniously and forcefully removed from the United States and taken back to the peon villages of interior Mexico. Chavez, clearly a Mestizo, got his start within the Mexican American Community Service Organization (CSO), which supported LULAC principles of getting Hispanics involved in language and citizenship classes and registered to vote in local and state elections. Together these efforts were termed *La Causa* during the 1950s court battles. The ultimate goal of these organizations was getting Hispanics elected in communities in the Borderland regions of Texas, New Mexico, Arizona, and California.

But Chavez took the CSO in California in a different direction, focusing on labor issues. He essentially shifted the Hispanic focus away from middle-class "other white" Mexican Americans to the brown Indian and Indian-mix Mestizo. This departure led the CSO board to abandon Chavez in 1961, attesting to the intragroup prejudices existing among Mexican Americans themselves. Chavez's affiliation with farmworkers began in 1965 when he became leader for both striking Filipino and Mexican workers in the vineyards of California (this included both Filipino and Mexicans who were citizens as well as guest workers). The prolonged strike gave Chavez and the National Farm Workers Organization national and international attention and support. In the fall of 1970, the last holdout agreed to the farmworkers' demands for a minimum wage. This attention occurred at a time when numerous other groups were demonstrating and protesting across the country for civil rights for minorities and against the Vietnam War. Groups that rallied with the Filipino and Mexican farmworkers included college students, African Americans, and those of draft age. With this support and notoriety, Chavez and the farmworkers took their battle to the fruit and vegetable fields and orchards throughout California. This attention to Mestizos ignited a spark in the barrio ghetto slums of Californian cities, leading to the larger Brown Power movement.

Chavez's farmworkers movement focused attention on the gap created by ending the Bracero Program that once provided some protections for Mexican farmworkers. With the Bracero Program's demise, new waves of immigration flooded the U.S. borders, including Asians displaced by the Vietnam War and Hispanics from Central and South America as well as Mexico. This new wave of immigrants, legal and illegal, flooded Southern California, adding to the overcrowded conditions of the economically challenged inner cities already occupied by African Americans, Hispanics, and the recently "relocated" American Indians. These interracial tensions forced each ethnic subgroup to fight for their territory and limited resources, as well as forcing the groups to assert their cultural identity within this conflicting ecosystem. Hence, the rise of the Brown Power movement.[32]

A professional boxer from the barrio of Denver is credited with igniting the bronze element of the Mexican American community. Rodolfo "Corky" Gonzales was a well-known Hispanic boxer whose status was critical in inspiring the more radical elements of the Brown Power movement of the 1960s and 1970s. In this sense, he played a role similar to Muhammad Ali and the Black Power movement. While both organizations were started by nonviolent protests, initiated by Martin Luther King Jr. and Cesar Chavez, the next step in the ethic protest movement was a more aggressive one that included the long-suffering urban youth. Gonzales broke away from his role with the Crusade for Justice organization in Denver in 1965. His stance was not integration, like those espoused by LULAC, but rather one that advocated for a separate Chicano movement. In 1968, he advocated for a Brown Power orientation for Chicanos within the larger dominant white society much like the Black Muslims advocated for African Americans. The vehicle for the separatists-oriented Brown Power movement was the La Raza Unida Party (LRUP), which aligned itself with the more radical elements of social discontent at the time, including the Black Panthers.

LRUP was short lived due to its failure to align with either Gutierrez's or Chavez's organizations. This weakness came to light at the four-day conference Gonzales called for in September 1972. At this time, a campus-based movement was underway much like the Anglo SDS movement. The Hispanic college students did not feel welcome in the SDS; instead they created their own group, MECHA (El Movimiento Estudiantil Chicano de Aztlan). MECHA originally was an outgrowth of the Chicano Youth Liberation Conference held in Denver in March 1969 with the plan now designated the Plan de Aztlan. MECHA originally was an ally of LRUP but then moderated their views by the early 1970s. By this time, the Brown Berets, the radical arm of the Brown Power movement, began to lose their radical edge. The cathartic event for the collective expression of Brown Power, collectively known as LRUP, was the National Chicano Moratorium March of August 29, 1970, held at Laguna Park in Los Angeles with representation from Hispanic organizations across the Southwest. Police reaction to the Moratorium March led to the death of three people, including *Los Angeles Times* columnist Ruben Salazar. Corky Gonzales was among the seventy arrested and jailed by the Los Angeles Police Department. Sixty-four police officers were injured in the ensuing riot that was clearly police instigated.[33]

Turmoil occurred in Mexico at this time as well, influencing the Brown Power movement in the United States. Students protesting in 1968 in Mexico City resulted in what became known as the Tlatelolco Square Massacre, where hundreds of unarmed protestors were shot. The prodemocracy student protest occurred on October 2 on the eve of the Olympics in Mexico City. The reaction of the police was one of the worst atrocities of the long-ruling Institutional Revolutionary Party (PRI) regime. Serious efforts to uncover the particulars of the PRI's dirty war were not uncovered until 2000 and the end of the PRI's seventy-one years of consecutive rule when President Vicente Fox appointed a special commission to investigate the student massacre. The investigation concluded that the military was involved in the violent suppression of leftist dissidents, including university students. Moreover, it was disclosed that the United States was involved, with the Pentagon sending military radios, weapons, ammunition, and riot-control-training support to Mexico before and during the crisis. Also, the CIA is shown to have provided reports on developments within the university community from July to October 1968.

In the Tlatelolco Square Massacre, 360 sharpshooters fired from surrounding buildings directly into the protestors, resulting in over three hundred known deaths. These deaths were not attributed to armed protestors, which the PRI press release indicated at the time. On October 2, 2008, thousands of protesters marched across Mexico City demanding justice for the 1968 student massacre by government troops, chanting "Dos de Octubre! No se olivide." Also on the fortieth anniversary of the massacre, Amnesty International joined the call to President Calderon to establish an independent inquiry into this dark chapter of Mexican history, an event that was felt across the U.S.-Mexico border, further inciting Hispanics in the United States.[34]

There is little doubt that the massacre in Mexico City in 1968 had a chilling effect on Hispanic protestors in the United States. Perhaps fearing a similar massacre in the United States, a gathering of Hispanic organizations met just across the Mexican border in El Paso, Texas, in 1972. Three thousand delegates met to determine the direction of the national La Raza Unida Party. Hispanics from the entire Southwest and adjacent regions were represented, and in the end, the moderates, those advocating peaceful change via the ballot box, prevailed. Jose Angel Gutierrez, of the Mexican American Youth Organization, with the backing of Cesar Chavez and the United Farm Workers, beat out Corky Gonzales for the party chairman position. The major outcomes of the La Raza Unida Convention were support for a guaranteed annual income for Latino workers, national health insurance, bilingual education, parity in employment, increased quotas for admission to medical schools, parity in jury selection, support for organized farmworkers, and enforcement of the land grant conditions of the 1848 Treaty of Guadalupe Hidalgo. Essentially this outcome was in concert with the goals of LULAC and the antithesis of violent interventions hinted at by Brown Power separatists.[35]

THE RISE OF THE AMERICAN INDIAN
MOVEMENT AND GOVERNMENT BACKLASH

An unintended consequence of the dual policies of cultural genocide enacted during the Eisenhower administration, *termination* and *relocation*, was the emergence of the *Pan-Indianism* and the *American Indian Movement* (AIM). Like their black and Hispanic counterparts, this was an effort for self-determination. The self-determination movement grew out of the civil unrest of the 1960s and 1970s, which also saw radicalism among both urban Indians and traditional reservation Indians. The early 1960s witnessed a movement against the combined effects of termination and relocation and the emergence of AIM. AIM, an urban militant organization founded in Minneapolis in 1968, was seen as a radical faction of the National Indian Youth Council (NIYC), a pan-Indian organization founded in 1961. In this sense, its radicalism was patterned after the Weatherman faction of the SDS, the Anglo-American college-level counterpart to the NIYC and the Black Panthers.

This radicalism influenced the takeover of Alcatraz prison on November 9, 1969. On that date, seventy-eight American Indians made a dramatic predawn raid on Alcatraz Island, home to the closed federal prison, focusing worldwide attention on the new Indian protest movement. At its peak, on November 30, 1969, about six hundred Indians, representing some fifty tribes, occupied the island. These numbers declined after electricity, water, and telephone services were cut off. All Indian occupants were forcefully removed eighteen months later. The capture of Alcatraz came to symbolize the Indian struggle for land and sovereignty and gave rise to a growing unrest that in 1972 resulted in the march across the country to Washington, DC, known as the *Trail of Broken Treaties*, and the occupation of the BIA offices in Washington, DC. Yvonne Bushyhead describes the motive for the Trail of Broken Treaties trek:

> The intent of the hundreds of Indians who caravanned to Washington, D.C. on the eve of the 1972 election was to present the two presidential candidates with a twenty-point program for reorganizing Indian-government relations and investigating treaty violations. After receiving a cold shoulder from the BIA and learning of an Interior Department memo instructing the BIA to offer "no direct or indirect assistance," they seized the BIA headquarters. After a week, participants were offered a response to their twenty-point proposal, and amnesty from prosecution, if they would leave. The promised response came in January, 1973, touting Nixon's new Indian policy, and rejecting wholesale the possibility of treaty reform. While no one was charged in connection with the takeover, AIM leaders, including Leonard Peltier, were targeted by the FBI under its Counter-Intelligence Program for surveillance and "arrest . . . on every possible charge, until they can no longer made bail," according to a memo leaked from then-Attorney General Saxbe's files. . . . The Bureau (BIA) activity during this period later came under close scrutiny, culminating in the 1975 report of the Senate Select Committee on Intelligence, headed by Senator Frank Church. The Bureau's actions were blasted by the Committee, which noted: "the chief investigative branch of the Federal Government, which was charged by law with investigating crimes and preventing criminal conduct, itself engaged in lawless tactics and responded to deep-seated social problems by creating violence and unrest." The report clearly established that the FBI was

capable of going beyond its intended investigatory functions. During the late 1960s and early '70s, the FBI was actively engaged in the systematic harassment, surveillance and infiltration of the American Indian Movement (AIM), the Black Panther Party, National Association for the Advancement of Colored People (NAACP), the National Lawyers Guild, and numerous other groups expressing political dissent. This covert program against activities in the United States, dubbed COINTELPRO, ran officially from 1953 to 1971, but the disruptive tactics continued past that date.[36]

The long-held U.S. practice of creating intratribal division manifested itself during this period, pitting government-sponsored "middle-class" Indians against the traditionalists. In a repeat of the past, these events unfolded on the Pine Ridge, South Dakota, Sioux reservation, much as they did in the winter to 1890 with the Wounded Knee massacre. The government puppet in the early 1970s was Dick Wilson, who as tribal chairman was protected by federal officers (BIA police, U.S. Marshals, FBI) as well as his own private police— the "Guardians of the Oglala Nation" aka as the GOON squad. *Wounded Knee II* is the term used in Indian Country for what the U.S. government calls the "Wounded Knee incident." The "incident" occurred from February 27 to May 8, 1973, at the Wounded Knee community on the Lakota Pine Ridge Reservation. Traditional Sioux leaders were upset with the corrupt and heavy-handed tactics and practices of tribal chairman, Richard "Dickie" Wilson, a mixed-blood, so-called progressive. The traditionalists, most full-bloods, formed the Oglala Sioux Civil Rights Organization (OSCRO) that was not successful in their effort to impeach Wilson. OSCRO members then took their protest to Wounded Knee, the site of the last major battle (massacre) during the long Indian Wars (1862–1890).

Knowing that they were no match for Wilson's GOON squad, the traditional elders sought AIM's support if only to bring attention to their plight. Under Wilson's rule most traditionalists did not share in tribal-directed, federally funded programs. Instead the reservation was split between the "haves" and "have-nots," with the latter relegated to dire poverty. In desperation, the traditional elders sought AIM's support in airing their grievance before the public. In response, AIM leaders Dennis Banks, Russell Means, Clyde and Vernon Bellecourt, and Leonard Peltier lent their support to the traditional Sioux protestors. On February 27, 1973, AIM occupied the town of Wounded Knee—the site of the army massacre of Chief Big Foot and his band in December 1890—and within three weeks, declared the independence of the Oglala Nation. For seventy-one days, the people of Wounded Knee withstood the onslaught of federal troops, SWAT teams, FBI agents, and U.S. Marshals equipped with Vietnam-era weapons (M-16 rifles, M-60 machine guns, and the like), armored personnel carriers, and helicopters. The Pentagon labeled this occupation as a "war game" coded "Garden Plot," under the military's Joint Chief of Staff. Indian casualties included two dead and many wounded. Finally, in exchange for congressional and White House talks focusing on the conditions on the Pine Ridge Reservation, the Wounded Knee protestors disbanded. Unfortunately, the talks became yet another in the long list of broken promises by the U.S. government. Instead, Wilson consolidated his despotic reign and the federal government, with the illegal tactics of the FBI, geared up to prosecute and dismember AIM.[37]

The 1974 trial of AIM leaders Dennis Banks and Russell Means was dismissed due to massive FBI misconduct:

> The misconduct by the FBI in this case included withholding and doctoring FBI files, the placing of an informer (Douglas Durham) within the defense team, and subornation of perjury. These actions were part of the Bureau's arsenal of techniques for the disruption of groups during the official span of COINTELPRO, although they occurred three years after COINTELPRO allegedly ended. Attorney William Kunstler further described the prosecution's misconduct as including failure to verify the testimony of a key witness in light of overwhelmingly contradictory information; failure to inform the court of the FBI's intervention in a rape investigation of that same witness; offering testimony which was directly contradicted by a document in its possession; and failure to provide relevant information regarding the extent of the United States military involvement in the occupation. (Based on this misconduct) the trial judge, Chief Justice Fred Nichol, dismissed charges against the defendants after concluding that the prosecution had acted in bad faith. One of the instances of improper conduct that particularly troubled Judge Nichol was the misrepresentation of [FBI] Special Agent Trimbach that there were no wiretaps at Wounded Knee.[38]

The conflicts at Pine Ridge did not end with the 1973 occupation of Wounded Knee or the 1974 acquittal of Dennis Banks and Russell Means. The traditional elders were still protesting Tribal Chairman Wilson's continued harassment by his GOON squad. These cases of abuse were ignored by the FBI, which held original law enforcement jurisdiction over Major Crimes committed in Indian Country. Aggravating the situation, the FBI, in April 1975, conducted what it called its "paramilitary operations preparedness on Indian Land" activities on Pine Ridge. The FBI used this as an excuse for increasing its presence on the Pine Ridge Reservation, ostensibly to provide support to Wilson and his GOON squad. Things came to a head on June 16, 1975, when a firefight between the FBI agents and AIM members erupted, resulting in the death of one Indian (Joseph Stuntz) and two FBI agents (Jack R. Coler and Ronald A. Williams). On November 25, 1975, four Indian males, Robert E. Robideau, Darrelle Dean Butler, James T. Eagle, and Leonard Peltier, were indicted for the death of the FBI agents. Complicating these events was the unsolved murder of Canadian Indian, Anna Mae Aquash, an AIM supporter who the FBI thought had information concerning the deaths of the FBI agents.

In their trial, two of the defendants, Robideau and Butler, pleaded self-defense for returning fire during the FBI assault on their compound. In July 1975, they were found "not guilty" again due to the sparse evidence against them and the FBI's continued misconduct during the trial. The Department of Justice then dismissed the charges against the youngest defendant, James T. Eagle. This left only Leonard Peltier, who had fled to Canada to avoid prosecution. Peltier was extradited based on what was later determined by both U.S. and Canadian justice officials as false evidence manipulated by the FBI from a dubious "witness" to the FBI agent's death. Tried in federal court in Fargo, North Dakota, Peltier was found guilty on April 18, 1977, of two counts of murder and sentenced on June 1, 1977, to life in prison. Fearing a planned assassination in prison, Peltier escaped from Lompoc Federal Prison on June 20, 1979, was recaptured, and is currently serving his "life sentence" at the federal prison in Kansas.[39]

Not everyone in Indian Country sided with AIM or its tactics. Others attempted to work within the existing political structure to bring about change on the reservations. One such organization was the Native American Rights Fund (NARF). Congress' contributions, on the other hand, included passage of the Indian Self-Determination and Education Assistance Act and the comprehensive review of Indian policies with the Task Force Reports of the American Indian Policy Review Commission. These inquiries followed passage of the Civil Rights Act of 1968. Titles II through VII of the act addressed expanding the Bill of Rights to Indian citizens residing in Indian Country, as well as establishing guidelines for the Courts of Indian Offenses.

The Indian Civil Rights Act of 1968 (ICRA) was made possible due to the influence of President Lyndon Johnson. A month prior to its passage, President Johnson set the stage for the new era in U.S.-Indian policy—that of "self-determination." In his special message to Congress on March 6, 1968, he proposed "a new goal for our Indian programs: a goal that ends the old debate about 'termination' of Indian programs and stresses self-determination; a goal that erases old attitudes of paternalism and promotes partnership self-help."[40] With its passage, the Civil Rights Act of 1968 finally extended to American Indians and Alaskan Natives the constitutional rights already granted to the rest of the country's citizens.

A special provision of the Indian Civil Rights Act ended the unilateral encroachment of jurisdiction by local and state agencies and authorities provided under Public Law 280. It also allowed Public Law 280 states to retrocede previous jurisdictions back to the federal government. It also set the stage for a critical review of the anti-Indian policies established under House Concurrent Resolution 108, notably termination and relocation. Indeed, in his Special Message on Indian Affairs (July 8, 1970), President Richard M. Nixon continued his predecessors' lead, declaring termination a failure and calling on Congress to repudiate this policy. (Interestingly, these devastating policies were enacted and directed by President Eisenhower when Nixon served as vice president.) Accordingly, in 1973 Congress passed the Menominee Restoration Act, effectively ending the failed policy of termination. Under the Nixon administration, Congress passed the Indian Education Act of 1972; the Indian Financing Act of 1974; the Indian Self-Determination and Education Assistance Act of 1975; while extending Indian preference in employment within the BIA.

ICRA also provided the impetus for the rise of Indian-interest legal and advocacy agencies such as NARF situated in Boulder, Colorado. These agencies provided needed legal representation for clients within Indian Country due, in part, to the complexities surrounding passage of the Indian Law Enforcement Improvement Act of 1975, issues articulated by U.S. Senator James Abourezk:

> I know of no other problems in the Indian field today that are as complex and difficult to resolve as those found in the area of jurisdictional concern in Indian country. Contributing to this dilemma is the tangle of overlapping or mutually exclusive jurisdictions—Federal, State, tribal—which govern law enforcement in Indian country. An outgrowth of the discredited "termination" policies of the 1950s resulted in congressional approval of Public Law 83-280, which served to exacerbate the problems emanating from law enforcement on Federal Indian reservations. Public Law 280 was adopted by the 83rd Congress and signed into law by President Eisenhower on August 15, 1953. The express purpose of that public law was to grant broad discretionary authority to the States to assume civil and criminal jurisdiction over Indian reservations within their borders. Unfortunately the Public Law 280 legislation was approved by Congress in the face of strenuous Indian opposition and denied consent of the Indian tribes which were affected by the act. In its final form the statute gave five States civil and criminal jurisdiction over all but three tribes within those States, and gave the United States authority to grant similar jurisdiction to all other States. The Indian community has consistently opposed implementation of Public Law 280 since its enactment. Tribal leaders allege that Public Law 280 has failed to achieve the objective of improved law enforcement and justice on Indian reservations through the assumption of civil and criminal jurisdiction by the States. In the face of these circumstances, I can readily understand

why major Indian organizations have established the repeal of Public Law 280 as high priority on their legislative agenda.[41]

The next significant policy action relevant to the ICRA was the revision of the federal statutes established under the 1883 *Crow Dog* dilemma and the establishment of the Major Crimes Act (1885) in Indian Country. The testimony before the Congressional Committee on the Judiciary-Criminal Jurisdiction in Indian Country session of March 10, 1976, included the remarks of Morris Thompson, commissioner of Indian Affairs (May 20, 1975). Thompson provided the following overview of what he considered serious defects of federal prosecution in Indian Country:

> The Major Crimes Act (18 USC.-1153) provides that 13 enumerated offenses committed by Indians within Indian country (as defined by 18 USC.-1151) shall be subject to the same laws and penalties applicable within the exclusive jurisdiction of the United States. However, in 1966 the Act was amended to provide that certain of these offenses—namely burglary, assault with a dangerous weapon, assault resulting in serious bodily harm, and incest—shall be defined and punished in accordance with the laws of the State in which such offense were committed. This Act applies exclusively to Indians whether the victim be Indian or non-Indian. A non-Indian committing these identical offenses against an Indian in Indian country is subject to the provisions of 18 USC.-1152 which extends Federal criminal jurisdiction over such non-Indians, and provides that punishment will be defined by Federal Law. Because of the disparities between Indians and non-Indians in penalties given, both the Eighth and Ninth Circuits recently declared portions of the Major Crimes Act to be unconstitutional. . . . Therefore, the Federal Government is now unable to prosecute Indians who commit assault resulting in serious bodily harm in Indian country in either of these two jurisdictions, which encompass a major portion of Indian country under Federal criminal jurisdiction. The problem is acute and leaves Indian communities without the protection not only of Federal law but of any law except in the sense that a person might be prosecuted for a lesser included offense. Tribal courts are restricted to jurisdiction over misdemeanors by the Indian Civil Rights Act of 1968. . . . H.R. 7592, a bill proposed by the Department of Justice, would restore the ability of the Federal Government to prosecute certain serious offenses by Indians under 18 USC.-1153 which was lost as a consequence of the recent court decisions.[42]

Thompson's input resulted in passage of the Indian Crimes Act of 1976 and expanded the Major Crimes Act of 1885 number of federal *Index Crimes* to fourteen: murder; manslaughter; kidnapping; rape; carnal knowledge of any female not his wife, who has not attained the age of sixteen years; assault with intent to commit rape; incest; assault with intent to commit murder; assault with a dangerous weapon; assault resulting in serious bodily injury; arson; burglary; robbery; and larceny.[43] Tribes felt that the changes brought about by the ICRA of 1968 eroded tribal sovereignty leading to Congress passing Public Law 102-137, which amended the ICRA, reinstating the authority of tribes to exercise misdemeanor criminal jurisdiction over all Indians, regardless of tribal enrollment status, within their tribal jurisdiction.[44]

BIA police training intensified following passage of the ICRA, with the Indian Police Academy (IPA) established in Roswell, New Mexico, in 1969. The IPA moved to Brigham City, Utah, in 1973, and then to Marana, Arizona, in 1985. In 1992, the IPA moved to its present location as part of the Federal Law Enforcement Training Center housed in Artesia, New Mexico. This facility also serves as the liaison with other federal (FBI, U.S. Marshals, border patrol, and the like), state, and local law enforcement agencies. The Federal Law Enforcement Training Center itself is the largest police training facility in the United States. As for Indian law enforcement, Indian police have jurisdictional authority over misdemeanor crimes committed by Indian against Indians, civil law violations, juvenile matters, and tribal ordinances, and they can conduct preliminary investigations for felonies while awaiting federal law enforcement intervention (generally the FBI). Indian police, however, are prohibited from arresting non-Indians who have offended against an Indian given that this falls within federal authority, or getting involved in crimes committed by non-Indians against non-Indians in Indian Country, since this generally falls under state jurisdiction.

III

CIVIL RIGHTS AFTERMATH

Increased Militarization and
Racial Myths Enhancement

• 8 •

The Omnibus Crime
Control and Safe Streets Act

Clearly the unrest of the 1960s and 1970s, manifested by both its intensity and duration, left a considerable void within American society. With the Vietnam War raging and civil rights being implemented, a wide array of youth of all races, ethnicities, and classes were challenging the status quo. Yet the political order, including those heading the major crime fighting apparatus, the FBI, DEA, and CIA, were bent on not only maintaining the status quo, but also increasing their control over these disruptive groups. This was the "law and order" cadre. Their sentiments were also shared by the governors of the two largest states, New York and California. Once the Vietnam War diminished in importance, a new rallying cry emerged from the law and order group—that of the War on Drugs—again targeting disruptive college youth and minorities. Moreover, the various "blue ribbon" committees, mandated to find the cause of the riots, provided fuel for better training and arming of law enforcement at both the federal and state levels, a process that contributed greatly to the further militarization of the police.

Richard Quinney noted that the various riot and violence commissions were stacked with representatives of the power elite whose interest was to protect the status quo. He quotes Anthony Platt, who addressed the politics of riot commissions:

(1) Commissions appear to be composed of and balanced by elite representatives from all established interest groups. *In fact*, representatives from politics, industry, and law predominate the composition of commissions. (2) Commissions appear to be composed of persons who unequivocally represent established interest groups. *In fact*, their representativeness is often disputed by their alleged constituencies. (3) Commissions appear to operate on the basis of an adversary system of conflict resolution. *In fact*, commissioners

generally work harmoniously and cooperatively as a result of their similar class backgrounds, interchangeability of interests, and mutual ideology.[1]

Criticism aside, the Eisenhower Commission on Violence in America was critical of J. Edgar Hoover's deceptive presentation of crime statistics and the "rise of crime" in America:

"Trends—it is the trends in crime statistics that count," declares Mr. Daunt [Jerome Daunt, chief in charge of FBI crime statistics at the time], "and we have been right on the trends." . . . The most valid complaint against the FBI is not that its figures have been soft, but that the Bureau has not presented them honestly to the public. When the FBI first began to sound the alarm about rising crime a decade ago, the overall increase was small and the violent crime rate was actually frequently in decline. In 1961, for instance, the crime rate for violent offenses, decreased across the board. Murder, forcible rape, robbery, and aggravated assault all declined. Yet the overall crime index rate rose by 3 percent because of a modest increase in property crimes. J. Edgar Hoover darkly announced that "major crimes committed in the United States in 1961 have again reached an all-time high," adding that during the year there were "four serious crimes per minute." The reason for the rise was that then, as now, about 9 out of 10 offenses included in the crime index do not involve violence, so that even a modest rise in property offenses can lift the entire crime index. . . . Another complaint about the FBI's crime-reporting system is its tendency to tempt exaggeration, oversimplification, and even manipulation of the crime increase. By taking the population increase over a given stretch of years and dividing it into the percentage of crime increase, it can be said that crime is growing many times faster than the population. . . . An even more warped impression is given by the "crime clocks" that the FBI publishes each year. This baffling presentation, year after year, of the shrinking average interval between the commission of various offenses across the country, seems to have no purpose other than sheer terror. . . . The "crime clock" device lends itself to shocking conclusions that means nothing, as a published interpretation of the 1966 figures show: "An American woman is raped every 12 minutes. A house in the United States is burglarized every 27 seconds. Someone is robbed every 4 1/2 minutes in this nation." By reducing crime to these terms, the "fear of stranger" [aka minorities] syndrome is justified in a way that is not borne out by the risks of everyday life.[2]

In retrospect, it became clear that Hoover was gaming the U.S. Congress to provide more funding and authority to the FBI and to recognize it as the steward of American law enforcement—factors that led to passage and continued funding for the Omnibus Crime Control and Safe Streets Act of 1968. Hoover's control over crime trends in America also allowed him to parasitize his race-based biases that ultimately played a significant role in the ensuing War on Drugs and harsh sentencing, especially for racial minorities. Unfortunately, like many government documents, the Violence in American commission report apparently was not read carefully, if at all, by members of Congress, resulting in J. Edgar Hoover's continued influence over crime control in America. Unfortunately, this trend continued with his successors following his death in 1972 at age seventy-seven. Eventually, exposés in the *New York Times* and the *Washington Post* fostered congressional inquiries into Hoover's secret files. The Watergate debacle and President Nixon's resignation also fueled further investigation into Hoover's FBI. In 1975, Hoover's files on political figures was disclosed:

> Washington, DC, Feb. 27: J. Edgar Hoover, the late director of the Federal Bureau of Investigation, made improper use of files that he collected on political activists, a House of Representative subcommittee was told today. Attorney General Edward Levi said that Hoover, who died in 1972, kept documents with derogatory information on presidents, on congressmen and on a variety of prominent people. The Attorney General's testimony indicated that at least three Presidents—John Kennedy, Lyndon Johnson and Richard Nixon—had data collected regarding congressmen and senators who opposed them (May 19, 1976).[3]

Also, in 1975, CIA abuses were also disclosed:

> C.I.A. is accused of domestic spying; Washington, DC, June 10: The Central Intelligence Agency whose charter bans "internal security functions, systematically spied on alleged radicals during the administration of Presidents Johnson and Nixon. According to the report of an eight-man panel headed by Vice President Nelson Rockefeller, the agency amassed 13,000 files on domestic dissidents by illegally scrutinizing mail from the Soviet Union. It used wiretaps and breakins to police its own employees and held a defector in solitary confinement for three years. But the panel blames the Presidents, not the C.I.A. Johnson, for one, insisted that foreign money was behind the student anti-war effort. Rockefeller says the violations were "not major." But Senator Frank Church, who is investigating the C.I.A. on foreign assassinations, disagrees. "Ours is not a wicked country," he said, "and we cannot abide a wicked government" (May 19, 1976).[4]

With exposés of federal law enforcement agencies, it became readily apparent that standards across all law enforcement agencies were in dire need. During the riots of the 1960s and 1970s, the Army National Guard became the de facto reliable state or federal police force to be called upon by both governors and the president in times of crises, mainly due to the standardization of training and discipline these soldiers had. And, in most instances, they were not specifically trained in law enforcement—military or civilian. The National Guard highlighted the vast differences existing among state, county, and local law enforcement, whether it be a race-based police force in the Jim Crow South or the nepotistic practices long held by elected county sheriff departments nationwide, or the "Mayberry" small-town forces depicted by the popular Andy Griffith television show. Undertrained, incompetence was not the only issue. Endemic corruption was also a concern, a factor highlighted by the 1970 investigation of the New York Police Department (NYPD), the largest municipal law enforcement agency in the United States.

THE KNAPP COMMISSION: REPORT ON POLICE CORRUPTION

New York City Mayor John Lindsay established the Knapp Commission, headed by U.S. Federal District Judge Whitman Knapp, in 1972 following the Frank Serpico disclosures about corruption in the police department and the measures that bad cops would take to preserve their domain. The Knapp Commission, funded by a substantial Law Enforcement Assistance Administration (LEAA) grant ($215,037.00), also noted the delicate issue of police morale, secondary to the dissemination of their findings:

> A word about a few things that are not in this report. Police Officers, wounded by criticism which they feel was generated by the Commission's disclosures rather than by the conditions which were disclosed, have objected that too little attention was paid to the good work they do and to corruption elsewhere in a society from which they feel singled out. Both subjects are, in fact, dealt with in the Commission's report. Neither is dwelt upon at length because, quite simply, it was not the Commission's job to do so. The Commission was charged with investigation of a single problem, corruption, in a single city agency, the Police Department. Having found police graft to be a serious problem, it was obliged to focus in its report upon the reasons for its findings and the steps that are being and might be taken by way of remedy. . . . Another thing the report is not is a blanket indictment of all police officers. This charge has been made by some who misinterpret in order more easily to attack—even at the cost of perpetuating in the public mind the very impression to which they object. When the president of the Patrolmen's Benevolent Association complains that the Commission report condemns the entire police force many people accept his characterization—and tend to believe it. Anyone seriously interested in evaluating the Commission's efforts must begin—as the PBA president did not before making his public observations—by reading the report. The report describes in specific detail patterns

of corruption which no knowledgeable police officer or law enforcement official has challenged, which the Department's new leadership acknowledges, and which recent indictments confirm.[5]

The climate of injustice at this time in New York City was further elaborated upon by Robert Daley, the then deputy police commissioner. In his book, *Target Blue*, he describes the murder attempt on officer Frank Serpico. Officer Serpico received a bullet to the head at the hands of fellow officers. He survived, and it was his efforts and those of his partner, police Sergeant David Durk, that led to the Knapp Commission investigation on corruption in the NYPD. Daley provided background as to the situation with New York City's justice apparatus that tolerated such a level of corruption. Part of that atmosphere was the turbulent waves of unrest within the country at that time, including antiwar and race protests; assaults by the Black Liberation Army; and prison unrest such as happened at Attica:

> New York was a city that had loved its cops in the old days, but mocked or feared them now. Ten times as many cops would be bitten that year as the year before. Twice as many would be kicked. There would be double the number of bomb threats and 12.7 percent increase in reported major crime: homicides, rape, armed robbery, and the like. Forty-five cops would be shot and seven murdered before Christmas, and ten more would be cut down before [Patrick Vincent] Murphy [NYPD Police Commissioner] had completed twelve months in office. New York policemen would make a quarter of a million arrests that year. Over, 120,000 people would pass through the city's 13 jammed jails. There were fewer than 100 judges, who accorded each case an average of two and a half minutes. For a misdemeanor the average miscreant spent 35 days in jail awaiting trial, for a felony, the average was five months. Despite the vast numbers, there were only 552 felony trials in the entire city that year. The rest was fallout, due to plea bargaining, dropped charges, failure of witnesses to show up or testify. There was a massive imbalance of the criminal justice dollar: 80 percent went to the police, only 20 percent to pay for the courts, the jails, the virtually nonexistent rehabilitation programs. About 80 percent of the criminals in New York's jail had been there before. The courts and jails turned them out fast, because there was no room.[6]

The Knapp Commission noted another factor about law enforcement's *Blue Code of Silence*—not to disclose any imperfection within law enforcement at any cost. Although addressed in chapter 23 of the commission report, clear evidence today, in the twenty-first century, shows that this attitude still prevails:

> The Commission found that corruption within the [NYPD] Department was so pervasive that honest rookies joining the police force were subject

to strong pressures to conform to patterns of behavior which tended to make cynics of them and ultimately led many of them into the most serious kinds of corruption. This situation was the result of an extremely tolerant attitude toward corruption which had existed in the Department for the better part of a century and had flourished despite the efforts—sometimes vigorous and sometimes not—of police commissioners and various law enforcement agencies.

Two important factors which perpetuated this attitude were: (1) a stubborn belief held by officials of the Department and of other law enforcement agencies that the existence and extent of police corruption should not be publicly acknowledged, because it might damage the image of the Department, thus reducing its effectiveness; and (2) a code of silence, honored by those in the Department who were honest as well as those who were corrupt, which discourages officers from reporting the corrupt activities of their fellows and which sometimes seemed to mark the reporting of corruption as an offense more heinous than the practice of corruption.

The effect of these attitudes was compounded by the fact that law enforcement agencies concerned with police corruption traditionally were commanded by persons who substantially agreed that it was contrary to the public interest to acknowledge the full extent of police corruption, and relied for their investigative efforts upon police officers who themselves were sympathetic to the code of silence.[7]

A PROFILE OF COUNTY CORRUPTION— THE JOANN LITTLE CASE

Nepotism and selective hiring with little regards to qualifications was pretty much the norm prior to the efforts put forth by the Omnibus Crime Control and Safe Streets Act. Commonly, elected high sheriffs would staff the deputy ranks and those of the county jail with friends and relatives, a situation that played out at the local-level police departments as well. The possible exception were state police departments, although race, gender, and sectarianism played a role in their hires, as is attested by the state police involved in Civil Rights and antiwar protests throughout the country. The North Carolina case of Joann Little, a young adult black female, illustrates this phenomenon. Joann Little's case, involving the death of a white jailer, gained national attention in the mid-1970s. She was held in the Beaufort County jail for three months awaiting her appeals of a breaking and entering and larceny conviction in August 1974. While in jail, she was charged with the ice-pick slaying of the sixty-two-year-old white jailer, Clarence Alligood, who was forcing her to perform oral sex on him while threatening her with an ice pick. Once he ejaculated, Ms. Little took the ice pick, stabbed Alligood, and fled, fearing for her life. The ice pick was the property of the jail, and Ms. Little had no access to it but Mr. Alligood did. Indeed, the ice pick was found in the dead jailer's hand when he was found in her cell on the bunk unclothed from the waist down and with evidence of his seminal fluid on his body and clothes. Given that Alligood was related to the county sheriff, Ms. Little, fearing for her life, left North Carolina, which still had a law allowing anyone to bring in any fugitive, "dead or alive." A murder warrant was issued, and it was her flight that drew attention to her legal plight.

It was due to the efforts of civil rights groups and the Black National Bar Association that Ms. Little surrendered, and under the national spotlight, she managed to obtain a fairer trial than the death sentence that was sure to await her if her fate was left to Beaufort County kangaroo justice. With a change of venue, Ms. Little's self-defense trial was successful. Justice was not "fair" or impartial for blacks incarcerated in North Carolina at this time. Change was slow coming to Southern states, where black offenders had a far greater chance of being incarcerated. Even then black females fared worse than their male counterparts. They were forced to work in virtual "sweat shops" eight hours a day, doing laundry and sewing police and correctional uniforms while working at pedal-powered sewing machines. Add to this list of abuses compulsory pelvic examinations, forced sterilization, and sexual assault, and one can see why such efforts were made on Ms. Little's behalf, if she even lived to reach North Carolina's notorious women's prison.[8]

THE LAW ENFORCEMENT ASSISTANCE ADMINISTRATION (LEAA) INITIATIVE

The *Omnibus Crime Control and Safe Streets Act of 1968* was the outgrowth of President Lyndon Johnson's 1967 President's Commission on Law Enforcement and Administration of Justice Task Force reports. The act was originally known as the "Law Enforcement and Criminal Justice Assistance Act of 1967." Public Law 90-351 was: "An Act to assist State and local governments in reducing the incidence of crime, to increase the effectiveness, fairness, and coordination of law enforcement and criminal justice systems at all levels of government, and for other purposes."[9] The major vehicle for changes implementing the Omnibus Crime Control and Safe Streets Act was LEAA. Funding would be block grants provided to all the states and administered under the direction of the newly established Governors Crime Commissions. The country was further divided into ten funding regions in order to better accommodate geographical differences and needs. Each LEAA regional office had its own administration with a director, deputy director, administrative services, technical assistance, and operations division. Accordingly, 25 percent of the annual block grant could be used at the state-level while 75 percent was to be doled out to local law enforcement (police, judiciary, corrections, and the like) agencies via submitted grant applications. The LEAA block grants provided the incentive for a more standardized criminal and juvenile justice system, setting up standards for police academies as well as standards and training for judges and prosecutors. Training was also provided for riot control.

The LEAA transformed the haphazard array of police, courts, and correctional facilities scattered across the nation. Many local law enforcement facilities (police, lay judges, jailers), as well as county, municipal, and state agencies, had their own set of rules and norms governing their perception of "justice," some of it blatantly discriminatory. Moreover, many criminal justice personnel were inadequately trained for their positions, most of which were based more on racial, ethnic, and cultural factors than on qualifications. The riots and protests of the 1960s and 1970s drew public attention to the wide discrepancies within the criminal justice system, from Jim Crow governors to big city bosses. Besides, the Civil Rights Acts fostered a number of legal challenges and changes, including capital punishment. Appropriate training for police and judges alike was required if these laws were to be enacted as intended.

In *Gideon v. Wainwright*, the U.S. Supreme Court ruled that indigent defendants have the right to Sixth Amendment protection, that is to counsel, especially when charged with major crimes that may result in the deprivation of one's life, liberty, or property. What resulted from this decision was the availability of counsel to any defendant, especially those who could not otherwise afford an attorney, with the government paying for indigent clients. Three years later in 1966, *Miranda v. Arizona* led to the police obligation of reading all suspects their rights against incrimination and the availability of counsel prior to making disclosures that may be incriminating. Together, Gideon and Miranda addressed a long-held tradition within some police agencies of using the "third degree," abuses tantamount to psychological and/or physical torture.[10]

In 1967, *In re Gualt* provided a milestone for the rights of juveniles suspected of delinquency or crimes. Here, the U.S. Supreme Court strongly suggested that due process provisions be extended to the juvenile justice system, one heretofore reliant on judicial paternalism—a process wrought with adult prejudices, especially against minority youth. The high court reached this decision mainly due to the dire failure of the rehabilitation philosophy that long held sway over juvenile justice. Now, the high court strongly recommended three due process procedural requirements, redefining the juvenile justice system: 1) the timely notice to parents and children of the nature and terms of any juvenile adjudication; 2) sufficient notice to provide counsel adequate time to prepare for these proceedings with counsel appointed for the indigent; and 3) maintenance of a written record, or its equivalent, adequate to allow for review for appeal purposes or for collateral proceedings. The U.S. Supreme Court felt that these requirements addressed the Fourteenth Amendment guarantees and, with the exception of a petit jury trial, afforded juveniles the same rights to which adults are entitled.[11]

Another component of the LEAA mandate was to allow for federal coordination of law enforcement agencies at all levels in the ongoing battles within the U.S. War on Drugs. Toward this end, in 1970, the U.S. Congress passed the *Racketeer Influenced and Corrupt Organizations* Status known as RICO. RICO reflects a major revision of the 1934 Anti-Racketeering Act (Hobbs Act) in the federal arsenal used in combating drug crimes. It is an unusual statute in that it now views business (white-collar) offenses as criminal activity punishable with stiff penalties in addition to property forfeiture, divestiture, and corporate dissolution and reorganization. Such federal authority over capitalist corporate enterprises had not been exercised outside of the quasi–martial laws enacted during times of national crisis such as times of war.

At the same time, the nation was undergoing a critical debate on the status of the death penalty, especially in light of the abuses in the Jim Crow South brought forth by the media during the civil rights protests. In 1972, the U.S. Supreme Court, in a narrow five to four decision in *Furman v. Georgia*, held that the imposition of the death penalty, as it had been administered, constituted cruel and unusual punishment in violation of the Eighth and Fourteenth Amendments of the U.S. Constitution. Nonetheless, public sentiment for the death penalty, especially in the former Jim Crow South, prevailed, and in making the necessary adjustments stated by the high court, three states successfully petitioned the court for reinstatement of capital punishment in 1976—Georgia, Texas, and Florida. The U.S. Supreme Court allowed for reinstatement of capital punishment as long as it was for serious offenses, notably first-degree murder, and consisted of a two-stage process. The first stage is the "guilty phase," while the second stage requires the separate review of both mitigating and aggravating circumstances prior to a determination of a death sentence. The petit jury is to determine the outcome, not the judge. The same jury members attend both phases of the death-qualifying process, requiring a unanimous decision in both phases.[12]

· 9 ·

Role of Academia in Validating "Institutional Racism"

A major component of the Law Enforcement Assistance Administration (LEAA) was funding police academies, as well as college-level criminal justice and correctional curricula. In this sense, academicians held a powerful sway on theories of crime causation and control. Unfortunately, inherent in this process was the flawed FBI data under the leadership of J. Edgar Hoover and a "white supremacy" (WASP) male-dominated perspective long held by the college and university elite regardless of their political orientations. Consequently, an internal debate emerged among the academic elites regarding not only causes but outcomes of crime and deviance, based on their liberal or conservative leanings. The fallacy of this thinking was that both camps thought that they knew what was best for the lesser classes, those most impacted by crime and violence. This theoretical pontification dominated the post–civil rights, anti-war, LEAA era and became inculcated in the textbooks of the era. With the advent of federal largess, textbooks on criminology, criminal justice, delinquency, and deviant behavior flooded the academic market, along with their theories and research. Indeed, LEAA fostered the birth of an independent discipline of criminal justice along with doctoral-degree programs. Prior to this, graduate-level criminology programs were generally housed within sociology departments while lower-level police training programs were associated with police academies or community colleges, aka "cop shops."

Richard Quinney came to represent the left-leaning element of radical sociologists as is evident of his critique of the LEAA:

> The modern era of repression has been realized in the rationalization of crime control. The legal order itself, as a rationalized form of regulation, continues to demand the latest techniques of control. It is only logical, then, that science should come to serve the state's interest in crime control. And this use of science makes the modern legal order the most repressive

159

(and rational) that any society has known. American society today is well on the way to, or has already reached, what may well be called "the police state." What we are experiencing is the "Americanization of 1984," a police state brought to you with the aid of science and modern techniques of control. . . . The move to apply the latest in science and technology to crime control by the state was made in the mid-1960s with the President's Crime Commission (the Commission on Law Enforcement and Administration of Justice). The state's application of science and technology to crime control was probably inevitable, however, given the tendency to rationalize all systems of management and control. . . . The message of the task force's research and analysis is 1) that crime control must become more scientific, 2) that crime control must utilize the kind of science and technology that already serves the military, and 3) that the federal government must institute and support such a program. In the traditional view, science and technology primarily means new equipment. . . . The similarities between military operations and domestic crime control are made clear, and the Crime Commission is advised to pursue the militarization of crime control.[1]

The problem with the scientific approach, one that found its way into the textbooks of the time, was a flawed methodology that had plagued sociologists and criminologists since the early 1900s—the ex post facto analysis. The "positivists" school, in turn, supported the eugenicist movement within academia, especially the elitists "Ivy League-type" schools of the twentieth century. America's academic elite built upon the social philosophers of the late nineteenth and early twentieth centuries such as Emile Durkheim, Herbert Spencer, Georg Simmel, and Max Weber. This new theory class emerged mid-twentieth century with the works of Edwin Sutherland, Robert K. Merton, Donald Cressey, Richard Cloward, Daniel Glazer, Edwin Schur, Thorsten Sellin, Gresham Sykes, Marvin Wolfgang, and others. Together these theories created a justification for the existing social order, providing a foundation for more effective social control over the inferior classes, often described as being impoverished, semiliterate, lazy, and "on the dole." The idea was that "these people" were inferior and posed a threat to the larger society in terms of violence and economics. The idea that the underclasses may be due to an unfair social structure that served to perpetuate these circumstances was not seriously entertained by the major schools of social theory, although Robert K. Merton did offer a differential association model that was more sophisticated than that of Edwin Sutherland—one that addressed the likelihood of conformity relevant to one's means to society's success goals. The more conservative criminologists separated themselves from the more liberal-leaning sociologists of the time, creating their own academic association—the American Society of Criminology (ASC). The

ASC was founded in Berkeley, California, in 1941 by August Vollmer, the city's former chief of police who went on to retire as professor of police administration at the University of California. The initial goals of the ASC were 1) to associate officials engaged in professional police training at the college level; 2) to standardize the various police training curricula; 3) to standardize, insofar as possible, the subject matter of similar courses in the various schools; 4) to keep abreast of recent development and to foster research; 5) to disseminate information [journals, annual conferences]; 6) to elevate standards of police service; and 7) to stimulate the formation of police training schools in colleges throughout the nation. These goals and objectives are similar to the ones adopted by the LEAA component of the 1968 Omnibus Crime Control and Safe Streets Act. In 1946 the organization was called the Society for the Advancement of Criminology, the forerunner to its current title—the ASC. Sociologists saw the ASC as an avenue for their research and it soon became dominated by theoreticians, leaving the police practitioners, the original audience, behind. The Academy of Criminal Justice Sciences (ACJS) emerged in 1963 in order to fill this void. The ACJS focuses more on police science and the role of the practitioner in both law enforcement and corrections while the ASC became more erudite, elitist, and theoretical. Both group of academicians subscribed to the positivists approach especially when LEAA funds (federal monies) became readily available in the 1970s.

The neo-positivists relied/rely heavily on emerging statistical methodologies, as the means to the end, instead of drawing on the volumes of work conducted during and immediately following WWII, such as Gunnar Myrdal's study of post-slavery blacks in American society, and Samuel A. Stouffer's group's comprehensive study of American soldiers and how GIs coped under stress, or the work of Erich Fromm describing social conditions leading to alienation. With the Positivists, the focus is mainly on an inductive statistical study of a segment of crime in real time often relying on "canned" data— data that may, in fact, pass through layers of biased attrition prior to its final outcome. And from this biased attrition or questionable subjective "surveys," contemporary criminologists infer to the larger population from which these subsamples are drawn, hence the *Lombroso fallacy*.

Cesare Lombroso, an Italian criminologist/penologist and proponent of social Darwinism, purported an atavistic theory of potential violent criminals, one that closely supported Terman's theory of innate human inferiority. The enduring quality of the Positive School was the easily recognizable physiological features of the inferior populace. J. Edgar Hoover, Harry Anslinger, and others readily applied this inherent inferiority to minorities, hence constituting the theory of a subculture of violence. According to the Positive School, the criminal is a throwback to a more primitive form of human being characterized by atavistic features. In Lombroso's study, this included a large jaw, facial asymmetry, large ears, beady eyes—features that would readily identify the born criminal, allowing for preventive actions to be taken prior to their expressions of violence. Chester Gould aided J. Edgar Hoover in depicting the potential criminal as a social misfit, doing so in his long-running comic strip, *Dick Tracy.* Lombroso's research was conducted on violent inmates incarcerated in Italian prisons. It was later disclosed that most of the inmates in his study were, in fact, of Sicilian ethnic heritage, a culture quite different from mainland Italy. Also omitted was the Sicilian "blood vengeance," a cultural norm long held within their traditional tribal system of justice. The exposure of this methodological fallacy did little to deter the Positivists from continuing to promote their theories of a criminal subculture composed of inherently inferior humans, notably people of color.[2]

Indeed, studies at the University of Pennsylvania, a prominent Ivy League member, set the stage of a renewal of the Positive (evidence-based) School's subculture of violence theme, under the direction of Thorsten Sellin, a prominent criminologist/sociologist of the twentieth century. Marvin Wolfgang did his sociology doctoral degrees at the University of Pennsylvania, where he later taught and directed similar doctoral research, under Thorsten Sellin, using police records, that is ex post facto analysis of "canned data," and passing this off as viable empirical research. Given Sellin's status in criminological sociology, the results of Wolfgang's dissertation outcome became widely promulgated in sociology and criminology texts, at a time when criminal justice was blossoming as a popular major, due largely to the LEAA funds colleges and universities were receiving through grants. To illustrate, Marvin Wolfgang cited these dissertation results in a chapter, "Victim-Precipitated Criminal Homicide" in the popular Cressey and Ward textbook, *Delinquency, Crime, and Social Process*:

> Empirical data for analysis of victim-precipitated homicides were collected from the files of the Homicide Squad of the Philadelphia Police Department, and included 588 consecutive cases of criminal homicide which occurred between January 1, 1948 and December 31, 1952. Because more than one person was sometimes involved in the slaying of a single victim, there was a total of 621 offenders responsible for the killing of 588 victims. The 588 criminal homicides provide sufficient background information to establish much about the nature of the victim-offender relationship. Of these cases, 150, or 26 percent, have been designated, on the basis of the previously stated definition, as VP [victim-precipitated] cases. The remaining 438, therefore, have been designated as non-VP cases, Because Negros and males have been shown by their high rates of homicide, assault against the person, etc., to be more criminally aggressive than whites and females, it may be inferred that there are more Negroes and males among VP victims than among non-VP victims. The data confirm this inference. Nearly

80 percent of VP cases compared to 70 percent of non-VP cases involve Negroes, a proportional difference that results in a *significant* association between race and VP homicide.[3]

MARVIN WOLFGANG

Marvin Wolfgang was a major influence within the field of criminal justice during the time when it was emerging as a separate discipline from its traditional roots as a subset of sociology. It was the timing of these circumstances, coupled with Wolfgang's privileged education at the University of Pennsylvania and the ensuing civil rights movement, which ensured him his position of prominence, albeit questionable, in criminology and criminal justice.

Born on November 14, 1924, in Millersburg, Pennsylvania, a rural Dutch community, Wolfgang first attended Pennsylvania State University, as the first in his family to attend college. Service in the U.S. Army during World War II interrupted his education. However, this experience introduced him to Italy, where his research endeavors and interests took him during his professional career. Once released from the army, Wolfgang continued his college education at Dickerson College in Carlisle, Pennsylvania, graduating with a bachelor of arts degree in 1948. He then pursed his masters of arts degree at the University of Pennsylvania, earning an MA in 1950 and continuing on for the PhD under the tutelage of Thorsten Sellin, one of the leading criminologists at the time. Wolfgang received the PhD in 1955 and married Lenora Poden, a faculty at Lehigh University, in 1957. Wolfgang remained at the University of Pennsylvania for his entire career, spanning forty-five years, benefitting greatly from his affiliation with Thorsten Sellin. One of these benefits was serving as president of the American Academy of Political and Social Sciences from 1972 until 1998, where Sellin was the long-term editor of the academy's journal, *The Annals*, serving in this capacity from September 1929 until July 1968. Wolfgang went on to direct the Sellin Criminology Center for Studies in Criminology and Criminal Law from 1962 until his death in 1998. He also served a term as president of the ASC and was the recipient of numerous awards.

Nonetheless, Marvin Wolfgang's *fame* and *shame* centered about his doctoral dissertation research conducted under Sellin's supervision. His secondary (ex post facto) analysis of Philadelphia's homicide data from January 1, 1948, until December 31, 1952 (which was published by the University of Pennsylvania Press in 1958) propelled Wolfgang to the national scene and prominence within the fast-growing field of criminal justice. *Patterns in Criminal Homicide*, a book based on the 588 homicide cases presented in his dissertation, made it into all the major criminal justice textbooks of the time, overshadowing other competent research, including that of his mentor, Thorsten Sellin, as well as the works of Eleanor and Sheldon Glueck, Frank Tannenbaum, Stuart Palmer, Robert E. Park, John Dollard, Richard Quinney, Joe Himes, Franklin Frazer, and Kenneth Clark, to mention a few. His research, based on biased data, coupled with the unraveling of social discontent (civil rights movement; anti–Vietnam War demonstrations) made Wolfgang a leader of the emerging conservative "law and order" movement that inadvertently demonized blacks and other minorities, including protesting students.

Essentially Wolfgang's (1958) homicide study along with that of his student Menachem Amir's (1967) rape study became classics within criminal justice, serving as unchallenged models of society's most serious forms of violence. Both studies came out of the criminology program at the University of Pennsylvania and involved secondary analysis of Philadelphia police data. From his data set, Wolfgang found that 621 offenders killed 588 victims, and that 26 percent of these cases (150) involved victim precipitation, thus concluding that homicides, in general, are characterized by: 1) Negro victims; 2) Negro offenders; 3) male victims, and the like. Amir's data (for the calendar years 1958 and 1960) concluded that blacks are overrepresented in rape statistics, both as victims and as offenders, and that extremely violent rapes usually involve black men and white women.

Both these studies have been widely cited in criminal justice, criminology, deviance, and social problems texts, among others, with attention usually limited to their summary characteristics and with little attention paid to the methodology or the limitation of these studies. These studies were portrayed as being representative of the United States in general. A consequence of this dissemination has been a general misconception among college and university students, especially in white schools, across the nation and beyond. Hence, blacks are commonly associated with criminal violence such as murder and rape, contributing to the rapid emergence of *racial profiling*. Moreover, Wolfgang's continued focus on the black subculture of violence, based on these oversimplified profiles, contributed greatly to a general fear of blacks by whites within American society, influencing passage of the *Omnibus Crime Control and Safe Streets Act* (PL 90-351) in 1968 and subsequently to the overrepresentation of blacks in U.S. prisons and on death row.

The limitations of Wolfgang's dissertation data and subsequent research is that it did not attempt to control on intervening factors such as racism and prejudice within the Philadelphia police department at this time, or the biases of J. Edgar Hoover as director of the FBI who collected, compiled, and disseminated local *Index Crime* data in his annual *Uniform Crime Report*. It is now common knowledge that the Uniform Crime Report data was biased and unreliable prior to 1958 and that Frank Rizzo, the chief of police of Phila-delphia and later mayor, was a racist. Francis "Frank" Rizzo was cut from the same cloth as J. Edgar Hoover and had the same racist bias. He joined the Philadelphia police department during WWII (1943) and served for twenty-eight years. He was the police commissioner from 1967–1971 and later served as mayor of Philadelphia (1972–1980). Rizzo's relationship with the African American population in Philadelphia was notorious, a factor that helped get him elected mayor. Under his leadership, black neighborhoods were targeted, leading to a disproportionate number of arrests and convictions, a fact that greatly skewed the data Wolfgang used for his infamous theories portraying blacks as violent-prone and living in subcultures of violence due to their in-herent inferiority, hence a population that police needed to be wary of.

Ironically, Marvin Wolfgang, who strongly associated himself with the Italian school of criminology, replicated the *Lombroso fallacy*—that is, inferring from a selective, biased data set to the general population. In 1967, Wolfgang and his Italian colleague, Franco Ferracuti, put forth their work on the *subcul-ture of violence*, again using black Americans as an example of this phenomenon. Absent from their work was mention of the surge of violence precipitated by law enforcement and the military (National Guard) mainly toward nonviolent protests by African Americans. Wolfgang's work remained unchallenged until the Department of Justice initiated and funded the *Education Project in Criminal Justice* in 1977 at the State University of New York at Albany (SUNY-A). This program was intended to develop a minority criminal justice curricu-lum to be used in college and university programs. Toward this end, twenty "college instructors," representing minority faculty from across the country, were to be tutored by a select group of *major professors* from leading criminal justice programs. The major block of college instructors (sixteen) represented the country's HBCUs (Historical Black Colleges and Universities) while the major professors represented the SUNY-A faculty and other associates led by Marvin Wolfgang. The condescending arrogance of Wolfgang and company with their contention that they were there to teach the minority perspective led to a revolt among the minority participants (author included). The pro-gram's outcome assessment stated that: "the patronizing elitism of the Major Professors and their associates obviated the two-way communication neces-sary for a project like this to succeed. The program evaluators, the National Council of Black Lawyers, concurred with this assessment. This project pro-vided notice to the white-dominant, basically conservative, criminal justice educators, practitioners, and organizations (ASC, ACJS, and the like) that the Wolfgang model was not a viable one and that it would continue to be chal-lenged. Marvin Wolfgang died without publicly acknowledging his negative impact on minority justice in the United States.[4]

MINORITIES AND CRIMINAL JUSTICE CURRICULUM

The Reagan era as governor of California (1967–1975) in conjunction with Richard M. Nixon's Presidency (1969–1974) greatly influenced the conservative movement toward policing in the United States at this time. Their influence carried into academia, leading to an explosion of "cop shop" programs funded by the LEAA. Colleges and universities in conservative states, public and private, began removing criminology from sociology and social sciences, instead creating new criminal justice, security, and police science departments. One such program was the federally funded "College Instructors Program Education Project in Criminal Justice" held at SUNY-A in 1978 and 1979. French described this project in a 1987 special minority justice issue of the *Quarterly Journal of Ideology*:

> Minority justice, long an area of academic interest, spilled into the public areas following the bloody riots of the 1960s (Bronx, Watts, Detroit, Newark . . .). Adverse public reaction led to numerous blue-ribbon commissions including the 1967 President's Crime Commission Report, the Kerner Commission (Riot Commission), and the Eisenhower Commission (Violence Commission). The ensuing authorization for controlling these disruptive forces (minorities, anti-war activists) was passage of the Omnibus Crime Control and Safe Streets Act of 1968. Its enforcement arm, the Law Enforcement Assistance Administration, began in 1969, (LEAA). As an agency within the Department of Justice, the LEAA provided federal influence at the state and local level throughout the United States, an experiment that lasted from 1969 to 1980.
>
> During this time, universal police standards were established as well as a national criminal information network among other positive contributions. These federal monies were also funneled into research and training programs bringing the Justice Department influence into colleges and universities. Unfortunately, in their quest for these lucrative federal monies, academic quality was often compromised with the Federal Justice Department becoming the weakest program within the school. Many of these degrees from the Associate of Arts to the Doctor of Philosophy became known as "Mickey Mouse" degrees. Consequently, a greater proportion of criminal justice practitioners, notably in law enforcement and corrections, acquired college and/or graduate degrees. Besides, during this era there emerged a substantial influx of new criminal justice departments to meet this new demand.
>
> At the same time the minority perspective was shouting to be heard. Certainly, this was not an unwarranted response given that this federal windfall was predicated upon minority unrest. Nonetheless, attempts to introduce a viable minority component within criminal justice curriculum

fell short of any realistic epistemological expectation with these programs rarely becoming a permanent part of the regular curriculum. In 1978, a nationwide minority project was conducted at the State University of New York at Albany (SUNY Project). However, without federal incentives for even token attention to minority issues and minority justice, since 1980, a marked decline in minority studies and the minority perspective has occurred within academe. This decline is especially noticeable in criminal justice programs and at professional meetings such as the Academy of Criminal Justice Sciences (ACJS) and the American Society of Criminology (ASC).[5]

Instead of providing a nationwide minorities in criminal justice curriculum, the SUNY Project (LEAA funded at over $400,000 per annum) failed due to its elitist pretense that Marvin Wolfgang and company were going to tutor minority faculty from mainly minority-serving colleges and universities on how to teach their African American, Hispanic, Asian, and American Indian students the ideal tenets of criminal justice, law enforcement, and corrections. The program was highly stratified by design, with the mainly white "Major and Associate Professors" instructing the mainly minority college instructors on how to teach criminal justice in minority-serving institutions of higher education. Marvin Wolfgang, Donald J. Newman, Fred Cohen, Michael Hindelang, and Marquetite Warren were the "Major Professors," assisted by their chosen "Associate Professors" who were not SUNY-A faculty: Roy Austin (Pennsylvania State University); Robert Jackson (Rockhurst College); Gary Perlstein (Portland State University); Vincent Webb (University of Nebraska–Omaha); Laurin Wollan Jr. (Florida State University); Patrick McAnany (University of Illinois–Chicago Circle); William Wilbanks (Florida International University); and Tom Phelps (Sacramento State University). Roy Austin was the prominent black among the "Professor Associates." The twenty "College Instructors," on the other hand, comprised of nine African American males and three African American females; two Hispanics (Cuban and Mexican descent); an Asian (Chinese descent); an Arab; and four non-Hispanic whites. The black "Instructors" were from HBCUs, as was one of the white instructors and the Arab instructor (S. N. Wailes—Jackson State University; Khayrallah Safar—Florida A&M University). The Chicano was from Cal State–Long Beach) while the white-Hispanic was from Florida International University. The Asian was from Chaminade University in Hawaii. Clearly, the Jim Crow style of rank and status did little to facilitate a cooperative and productive milieu. Needless to say, the "College Instructors" along with Roy Austin and staff assistants, Daniel Georges and Scott Christianson, challenged Wolfgang and company on their ownership of theories of minority justice, especially the concepts of the violence-prone minority male and the inherent racial nature of subcultures of violence.[6]

The Quinn Bill in Massachusetts illustrates the level of abuse that occurred within certain academic settings relevant to LEAA funding for police training. Established during the LEAA era (1970), the Police Career Incentive Pay Program (Quinn Bill) has come to represent not only "status inflation" but bogus degrees offered by otherwise legitimate schools of higher education. Its end-oriented focus (pay raises) led to the proliferation of phony extended university campuses, mainly located near or at police stations and staffed by fellow police offers serving as "adjunct faculty." With both enrollment and payment guaranteed, many colleges and universities in Massachusetts and surrounding states quickly abandoned academic ethics and standards for this financial (cash cow) windfall. Incredible as it seems, given that these programs apparently underwent both state and regional accreditation reviews and constant criticism and exposes in the *Boston Globe*, these diploma mills continue in some form to the present.

One of the worst offenders was Western New England College, which apparently inherited their "cop shop" program from New Hampshire College (now Southern New Hampshire University). It had twelve off-campus sites at the turn of the century, administered through its Office of Continuing Education, with eleven off-campus sites offering either the bachelor of science or master of sciences degrees, or both, in criminal justice administration. The exception was the program in Natick, Massachusetts, where the campus site is the Natick Army Laboratories. The *Boston Globe* exposed a number of problems with these programs, including the fact that many, if not most, of these courses are taught by part-time adjunct instructors, often fellow police officers. Moreover, the *Globe* pointed out the lack of quality control over course content and delivery while credit is liberally given for nonacademic "lifetime experiences" and for regular training such as attendance at the Police Academy, CPR courses, and the like. The *Globe*'s exposure of this sham finally led to a review in 2000, thirty years after the Quinn Bill. Ironically, the long-delayed review was by the Massachusetts Board of Education, the same board that supervises the curriculum of Harvard, Tuffs, Boston College, Boston University, Brandies University, the University of Massachusetts campuses (Amherst, Boston, Lowell), and Northeastern University.

The politics associated with the Quinn program is equally interesting. First, the president of the University of Massachusetts campuses at this time was former Senate President William Bulger, the brother of the now-captured and convicted notorious James "Whitey" Bulger, former crime boss of the Winter Hill Gang. William Bulger lost his lucrative position when, in December 2002, he pleaded the Fifth Amendment during a federal subpoena when asked if he knew the whereabouts of his brother. Facing serious cuts statewide due to Governor Mitt Romney's proposed budget, the Quinn Bill was spared mainly due to the support Romney received from the law enforcement/police lobby. Hence, police continued to receive a guaranteed 10 percent raise for obtaining an associate degree, 20 percent increase for the bachelor's degree, and between 25 and 30 percent increase for a graduate (master's) degree, which many obtained from these fraudulent programs, adding an average of ten thousand dollars a year to their salary in addition to padding their pension as well. The pay increase was in addition to free tuition, costing the commonwealth tens of millions of dollars extra per year for bogus, empty degrees.[7] The continued popularity of criminal justice and police sciences degrees continues unabated throughout academia, again with many being taught by adjunct (aka clinical faculty) instructors, many with law enforcement or judicial experience (JDs) but with minimal academic credentials, certainly not sufficient for regular tenure-track positions. Unfortunately, many initially saw the LEAA as providing incentives for better qualified law enforcement and correctional professionals so that they could transcend the conservative, often racist and sexists, biases long associated with these practitioners.

THE "BLAMING-THE-VICTIM" FALLACY

The Wolfgang minority violence perspective was cemented at the 1978 SUNY Project. He became the prophet of academic racism, adding another important level of support for the Hoover/Anslinger neo-Jim Crow racist bias within law enforcement. The SUNY Project was Wolfgang's venue for recruiting his disciples from within academia and both the ASC and the ACJS. The Wolfgang followers at the SUNY Project included "Major" and "Associate Professors" and at least one "College Instructor." The Wolfgang perspective also transcended academic disciplines, including psychology, public administration, and history, along with sociology, political sciences, and the newly emerging criminal justice and justice studies programs. This interdisciplinary approach allowed for the generation of their own data base promulgated through their "official" journals. The journal, *Criminology*, began in 1962, at the beginning of the Wolfgang era. Its editorial advisory board affiliations are a good listing of conservative "cop shop" colleges and universities, those that are most likely to be awarded federal research grants. In 2017, this included: Arizona State University; University at Albany (formerly SUNY-A); University of Missouri–St. Louis; Florida State University; University of Cincinnati; University of New Mexico; Pennsylvania State University; University of Texas, Austin; University of New Hampshire; Sam Huston State University; Rutgers University; University of Maryland; University of Miami; George Mason University; the University of California–Davis; and the like, in addition to Simon Frazer University, the University of Montreal, and the University of Toronto in Canada, and the U.S. Marshals service.[8]

It is surprising that the Hoover/Anslinger/Wolfgang race and violence perspective continues to have such a hold throughout American society, especially within criminal justice programs, law enforcement, the judiciary, and corrections, especially since there were important social psychology studies that clearly debunked these theories. Kenneth Clark's study in the 1950s was inadvertently supported with Philip Zimbardo's 1971 imprisonment study conducted at Stanford University. In his study, Zimbardo showed that it is the circumstances of the situation that leads to abuse of power over others under our control, abuses that engender cruel and violent behaviors. Extrapolating from this experiment, conducted with white, upper-class, college youth, similar outcomes would likely result regardless of race, ethnic, sectarian, or social class. Other social psychologists, from both sociology and psychology disciplines, have written on the psychologically devastating effects of poverty, especially that forced upon minorities by the larger dominant society. Using Zimbardo's research outcomes, whites forced into similar situations would face equal challenges. Robert K. Merton's paradigm of social adaptations offered two choices for the desperate entrapped in ghetto-like environments— "retreatism" (drugs, alcohol, and the like) or "rebellion" (gangs, crime, delinquency, and so on). Ostensibly, these socially engineered ghetto-environments create the same problems that Wolfgang, Hoover, and Anslinger predicted— hence, a self-filling prophecy and a call for a better-armed police. A greater problem is that Wolfgang and company portrayed the marginalized, often alienated, young minority male as reflecting all members of this ethnicity, leading to any male of color being suspected of being not only criminal but potentially violent. This, perhaps more than any other factor, has fueled the current Black Lives Matter movement, as well as the anti-Hispanic and anti-Muslim furor contaminating the U.S. image throughout the world.[9]

· *10* ·

The War on Drugs and Its Escalation

HISTORICAL ANTECEDENTS TO THE CONTEMPORARY WAR ON DRUGS

The "War on Drugs" can be traced to the U.S. era of *gunboat diplomacy* and the effort to extend American-based capitalism beyond the hemisphere. The standard federal history of policing mind-altering substances in the United States usually begins with the 1914 Harrison Narcotics Tax Act with little insight as to the race-related incidents that led up to the Harrison Act. This history extends to the early years of the republic with alcohol prohibition in Indian Country. Cultural ambivalence regarding drinking was institutionalized in U.S. Indian policy with the Indian Intercourse Act of July 9, 1832. This act not only made it illegal to sell liquor to Indians anywhere in the United States, it also established the first drug czar, the commissioner of Indian Affairs:

> Be it enacted . . . , That the President shall appoint, by and with the advise and consent of the Senate, a commissioner of Indian Affairs, who shall under the direction of the Secretary of War, and agreeably to such regulations as the President may, from time to time, prescribe, have the direction and management of all Indian affairs, and of all matters arising out of Indian relations, and shall receive a salary of three thousand dollars per annum. . . . Section 4. And be it further enacted, That no ardent spirits shall be hereafter introduced, under any pretense, into the Indian country.[1]

Intended as a mechanism for control over Native Americans, and not so much as a humanitarian or benevolent act, this federal intervention remained in effect until repealed in 1953. Even thereafter, federal influence was exercised to keep Indian Country dry. This process led to two highly profitable non-Indian enterprises in and around Indian Country, bootlegging and "drunk towns." Noted Indian leader Reuben Snake reported on the latent factors associated with Indian prohibition in his testimony before the 1976 Congressional Indian Select Committee:

> The reservation, although encased by specific boundaries, was still so vast and thinly populated that bootleggers and smugglers of liquor and other articles were never effectively controlled by the available enforcement officers and therefore left to flourish. Prohibition for Indians was to continue past the repeal of the 18th Amendment in 1933 even though they were granted full citizenship in 1924. The bootlegger and smuggler continued to peddle their intoxicating wares at great expense to the Indian people, both financially and legally. It is from this prohibition era in Indian history that both the patterns of drinking and causative factors for that drinking can be seen emerging. Gulp drinking and rapid ingestion of alcohol, as particular drinking patterns of the American Indian, are said to evolve strongly from this era. The very illegality of the drink "may have in fact increased its appeal, especially for the adolescent and young adults."[2]

A few years later following passage of the Trade and Intercourse Act that drew together previous federal conditions for white-Indian interactions within Indian Country, including the universal prohibition of alcohol, the United States became entangled in the British-China Opium Wars (1839–1842). These events are seen as being the foundation for the current narcotic-based War on Drug, leading up to the Harrison Act in 1914. China banned the opium trade with Britain in 1799, but the British refused to stop such a profitable endeavor leading to the Chinese destroying a year's supply of the British East Indian Company's opium supply. Using this as pretense for expanding their influence in China, Great Britain declared war in China in 1839, which was decided by the Treaty of Nanking in 1842 ceding Hong Kong to Great Britain on a 150-year lease as well as granting British merchants full rights to other major Chinese ports. Hong Kong reverted to Chinese control in June 1997.

The United States became involved two years later, benefitting from the Treaty of Wanghai (1844) also gaining access to Chinese ports. Fourteen years later, the 1858 Treaty of Tientsin expanded these trade rights for the United States and Britain, as well as expanding them to France and Russia. This was part of the gunboat diplomacy initiated during Franklin Pierce's presidency (1853–1857). This effort was to gain access to cheap labor from China to the United States, a needed commodity in the development of the West, especially the transcontinental railroad system, as well as for other dangerous and undesirable jobs like underground mining. But racism in the United States soon used these same drugs to open China to their colonial markets and to discriminate against these foreign immigrants. In 1900, the United States joined the other colonial powers in putting down the Boxer Rebellion, which was an effort by China to purge foreign influences. The U.S. Marine Corps again acted in the capacity of America's international police. The long history of racial discrimination against Asians began in San Francisco in 1875, eventually leading to the Harrison Narcotic Act of 1914. During the same time, Japan went to war with Russia in order to consolidate its colonial hold on China. Ironically, President Theodore Roosevelt, on December 10, 1906, became the first U.S. president to receive the Nobel Peace Prize for bringing a settlement to the Russo-Japanese War.

Related to race and substance use control was federal legislation regulating immigration. The enforcement arm for immigration control was established in 1891 with the establishment of the Bureau of Immigration, later to become the Immigration and Naturalization Service. In 1917, the Chinese Exclusion Act increased the Asian prohibition to include the Asia-Pacific triangle. The Quota Law of 1921 and the Immigration Act of 1924 further restricted the type of immigrants allowed into the United States. These race-based biases in immigration laws were not corrected until 1952 with the Immigration and Nationality Act, a century since President Pierce forced Asia to open its ports and exports (opium and peasant laborers) for U.S. exploitation. And when we no longer needed these resources, or felt that they were detrimental to U.S. interest, then we passed restrictive law targeting the same resources we once used force to acquire.

Abrams and Beale, in their comprehensive work *Federal Criminal Law and Its Enforcement*, trace the current War on Drugs to 1970 and the Omnibus Crime Control and Safe Streets Act following the turbulent antiwar and civil rights era of the 1960s and early 1970s. They noted that at the beginning of the twentieth century, heroin, opium, morphine, and cocaine could be freely purchased in the United States at local drug stores. This changed with passage of the Harrison Act in 1914. It was the first antidrug statute aimed at curbing the drug trade by forcing those dealing with these substances to register so that they can subsequently be taxed:

> Any sale or exchange of the drugs was required to be done pursuant to a written order on forms provided by the Commissioner of Internal Revenue. Criminal penalties applied to a failure to comply with any of these requirements or for possession of the specified drugs by an unregistered person or one who had not paid the tax. The Harrison Act included an exemption for the dispensing of drugs to a patient by a physician . . . in the course of his professional practice only.[3]

Abrams and Beale list the post–Harrison Act statutes up to the 1965 statute that was in place at the onset of the current War on Drugs:

The Narcotic Drug Import and Export Act of 1922, adding cocaine to the list of drugs forbidden entry and established a Federal Narcotics Control Board to administer the Act.

The Marijuana Tax Act of 1937, which applied a registration, taxing approach to the marijuana distribution chain.

The Vehicle Seizure Act of 1939, which made it unlawful to transport contraband drugs on any vessel, vehicle or aircraft and made mode of transportation subject to forfeiture.

The Opium Poppy Control Act of 1942, prohibiting any person not licensed by the Secretary of the Treasure to produce the opium poppy.

In 1946, legislation was adopted applying the federal government statutes on opium to synthetic opiates such as methadone.

The Narcotic Manufacturing Act of 1960 established a licensing system for narcotic drug manufacturers and applied a quota system for various drug categories.

1965 amendments to the Food, Drug and Cosmetic Act expanded the Harrison Act registration and record-keeping mandate to barbiturates, tranquilizers, stimulants and hallucinogens.[4]

Although treated separately from other mind-altering agents, alcohol placed a significant role in the policing of these substances. In addition to the trade and intercourse laws policing alcohol within Indian Country, the United States witnessed its Whiskey Rebellion early in its developmental years. In 1794, Scotch-Irish settlers resisted the federal taxation on their whiskey production resulting in President Washington sending a militia force of 13,000 men to quell the rebellion. One hundred and twenty-five years later, the United States passed the Eighteenth Amendment to the Constitution prohibiting the manufacturing, sale, or transportation of intoxicating liquors within the United States and all of its territories. The Eighteenth Amendment was seen by some scholars as an attempt to legislate morality, giving the implication that Protestant sects that prohibited alcohol among its members were both morally and legally superior to those religious sects that allowed alcohol, notably Roman Catholics, Orthodox Christians, and Jews. While a dire failure to either implement or police, the fourteen-year effort set the groundwork for policing substance abuse in America.

It also gave J. Edgar Hoover the opportunity to both grow and arm his Federal Bureau of Investigation. Moreover, it provided the United States an opportunity to test its border policing practices, this time with Canada.

Rum-running was a major problem during Prohibition given that the U.S.-Canada border still remains the longest open international border. Unlike the United States, Canada never enforced a nationwide prohibition. Instead, the federal government allowed the provinces to enact their own acts. Quebec was one of the first to opt out of prohibition, making it a major source of contraband entering the United States via the shared lakes and waterways, in addition to isolated land entry points. Even then, Canada never took on the stigma Mexico acquired in the current War on Drugs. With passage of the Nineteenth Amendment in 1933, alcohol consumption was no longer a federal offense. Nevertheless, prohibition remained a part of local government, notably in the South and West where counties could vote to remain "dry." Hoover and his colleague Harry Anslinger now turned to attacking marijuana, a cheap, readily available byproduct of the hemp industry, one more closely associated with minorities of color, notably African Americans, Hispanics, and American Indians.

THE EVOLUTION OF THE CONTEMPORARY WAR ON DRUGS

With passage of the U.S. civil rights laws, it was no longer legal to directly target certain groups for civil rights violations, including being subjected to police brutality, judicial biases, and disproportionate punishment. Hence, the process needed to be more oblique, instead singling out a behavior common to these once targeted populations. Drug abuse arrests and convictions played a large role in this redirection of discrimination. The 1968 Omnibus Crime Control and Safe Streets Act played the major role in transforming law enforcement and the judiciary in this redirection, providing support for an increase in the FBI's budget, providing training and material to "combat" crime, and providing a nationwide reorganization of police via the law enforcement and criminal justice assistance component.

Toward this end, Congress, in 1970, passed the Racketeer Influenced and Corrupt Organizations Statutes, known as RICO. This represented a major revision of the Anti-Racketeering Act of 1934 (Hobbs Act) and became a key federal prosecutorial tool in combating drug crimes. It is unique in that for the first time within the American capitalistic society, organizations could be targeted for criminal offenses, and not just the usually civil "cease and desist" orders commonly allowed for business corruption, no matter how significant the offense. But RICO is rarely used in white-collar corruption other than drug-related offenses, including money laundering.

The other major development stemming from the Omnibus Crime Control and Safe Streets Act was the Comprehensive Drug Abuse Prevention and Control Act, also passed in 1970. Abrams and Beale noted that this act created, for the first time, a single all-encompassing approach covering narcotics and other dangerous drugs, with a new approach based on commerce and not on taxation like the Harrison Act and subsequent modifications up until 1965:

> The Act made it criminal, when not in compliance with statutory requirements, to manufacture, distribute, dispense, import, export, possess with intent to manufacture, distribute, or dispense, or knowingly possess narcotics or attempt or conspire to do any of the foregoing. . . . A 1980 amendment of the Act criminalized drug-related conduct in a variety of sea-going and other extra-territorial contexts. The 1970 Act also penalized knowing use of a communication facility to commit a felonious violation of the Act. Engaging in a continuing criminal drug-related enterprise was punished; provision was made for sentencing persons as dangerous special drug offenders; additional penalties were provided for distributing drugs to persons under 21 years of age; and there were forfeiture provisions.[5]

The harsher approach toward drug law enforcement is often credited to perennial U.S. president candidate (1960, 1964, 1968) and governor of New York (1959–1973), Nelson Rockefeller. It is during his terms as governor that the infamous "Rockefeller drug laws" emerged as a model for stricter drug enforcement, contributing to the massive arrest and incarceration of mainly black and Hispanic drug offenders throughout the United States. Unfortunately, this stigma obviates his impressive record on civil rights during his term as governor. Rockefeller prohibited discrimination in housing and public accommodations, as well as in jobs, resulting in a substantial increase in African Americans, Hispanics, and women in state positions. The first woman admitted to the New York State Police occurred on his watch. Nonetheless, his 1973 drug laws did considerable harm not only to citizens of New York but nationwide as it became the new standard of discrimination against people of color in the United States. These laws included mandatory life sentences without the possibility of plea bargaining or parole for all drug offenders, including youthful offenders. The mandatory minimum sentence of fifteen years to life for possession of four ounces of narcotics was the same for second degree murder.

The New York Rockefeller law influenced a stricter federal response beginning with President Richard Nixon (1969–1974), who is credited with starting the federal War on Drug in 1971 when he pushed mandatory sentencing and no-knock warrants and placed marijuana as a schedule one dangerous drug. However, it was President Ronald Reagan (1981–1989) who set the stage for a racial division in drug law enforcement, making "crack" cocaine, used mostly by blacks and Hispanics, a more serious offense than "powder" cocaine used by whites and the middle classes. And the federal death penalty was reintroduced by President Reagan as part of the Anti-Drug Abuse Act of 1988. Abrams and Beale explain these changes in the Anti-Drug Abuse Acts of 1986 and 1988:

> In the Anti-Drug Abuse Act of 1986 Congress increased the penalties for most existing drug offenses. For example, 21 USC.; 841 was amended to require a 10-year minimum sentence for anyone convicted of distributing, manufacturing, or possessing with the intent to distribute one kilogram of heroin or five kilograms of cocaine. For persons who have previously been convicted of a felony drug offense, the mandatory minimum increases to 20 years. Under 841 an offense involving 100 kilograms of marijuana requires a mandatory minimum sentence of 5 years, with a maximum of 40 years. . . . The Anti-Drug Abuse Act of 1988 adopted new civil and criminal penalties. The new criminal penalty provision, codified as 21 USC.; 862, provided that a defendant convicted of either trafficking or possession of a controlled substance may be declared ineligible for certain federal benefits. This provision is of interest for several reasons. First, it applies to state as well as federal convictions, and thus implements the goal of integrating federal and state anti-drug efforts. Second, because this provision applies to possession as well as trafficking offenses, it targets users. Prior federal enforcement efforts focused principally if not exclusively on reducing supply; by providing a penalty applicable to users, this provision could also serve to decrease demand.[6]

In December 1999, the U.S. Congress passed the Foreign Narcotics Kingpin Designation Act, effectively expanding RICO standards beyond U.S. borders. This act addressed outside financial organizations that may be implicated in funding drug operations (money laundering). It also allowed for the international pursuit of major drug leaders. This law led to the January 2017 extradition of *El Chapo*, Joaquin Guzman Loera, alleged drug kingpin of the Sinaloa Cartel, to the United States for adjudication.[7]

Factors Contributing to the Militarization of the Police

Federal training of law enforcement agencies within the United States and beyond its borders began in earnest in an effort to curtail the influx of illicit drugs into America. Following Repeal of Prohibition in 1933, border policing changed from Canada to Mexico, especially following the successes in stemming the flow of illegal substances (mainly heroin and cocaine) from operations in Columbia and Southeast Asia. Given that the Columbian and Asian successes were due largely to joint military and police efforts, the focus of Mexico resulted in the recent remilitarization of the U.S.-Mexico border. The *War on Terrorism* that began following the September 11, 2001, attacks in New York and Washington, DC, led to another round of federal funding for state and local law enforcement through grants made available by the newly created Department of Homeland Security (DHS). Here, the border patrol, National Guard units, state, country, and local law enforcement act in unison against the perceived threats against the United States. Granted these coordinated efforts are needed and the end result has contributed to better law enforcement coordination and standards, nonetheless, some feel that these achievements have been at the expense of traditional community policing. The effectiveness of these coordinated efforts was clearly demonstrated with the manhunt subsequent to the 2013 Boston Marathon terrorist attack on April 15, which included both federal and state (Massachusetts and New Hampshire) law enforcement personnel.

UNDERSTANDING THE FOUNDATIONS OF AMERICAN POLICING

The change in policing in America stemmed mainly from the 1967 *Task Force Report: The Police* that was part of the President's Commission on

Law Enforcement and Administration of Justice, which, in turn, provided the foundation for the Law Enforcement Assistance Administration that emerged from the 1968 Omnibus Crime Control and Safe Streets Act. The report provides a short history of the influences on law enforcement in the United States:

> France and other continental countries maintained professional police forces of a sort as early as the 17th century. But England, fearing the oppression these forces had brought about in many of the continental countries, did not begin to create police organizations until the 19th century. . . . Primarily, the system encouraged mutual responsibility among local citizen's associations, which were pledged to maintain law and order; it was called the "mutual pledge" system. Every man was responsible not only for his own actions but also for those of his neighbors. It was each citizen's duty to raise the "hue and cry" when a crime was committed, to collect his neighbors and to pursue a criminal who fled from the district. If such a group failed to apprehend a lawbreaker, all were fined by the Crown.
>
> The Crown placed this mutual responsibility for group police action upon 10-family groups. Each of these was known as a "tithing." From the tithing, there subsequently developed the "hundred" comprised of 10-tithings. From this developed the first real police officer—the constable. He was appointed by a local nobleman and placed in charge of the weapons and equipment of each hundred. Soon the "hundreds" were grouped to form a "shire," a geographical area equivalent to a county. A "shire-reeve"—lineal antecedent of tens of thousands of sheriffs to come—thus came into being, appointed by the Crown to supervise each county. The constable's breadth of authority remained limited to his original "hundred."
>
> It was during the reign of Edward I (1272–1307), that the first official police forces were created in the large towns of England. These were called the "watch and ward," and were responsible for protecting property against fire, guarding the gates, and arresting those who committed offenses between sunset and daybreak. At the same time the constable became the primary law enforcement officer in all towns throughout England. In 1326, to supplement the "shire-reeve" mutual pledge system, Edward II created the office of justice of the peace . . . to assist the Sheriff in policing the county. . . . The constables, who retained the responsibility of serving as a major official within the pledge system . . . became an assistant to the justice, responsible for supervising the night watchmen, inquiring into offenses, serving summonses, executing warrants, and taking charge of prisoners. [By the end of the 14th century, the constable] was obliged to serve the justice. This essentially set the justice-constable patterns for the next 500 years.

American colonists in the 17th and 18th centuries naturally brought to America the law enforcement structure with which they were familiar in England. The transfer of the offices of constable and sheriff to rural American areas—which included most colonial territory—was accomplished with little change in structure of the offices. . . . The Crown-appointed Governors bestowed these offices on large landowners who were loyal to the King. After the revolution, sheriffs and constables tended to be selected by popular elections, patronage then being on the wane. . . . As American towns grew in size and population during the first half of the 19th century, the constable was unable to cope with the increasing disorder. As in England years before, lawlessness became more prevalent. Again, as in England, many American cities began to develop organized metropolitan police forces of their own. Philadelphia was one of the first (1833). In 1838, Boston created a day police force to supplement the nightwatch and other cities soon followed its lead. . . . Keen rivalries existed between the day and night shifts, and separate administrations supervised each shift. Recognizing the evils of separate police forces, the New York Legislature passed a law in 1844 that authorized creating the first unified day and night police, thus abolishing its nightwatch system. Ten years later Boston consolidated its nightwatch with the day police. . . . And by 1900s there were few cities of consequence without such unified forces.

These first formal police forces in American cities were faced with many of the problems that police continue to confront today. Police officers became the objects of disrespect. The need for larger staffs required the police to compromise personnel standards in order to fill the ranks. And police salaries were among the lowest in local government service, a factor which precluded attracting sufficient numbers of high standard candidates. It is small wonder that the police were not respected, were not notably successful, and were not known for their vitality and progressiveness. . . . Many of the problems that troubled these first organized metropolitan police forces can perhaps be traced to a single root—political control.[1]

In their comprehensive review of policing in America and its obvious failure during the turbulent 1960s, the 1967 President's Commission on Law Enforcement and Administration of Justice concluded that changes were needed, changes that provided the foundation for the 1968 Omnibus Crime Control and Safe Streets Act:

There are today (circa 1960s) in the United States 40,000 separate agencies responsible for enforcing laws on the Federal, State, and local levels of government. But law enforcement agencies are not evenly distributed among these three levels, for the function is primarily a concern of local government. There are 50 law enforcement agencies on the Federal level of government and 200 departments at the State level. The remaining 39,750 agencies are dispersed throughout the many counties, cities, towns, and villages that form our local governments. . . . 3,050 agencies are located in counties and 3,700 in cities. The great majority of police forces—33,000— are distributed throughout boroughs, towns, and villages.

Because the concept of local autonomy in enforcing laws has prevailed throughout our history and because the many local policing agencies have held firmly to their traditional jurisdictional authority, responsibility for maintaining public order is today extremely decentralized. This decentralization is further accentuated by the fact that a police officer's responsibility for enforcing law is usually confined to a single jurisdiction.[2]

When looking at the problems plaguing police agencies in the United States, the Task Force on Police made three basic observations:

1. There is a need to recognize the variety of functions which police perform today, particularly in the large urban community. The demands upon police are likely to increase in number and complexity rather than decrease.
2. Important and complex social, behavioral, and political problems can adequately be dealt with by American government only if there is room for administrative variation, innovation, and experimentation of a kind presently lacking in the police field.
3. To deal adequately with current law enforcement needs requires an explicit acknowledgment that police are one of the most important governmental administrative agencies in existence today. It requires also that major change be made to equip police to develop appropriate administrative policies and willingness and capacity to conform with these policies.[3]

The vehicle for addressing these shortcomings and the implementation of new standards was the Law Enforcement Assistance Administration (LEAA) component of the Law Enforcement and Criminal Justice Assistance Act. Block grants were provided by state and region, with the vast majority of monies going to the local law enforcement agencies. As stated earlier, police standards were now implemented at newly established police academies at both the state and federal levels. All police personnel were expected to be trained at these academies and certified allowing both lateral and upward mobility for law enforcement and correctional personnel. In addition to specific training, many police academies held articulation agreements with local community colleges whereby police candidates could earn at least an associate degree, if not a four-year degree. This element of the LEAA was quite successful in that many law enforcement personnel at all levels hold postgraduate degrees. Granted some are of dubious quality, such as those provided under the Massachusetts Quinn Bill or other questionable "cop shops" where local adjunct practitioners teach in lieu of bona fide academicians. Nonetheless, this is a far cry from the nepotistic hiring of the past and the blatant racist atmosphere within certain local jurisdiction, notably those associated with the Jim Crow South. But better armament, including firearms and military-style armored vehicles, were also purchased using LEAA funding.

THE MILITARIZATION OF LAW ENFORCEMENT

Again, the English provide the historical bases for the military structure that emerged within American law enforcement, especially in metropolitan police. In 1822, Sir Robert Peel, England's Home Secretary (similar to Interior Minister in European systems), began searching for a better metropolitan police force to protect London. Toward this end, Peel, in 1829, introduced An Act for Improving the Police In and Near the Metropolis, basing his innovative approach on a military-style structure. His "bobbies" would wear a distinctive uniform, not to be confused with military personnel. The Metropolitan Police Force proved so successful that Parliament enacted other police reform bills, including the establishment of a similar police force in the counties (1839) and in 1856 requiring every borough and county to have a police force based on the Metropolitan Police model. These local jurisdictions became known as "batches" while overall supervision rested at the Met's headquarters, Scotland Hall.[4]

Prior to the Omnibus Crime Control and Safe Streets Act, many law enforcement agencies in the United States were responsible for the purchase, if not the choice, of firearm. Following the U.S. War between the States, black powder revolvers were replaced with self-contained cartridge bullets, with the popular six-shot revolver usually in .32, .38, or .45 caliber. By the mid-twentieth century, the most popular sidearm was the .38 caliber revolver. And given that many law enforcement personnel also were members of their respective State National Guard units, access to high-power 30-06 caliber rifles (bolt-action Springfield rifle, the, Browning Automatic Rifle, and the M1 Garand) increased, although authorization for use of these weapons was greatly restricted, requiring a governor's or the president's authorization. The National Firearm Act of 1934 was designed to restrict the purchase and use of submachine guns, like the .45 caliber Thompson, as well as sawed off shotguns. Even then, these long-guns and shotguns were awkward to conceal and use. The change in military armament coincided with the advent of the

LEAA providing both law enforcement and the military with more versatile firearms. At the same time, large capacity (thirteen- to fifteen-round clips) semiautomatic pistols adopted by the military were in demand by police forces as well. Now the Beretta and Glock pistols rapidly replaced six-shot revolvers throughout the nation's police forces at all level.

The jungle warfare in Vietnam required another type of weapon, hence the emergence of the M16 rifle in caliber 5.56mm—a lightweight, rapid-fire assault rifle with a standard twenty-round magazine. Used selectively by the U.S. Army beginning in 1963, it became the standard service rifle for the U.S. military in 1969 and later was modified to fire three-round burst per trigger pull. The smaller version, M4 carbine, is used as well. The M16 rifle/M4 carbine played a significant role in the militarization of U.S. law enforcement in that they coincided with the advent of Special Weapons and Tactic (SWAT) teams devised during the 1960s in Los Angeles for riot control, and with the creation of LEAA, each state began creating its own SWAT teams for potential riot control, as well as to participate in the national War on Drugs. The LAPD SWAT team saw the advent of increased firepower vested in special police units. Here, SWAT units were equipped with submachine guns, assault rifles, breaching shotguns, sniper rifles, stun grenades, heavy body armor, ballistic shields, door rams, armored vehicles (BearCats and the like), night-vision devices, motion detectors, and, later, robots. The SWAT concept provided law enforcement agencies the same authority and firepower as a military Special Forces, Navy Seal, or Marine Corps unit. The police now transformed from an intracommunity protection unit to an "occupational" force justified in protecting against criminal subversives and terrorists. Part of this transformation was also manifested in the change in uniform from recognizable "blue" to combat black, along with all the apparatus indicating a combat situation. This was certainly the polar opposite of the initial intent of the Omnibus Control and Safe Streets Act. Now, more than ever, U.S. society was divided into acceptable versus criminally stigmatized, visibly recognized entities.

An even more intense militarization effort followed the September 11, 2001, terrorist attacks and the new *War on Terrorism*. Clearly, a major factor in the militarization of law enforcement in the United States was the creation of SWAT teams and their federal support through programs such as LEAA and Homeland Security.[5]

MILITARY RANK AND STATUS

An interesting outcome of the militarization of law enforcement is the corresponding rank/status phenomenon. Anthropologists and sociologists have long recognized that authority and privilege are associated with a person's status within the society. In this sense, all organized societies define the status hierarchy. Ralph Linton noted that cultures usually subscribe to two types of status—*ascribed*, based mainly on sex, age, and family/clan affiliation; and *achieved,* based on individual accomplishments or elective processes such as occupation, marriage, and the like. I would add two subcategories to the latter—*enhanced* and *fabricated*. Enhanced status is when an obviously legitimate status is elevated to something higher, while fabricated status is when someone creates a status far removed from their actual position.[6]

In societies like the United States where there are no inherited titles, military status ranks high. The military is based on a caste system that divides commissioned officers from enlisted personnel. The officer ranks (O-1 to O-10), in turn, are divided into two echelons with "field grade" ranks, that is major and above, being the most prestigious. Within this system, a captain (O-3) is the commanding officer (CO) of a company or battery while a battalion has a lieutenant colonel (O-5) as the CO and a major (O-4) as the executive officer (XO). Colonels generally head regiments, while brigadier generals are COs of brigades and major generals lead divisions and so on. Thus, a field grade officer can command anywhere from 1,000 to 10,000 military personnel, including entire armies or navies. The United States did not have a permanent four-star general until 1866 when this status was awarded to U. S. Grant. The Confederate army, however, created the four-star rank during the Civil War. When U. S. Grant became president, the sole four-star rank was passed on to William T. Sherman and then to Philip H. Sheridan, who was leading the Indian wars in the West. This permanent rank was not allocated again until 1919 when it was given to John (Black Jack) Pershing. The Second World War not only saw the proliferation of four-star generals and admirals but the creation of the five-star general; even then, only nine men held this rank—four admirals and five generals. This was a lifelong position and was retired in 1981 with the death of General Omar Bradley. George Washington was added to the list posthumously on July 4, 1976. Today, the head of the Joint Chiefs of Staff, the heads of the four military services (army, navy, air force, and marines), and the head of NATO forces, are four-star generals or admirals, albeit superior to other four-star officers serving under their command.

Civilian superiors, such as the secretary of the army, navy, and air force, do not hold military rank. Yet the use of military rank predominates within U.S. society, especially within the paramilitary police organizations. The military structure at the state level, on the other hand, occurs with the National Guard, which follows the regular military rank structure with the governor appointing the commanding general, usually at brigadier rank (0–9). However, the prolonged *wars on terrorism* in Iraq and Afghanistan, with greater reliance on the federalized National Guard, resulted in an upgrade to the rank with a major general in command of the overall National Guard and brigadier generals as heads of the basic components such as the Army National Guard and the Air National Guard. This inflation at the higher echelon of military rank has also afflicted the U.S. military in general.

Within the civilian criminal justice systems, both federal and state, the top law enforcement officer is the attorney "general." Within the state-system, the state police are the law enforcement agency assigned to the attorney general's office with statewide jurisdiction. At the federal level, the U.S. Marshal's office was designed in 1789 to act as the law enforcement unit for U.S. courts with a high marshal appointed to each state and territory, with the U.S. attorney general now being the top government law enforcement officer. State police agencies, on the other hand, usually follow the military rank structure with the director holding the rank of O-6 colonel acting under the direction of the AG (attorney general). State police forces often have "troops" located throughout the state's jurisdiction, again using the military rank model with a captain heading the troop.

When looking at the largest municipal police department in the United States, New York City, with a population of over eight million and covering 468.9 square miles in five boroughs, it becomes evident that a well-organized police force is justified. In the New York Police Department (NYPD), we again see the five-star rank, this time for the police commissioner, who supervises up to 40,000 personnel. Clearly, this falls under the enhanced status category while the basic rank hierarchy below the commissioner's office clearly follows a reasonable paramilitary format: chief of department holds four-stars; bureau chief, three-stars; assistant chief, two-stars; and deputy chief, one star. Inspectors are full-bird colonels; deputy inspectors, lieutenant colonels; while captains head precincts. Below Captains are lieutenant, sergeant, and patrolmen. Captains head the seventy-six precincts. The Los Angeles Police Department has jurisdiction for a similar geographic area as the NYPD but with half the population. The LAPD's (third-largest U.S. police agency—Chicago is second largest) rank structure has the politically appointed (by the mayor) chief of police holding four-star general status, with the assistant chief (deputy chief II) holding three-star general rank, while the deputy chief I is a two-star general, and police commanders hold one-star status. The intermediate field-grade military ranks (O-4 major/lieutenant commander; O-5 lieutenant colonel/commander; and O-6 colonel/captain) are omitted with the next highest rank being that of captain and then lieutenant, police sergeant II/police detective III (staff sergeants), police sergeant I/police detective II (buck sergeants); police detective I/police officer III (corporals) with police officers I and II having no military insignia.

Other police departments soon picked up on this military-style ranking, assigning themselves the rank of general regardless of the size or jurisdiction of their department. The proliferation of this fabricated status was soon demonstrated with heads of departments putting on general's stars (including four or five stars) regardless if their legal status was high sheriff or chief of police. This practice clearly speaks of "arrogance of position," raising serious questions concerning their commitment as public servants who are licensed to use lethal force in their role in securing public safety. Law enforcement represents a public-service agency, one licensed to use deadly force in protecting the public at large. Enhanced and inflated status has little to do with carrying out law enforcement functions. Instead, it can lead to a self-fulfilling prophecy whereby the chief or high sheriff comes to believe that they are, in fact, far superior to their fellow officers, an image conveyed to the public as well. Those police leaders posing as a high-ranking military officer project the image of heading an occupational force, an image not lost on minorities who are often disproportionately targeted by law enforcement. Law enforcement was not intended to be a high-status occupation. All that is necessary to convey their authority to the public is the uniform and shield or badge. The standard for any state should be the state police force, which has the broadest jurisdiction.[7]

POST–9-11-2001 AND THE FERGUSON EFFECT

Clearly, the LEAA addressed the issues of standardized training, communication, and equipment for law enforcement agencies across all levels of government. Its shortfall was in the area of defusing racial tensions both in the communities they served and within their own ranks. This became evident with the 1992 Watts Los Angeles riot following the acquittal of four white police officers who were charged with the beating of black motorist, Rodney King, which was captured in a widely distributed video. The acquittal was the catalyst for the latent racial tensions evident in Los Angeles. The three days of rioting in May 1992 resulted in dozens of deaths, over a thousand injuries, many serious, and property damages estimated at 600 million dollars, making it the deadliest U.S. riot since the turbulent 1960s and 1970s. President George H. W. Bush (1989–1993) federalized the National Guard and placed army and marine troops on standby. Interestingly, the jury that acquitted the four white police officers did not have any black members. Obviously, the costly measures advocated in numerous blue ribbon commissions failed in their efforts to lessen racial tensions.[8]

Gang activity and increasingly more lethal weapons available to lawbreakers were also highlighted within the Los Angeles jurisdiction when on February 28, 1997, two heavily armed men, Larry Phillips Jr. and Emil

Matasareanu, clad head-to-toe in military-style body armor, robbed a Bank of America branch of some 300 thousand dollars and then engaged in a forty-four-minute gun battle with the police, shooting at civilians and police within their sight, using armor-piercing bullets, and injuring twelve police officers and eight civilians. In all more than 2,000 bullets were fired in the widely televised forty-four-minute shoot out in the "battle of North Hollywood." Both gunmen died from their wounds, one self-inflicted. The clear message to law enforcement throughout the country was that there was the potential danger of confronting "bad guys" who were better armed than they were. This led to the rapid expansion of SWAT teams throughout municipalities, with rural SWAT teams comprised of local, county, and state police units with access to armor personnel vehicles (BearCats). The battle of North Hollywood also led to increased demand for military weapons like the M-16 or its civilian counterpart, the AR-15, and for rapid-fire, semiautomatic pistols with high-capacity magazines (thirteen to fifteen rounds) to replace the slower, six-shot revolvers long used as the standard police sidearm.[9]

The terrorist attacks on the United States on September 11, 2001, changed the nature of law enforcement, greatly increasing federal control over policing America at all levels and jurisdictions. The federal government created the DHS on March 1, 2003, with oversight over three agencies: U.S. Customs and Border Enforcement (CBE); U.S. Citizens and Immigration Services (USCIS); and U.S. Immigration and Customs Enforcement (ICE). Under this arrangement, the U.S. Border Patrol becomes part of the CBE while ICE now is responsible for deportation of undocumented (aka "illegal") immigrants. Under DHS, federal law enforcement has merged the War on Drugs with the War on Terrorism, with increased focus on security at the Mexico-U.S. border vis-à-vis the U.S.-Canada border. Indeed, since the establishment of the DHS, the vast majority of all arrests for illegal entry comes from the U.S.-Mexico border, known historically as the *Borderlands*. These efforts at curtailing illegal entry has led to an increased militarization of the Borderlands.

In 2006, President George W. Bush initiated *Operation Jump Start*, providing monetary enticements to the border states (California, Arizona, New Mexico, Texas) to deploy their National Guard forces at their respective state's Borderlands. This tactic, of not federalizing these National Guard units, bypassed the prohibition of using federal troops within the United States for domestic purposes. The components of *Operation Jump Start* include: *Operation Gatekeeper*, involving the California-Tijuana region of the Borderlands; *Operation Safeguard*, the term for the component at Nogales, Mexico–Douglas, Arizona; and *Operation Hold the Line* for the Juarez, Mexico–El Paso, Texas region. New Mexico has no major entry points with the Borderlands. These border operations resulted in an increase in U.S. Border Patrol agents in addition to the introduction of National Guard troops. Also, in 2006, the ATF (U.S. Bureau of Alcohol, Tobacco, Firearms, and Explosives) initiated its clandestine, five-year (2006–2011) *Project Gunrunning* sting operation, allegedly in order to trace U.S. weapons crossing the border into Mexico for use by gangs and cartels. Here, the ATF purposely allowed licensed firearm dealers, mainly in Tucson and Phoenix, Arizona, to sell assault-type weapons to illegal straw buyers in order to trace these guns to Mexican drug cartels. This was known as *gun walking*, with the largest of these projects known as *Operation Fast and Furious*. Of the 2,000 firearms involved in the *gun walking* project, only 710 were successfully traced. Moreover, some 150 civilian deaths in Mexico were traced to these guns, leading to a major investigation by Mexico's Attorney General's Office and a further distrust of U.S. law enforcement agendas.

The militarization of the U.S. borders in the name of homeland security continued under President Barack Obama. The September 11 terrorist attacks impacted travel at both U.S. international borders. On January 6, 2009, the *Western Hemisphere Travel Initiative* (WHTI) was initiated. Its purpose was to facilitate the free trade arrangements under NAFTA while at the same time increasing security to "others" attempting transborder entry into the United States. Here, approved NAFTA groups have access to Free and Secure Trade Express (FAST) passage while requiring official passports for all others, including North American Indians, many who do not possess U.S.-approved birth certificates required for passports. Effective June 1, 2009, as part of the Intelligence Reform and Terrorism Prevention Act of 2004 (IRTPA), WHTI requires U.S. and NAFTA partner travelers to present a passport or other documents that denote identity and citizenship when entering the United States.

This agreement does not recognize tribal-issued identification cards, such as tribal membership or enrollment cards, the sole identification for some North American Indians. Consequently, indigenous peoples, notably members of the forty tribal groups whose traditional lands transcend either the Mexico-U.S. or Canada-U.S. borders, are among those most affected by this increased security. Since September 11 and the creation of the Department of Homeland Security, the federal government has further intruded into the limited autonomy of tribal governance within Indian Country. Under these provisions the U.S. military can occupy tribal lands under the DHS Tribal Consultation Policy, a measure not taken since Wounded Knee II in the 1970s. Now the U.S. government can unilaterally intervene in Indian Country under any pretense that is authorized by DHS, including military intervention.[10]

President Obama, in May 2010, followed his predecessor's actions by ordering 1,200 National Guard troops along the U.S.-Mexico border. This was to augment the New Mexico National Guard component activated by

Governor Bill Richardson. DHS used the combined federal, state, and local law enforcement and the National Guard to augment the border patrol and coast guard in securing the country from illicit networks trafficking in people, drugs, illegal weapons, and money. The use of the military to provide support to law enforcement agencies challenges the long-held protections against such action vested in the Posse Comitatus Act. The main exception is when martial law is declared. However, the War on Drugs led to congressional language that appears to skirt this law by allowing the militarization of law enforcement if the military units are used primarily as support for civilian law enforcement agencies. This provision actually goes back to the Carter and Reagan administrations, having been crafted in the 1980s leading to its 1981 codification as Chapter 18 of Title 10 of the U.S. Code—Military Support for Civilian Law Enforcement Agencies. Under this law, the efforts begun under the 1968 Omnibus Crime Control and Safe Streets Act expanded the military influence on civilian law enforcement agencies through loans of equipment and facilities, as well as training. This service is curtailed only if providing such assistance adversely affects the Department of Defense's military preparedness. The National Defense Authorization Act of 1991, Section 1004, authorized the Department of Defense to extend military assistance to civilian law enforcement agencies requesting counterdrug assistance, including providing equipment and training. When federalized, the National Guard units become either the "Army National Guard of the United States "or the "Air Force National Guard of the United States."

However, in the War on Drugs National Guard units can serve a federal purpose while still under the control of the state's governor. This is known as "Title 32 Duty status" and is the situation under which Operation Jump Start was authorized. Moreover, federal funding and support can be provided to states for implementing drug interdiction and counterdrug activity, such as the Joint Counter Narco-Terrorism Task Force used in Arizona. Also following the creation of DHS, in 2004, Congress authorized the use of the National Guard for "homeland defense activity," which implies reaction to a threat or aggression against the United States. This allows for a wide array of situations, given the ambiguous nature of the worldwide War on Terrorism.[11]

These federal-state agreements extend beyond illicit drug trafficking and potential terrorists to include illegal immigrants per se. ICE agreements with states, such as the Rapid REPAT Program and Border Security Task Forces (BEST), use civilian law enforcement agencies to assist in the arrest and detainment of suspected illegal immigrants. The roundup of undocumented aliens, notably those charged with a criminal offense (including misdemeanors), accelerated under President Obama's administration and is being pursued even more rigorously under the presidency of Donald Trump. The problem of these assorted efforts purported to combat crime and terrorism is that they tend to demonize people of color, hence stereotyping entire racial groups as constituting an eminent danger to the public at large and law enforcement in particular. Here, discriminatory drug laws served in creating a self-fulfilling prophecy with the overrepresentation of race and ethnic minorities arrested, convicted, and incarcerated disproportionately to their representation in American society.

The divide between minority communities and police was further compromised by the increased militarization of civilian law enforcement agencies. SWAT teams, armored vehicles, assault rifles, and black garb does little to engender a sense of community policing, nor does the use of military rank, which connotes marshal law to many minorities in these "occupied communities." This divisiveness provides the stimulus for impulsive behaviors by both the public and the police, often igniting situations like that in Ferguson, Missouri, where the black community is seen by the police as not only "enemy territory" but as a source of monetary exploitation, much like that which existed in the *Jim Crow South* prior to passage of the U.S. civil rights laws a half-century ago. In March 2015, a U.S. Department of Justice report found blatant abuse by the police and courts in the Ferguson case including:

Racial profiling and bigotry by the police;
Profit-driven municipal court system that targeted minorities;
Fines and fees generated one-quarter of revenues with minorities targeted for minor violations, arrests, fines and incarceration for failure to pay fines while police and courts often "fixed" tickets for whites.

This is a common theme in many minority communities today, clearly indicating that while police armament has greatly proved equal to our well-suited military forces, racial biases and discrimination still persist and are institutionalized in many communities with substantial minority populations. In May 2015, President Obama started efforts to restrict the easy access of military armaments to civilian law enforcement agencies. This includes restricting the military transfer of grenade launchers, bayonets, tracked armored vehicles, weaponized aircraft and vehicles, firearms, and ammunition of .50 caliber or higher. President Obama said these military items can alienate and intimidate local residents and send the wrong message. An essay on law and disorder in the January/February *Smithsonian* addressed this issue:

You can debate why the United States has the world's largest inmate population with some 2.2 million people in prisons and jails (China is second, with 1.5 million), as well as the world's highest incarceration rate, with 690 out of every 100,000 people locked up (the next major nation is Russia, with 440). You can also debate, as scholars and criminal justice authorities do, why America's incarceration rate has shot up dramatically, more than six-fold over the past century. What can't be disputed, though, is that this phenomenon has acknowledged ripple effects that reach far beyond the inmates themselves—to their extended families, the wider social fabric, the nation's history.[12]

A ray of light existed during the previous administration when President Obama reiterated his call for overhauling sentencing practices for nonviolent drug crimes, convictions that disproportionately afflict minorities and constitute the bulk of our overcrowded prison and jail populations.[13] Toward this end, President Obama set a presidential record for commutations for nonviolent drug offenses, bringing his total number of clemencies to 1,715, including 212 pardons—more than the past twelve presidents combined. To the dismay of many Native Americans, President Obama denied clemency to AIM activist Leonard Peltier. Unfortunately, the Trump administration appears determined to contain, or even reverse, Obama's efforts.

IV

TWENTY-FIRST-CENTURY CONCERNS

Understanding Group Dynamics, Biases, Prejudices, and Discrimination

The elections of 2016 saw a widely divided American public with Trump's supporters rallying around his calls for a "Border Wall" and strict immigration restrictions for Hispanics, as well as for peoples of the Islamic faith trying to escape wars and poverty in the Middle East and Africa. Trump's supporters, although not in the majority but sufficient in numbers to give Trump the Electoral College score he needed, also appear to hold a strong distain for the "established elite," notably those seen as supporting Hilary Clinton's bid for the presidency. On the other hand, Clinton's elite disparaged Trump's supporters as "deplorable" and "basement dwellers." This rhetoric, labeling, and stereotyping is widely promulgated via the mass media so that each group knows how to recognize their public enemy—*the others*. Each group, in turn, seems determined to politicize their ideology within the laws that will tend to *legalize (legislate) their morality* or vision for America. Federal and state laws can either contribute to the ongoing de facto racial divides that have emerged since passage of the civil rights laws of the mid-1960s (ending de jure discrimination) or they can attempt to bridge this widening social divide. As is the case in any society, past or present, mechanisms need to be in place to ensure compliance with these rules. The Jim Crow South effectively enforced segregation contributing to a de jure legal system that discriminated against blacks and other nonwhites. Within any legal system, judges, prosecutors, law enforcement, and correctional personnel are compelled to enforce these laws. Herein lies a basic source of personal conflict for criminal justice practitioners, especially law enforcement personnel.

An understanding of group dynamics, including group conflicts, was posited early in the twentieth century by such noted social philosophers as Max Weber, Emile Durkheim, and Georg Simmel.[1] The dynamics of human behavior obviously have an impact on collective (group) behaviors. Common

themes include how we settle everyday conflicts like making choices or resolving seemingly unanswerable questions such as the meaning of life and what
happens to us in the afterlife: "Who am I?; Why am I here?; What's my purpose?" These issues lie in the physiology of the evolved human brain, which
allows us to perceive things that do not necessarily have hard and set solutions
or answers, hence the reliance on a collective interpretation. But even then,
questions will surface during the process of our everyday lives that require
selective interpretations that provides us with some sense of the meaning of
things at any given time. Social psychologists termed the process of resolving
everyday choices as cognitive dissonance. Here we tend to reduce multiple
choices down to an "either/or" process, much like the binary mechanism of
computer machine language. Otherwise, we would spend too much psychic
energy ruminating on all possible choices and solutions. Cognitive resolu-
tions to these issues often rely on our socialization and how those we associate with may perceive these issues. Once a choice is made, we tend to skew
our perception such that we look favorably at the stimuli associated with the
choice we selected and unfavorably at those we did not select. This is a form
of cognitive discrimination, a process we all engage in. Available choices are
rooted within the normative structure of the group that we belong or identify
with—our "reference" group." The reference group helps define the audience
that we are attempting to influence, the one from which we seek approval.
However, it is important to understand that members of the out-group, our
perceived antagonists, are also part of an audience in that we often act in such
a manner as if to send them "a message." This is best illustrated in retaliatory
acts during armed conflicts or when police from across the country come to
honor a fallen colleague, one they most likely never knew or would even associate with when he or she was alive. These displays are designed to reinforce
the image that law enforcement is a dangerous profession (for the in-group
audience) and that there is a united front confronting the criminal outlaw class
(perceived out-group audience).

The concept of cognitive dissonance gave rise to the theories of a general attribution bias and its various manifestations, such as the "risky-shift
phenomenon" that often results in an overreaction to perceived threats by
the out-group audience.[2] The general attribution bias is rooted in intergroup
dynamics, whereby a social-cultural distance occurs between the in-group
versus out-group(s). George Simmel postulated that "out-group hostilities
increase in-group cohesion" and that this process is an integral component of
boundary maintenance within groups since reciprocal antagonistic relation-
ships, both within and between groups, provide a valuable function by defining the group's boundaries of acceptable behavior at any given time. A function of reciprocal animosities between groups within a given society tends to

strengthen both groups' internal cohesion while at the same time maintaining the rigid class and/or caste lines and social distances that exist between these groups. Here the dominant group sets the rules, which label those outside the normative boundaries as being deviant. Competition for the same resources intensifies in-group–out-group biases. Accordingly, serious deviants are so defined and stigmatized as to warrant the group's most severe sanctions, which in many societies are the death penalty.[3]

Caste and class are common divisions within societies, with the former totally closed out from the dominant mainstream. Class, on the other hand, pertains to the stratification within a group regardless of caste. Social stratification, or division among in-group members, is a phenomenon that exists in all groups regardless of its manifest ideology, even those alleging a singular status ascribed to all members of the group. The French social philosopher, Emile Durkheim, noted that as societies change so does their moral and legal boundaries:

> Imagine a society of saints, a perfect cloister of exemplary individuals. Crime, properly so called, will there be unknown; but faults which appear venial to the layman will create there the same scandal that the ordinary offense does in ordinary consciousnesses. If, then, this society has the power to judge and punish, it will define these acts as criminal and will treat them as such. For the same reason, the perfect and upright man judges his smallest failings with a severity that the majority reserves for acts more truly in the nature of an offense. . . . Crime is, then, necessary; it is bound up with the fundamental conditions of all social life and by that very fact it is useful, because these conditions of which it is a part are themselves indispensable to the normal evolution of morality and law.[4]

Political communism and medieval Catholicism both assigned a common class status to its members within its ideological metaphysical epistemology, yet both societal models employed a stratified control apparatus where leaders held superior status and power. Even if everyone was assigned the status of proletariat worker, distinctions would be made by the workers according to occupation and other criteria. Interclass struggles, as well as those between members of the same class or caste, help define the acceptable boundaries of the group at any given time. Those excluded from privileged status are often seen as being outside these acceptable boundaries. The restrictive accessibility to education has long been the determining factor in maintaining class differentials. The emerging middle class in England was an unforeseen consequence of the *Black Death*, the widespread bubonic and pneumonic plague that decimated much of Europe and Asia during the fourteenth century. The successive waves of the pandemic brought with it social and economic changes to the feudal or manor system, including the availability of education to the lower strata of society. Recorders were sent throughout the country in order to document the extent of the plague's devastation on cities, towns, and villages. These were educated men who, in turn, became de facto instructors for the schooling of the children within these communities, giving England a high literacy rate in an environment where ignorance was once predominate among the masses. Hence, began the education of the masses in Europe, a model that the British brought to the American colonies. Even then, substantial hurdles still remained between common literacy programs and a classical education, where the latter was provided only for the ruling elite (clergy, nobility, American elite). American colonial class structure has its foundation in British history, culture, and customs, remnants which survive to the present.

The sociologist, Howard Becker, termed those members pushed outside the acceptable realm of society as being *outsiders*. Accordingly, social groups tend to label their outsiders as being sinners, heathens, infidels, deviates, terrorists, or criminals. The sanctions directed toward the outsiders, floggings, executions, excommunication, banishment, and the like reinforce the limits of the prescribed social boundaries at any given time. In the past, public humiliation and punishment, including executions, served this purpose. Since the early twentieth century, mass media coverage of these incidents provides the group with the news of the transgressions of these wayward outsiders. Conversely, these public events also help other members to identify with the out-group. Social change often is a result of the out-group membership substantially overwhelming the status-quo in-group.[5] William F. Ogburn, one of the founding fathers of the Chicago School of Sociology, noted that certain rituals associated with a cultural practice, especially those rooted in their creation myth, often remain as significant social rules long beyond their utility. This process of maintaining rituals that may even be counterproductive to the group's quality of life is known as *cultural lag*.[6] The prohibition against contraceptives or abortions by the Catholic Church and Evangelical Christian faiths even into the twenty-first century is a prime example of a cultural lag. There are also a number of class and gender biases within fundamental Islamic societies today that extend back to the Middle Ages, which, in effect, discriminate against women and children in order to maintain strong male-dominance and authority in their society. The prohibition against educating females, the forced sterilization of women, and bride murders are still common throughout many third world societies.

Following this framework on group dynamics and human behavior is such that we tend to perceive the actions of in-group members, those we identify with—our *reference group*—differently than those of out-group members. To illustrate, if someone within our group (in-group) succeeds at a task, we tend to attribute their success to inherent factors, while, on the other hand, if someone in the out-group succeeds along similar lines, we tend to attribute this to external factors including luck or unfair advantages. Likewise, if someone in the in-group fails, or is caught doing something bad or criminal, we tend to look for external factors and influences contributing to this situation, including "blaming the victim." However, if someone in the out-group fails, members of the in-group commonly attribute this behavior exclusively to the individual excluding any mitigating circumstances. This process pertains to law enforcement personnel, regardless if military or civilian, especially when the in-group perceives the out-group as being dangerous and acts accordingly. The perceived out-group, in turn, reacts with distrust of law enforcement, hence aggravating reciprocal antagonism. Similarly, *risky-shift behavior* is a form of group-think actions taken against perceived injustices committed by either group when confronting its perceived out-group. This explains police shootings of minorities as well as riots and demonstrations following such shootings. Here, the people involved in the decision-making process transcend their individuality and conform to the group leader's plan with no or minimal objections. In these instances, collectivism overpowers individualism during times of excitement. This phenomenon is associated not only with impulsive juvenile acts but with major international confrontations. Classic examples abound, including those leading to war such as the sinking of the *Maine* in Cuba leading to the Spanish-American War, the assassination of Arch-Duke Ferdinand and his wife in Sarajevo leading eventually to the First World War, or, more recently, the *Bay of Pigs* CIA-planned invasion of Castro's Cuba during the Kennedy administration that precipitated the 1962 Cuban Crises, as well as the "weapons of mass destruction" hysteria used to invade Iraq during the Gulf Wars. Absent from these events is any effort to produce a viable alternative that could serve to mediate the situation—someone playing *the Devil's Advocate.*

The intensity of intergroup antagonism generally follows two scenarios. One is calculating, and the other is spontaneous—while both types can revolve about a single incident. The intensity of these conflict situations generally is proportionate to the ideological divide between the groups and their members. Either way, the intensity associated with ideological mythology is a strong factor associated with group conflicts and aggression. Simmel noted two types of intergroup conflict situations. Objective or calculated conflict, what he termed *realistic conflict*, is directed toward tangible social objectives such as status, power, and resources. *Nonrealistic conflict* (subjective conflict), in contrast, stems from social frustrations exacerbated by group and/or societal divisions. In the former, conflict is viewed as a rational, calculated process directed toward the accomplishment of a specific goal, while in the latter, aggression becomes an end in itself. Examples of intragroup nonrealistic conflict are inter-Christian and/or inter-Islamic conflicts like *the troubles* in Northern Ireland and the schism between Islamic faiths in the Arab world. The other scenario involves diametrically opposing ideologies. This is illustrated by the communist (Second World) versus capitalist (First World) Cold War adversaries or the current Islam versus Christian conflict, often termed the *War on Terrorism*. A more compelling example is the five-hundred-year conflict between the white Euro-American Protestant ethic and the aboriginal, traditional Harmony Ethos of the original inhabitants of the Americas.[7] Social psychological studies have demonstrated how these mechanisms of group divisions play out in everyday life. Stanley Milgram's work shows how the demands of authority influences and overpowers the demands of individual conscience, explaining such phenomena as the acceptance of racism and discrimination when these policies are endorsed by the government or military. Neal Miller and Stuart Palmer addressed the role of socialization to the expression (direction) of individual and/or collective frustration, helping to explain the mistreatment of identified out-groups such as out-group gangs, civilian prisoners, or prisoners-of-war.[8]

In order to better understand the mechanisms of intense in-group–out-group relations we first need to understand the conceptual model that defines institutional racism and discrimination. These are the terms that help us understand intergroup relations.

- **Ethnocentrism:** The judgment of other groups, beliefs, and cultures through our cultural beliefs—judging ours to be superior to others.
- **Manifest Destiny:** The belief that God predesignated a particular group as being superior to all others—the foundation for racial, sectarian, and ethnic superiority.
- **Prejudice:** Negative feelings toward persons based solely on their membership in certain groups.
- **Discrimination:** Any behavior directed against persons because of their identification with a particular group.
- **Racism:** Discrimination based on a person's skin color or ethnic heritage.
- **Sexism:** Discrimination based on a person's gender.
- **Hate:** Intensely hostile aversion, compounded by anger, ignorance, and fear.
- **Tolerance:** Ability to understand the merits of other beliefs, cultures, and social groups.
- **Value System:** Our collective/shared way of seeing things—*epistemological methodology*.

- **Procedural Justice:** "Due Process" (fairness) under legal systems—adversarial vs. restorative systems of redress.
- **Distributive Justice:** The evaluation of the allocation outcome—distribution of goods and wealth within the group or society. Also, the relationship between authority and recipient (what people think they should have as against what they receive from those in charge of allocating collective resources).
- **Social Justice:** Procedural and distributive justice within a sociocultural context.

These social psychological factors need to be included in any viable assessment of law enforcement personnel regardless of affiliation (military, federal, state, county municipal, local). Some of these factors are intergenerational, hence institutionalized, fostering long-held animus between groups based on race, ethnicity, sects, gender, and social class. Hence, when suffering from extreme frustration, the perceived out-group becomes the target of this pent-up aggression. Although often transitory in nature, these "riots" or "protests" can ignite into collective actions directed toward the perceived cause of the situation or incident that ignited the collective outpouring of emotions in the first place. Here, a cursory understanding of the recent findings relevant to the neurophysiology of human behavior is needed for anyone participating within the justice system: law enforcement, corrections, judiciary, prosecution, and defense. The most important understanding is to discern between impulsive behaviors versus rational choices. This is especially true when looking at impulsive behaviors that occur prior to age eighteen, the age at which both skeletal (body) and neurological (brain) development is generally complete. Even then it takes another seven years for the neuropathways to be completely functional. Hence, the idea of rational action (mens rea) and culpability do not actually apply in these instances, regardless of how horrifying the acts committed. All too often, the public, police, and courts react to horrific acts as if they are premeditated when most occur in the "heat of passion." It has been only recently that the courts have come to recognize and discern between impulsive versus rational acts of violence. These considerations need to also be applied to police violence and violence against the police. It is not just the act per se but the mitigating circumstances surrounding these actions.

The divide between law enforcement and minorities has intensified during the Trump administration, as have the divisions within American society itself. The in-group versus out-group phenomenon has forced citizens into stereotypical groups, each with its own audience (reference group). The rhetoric addressing these groups exacerbates the attribution bias used respectively by each group to define its actions vis-à-vis those of their perceived out-group. This is especially true for law enforcement and its political allies. Clearly, the use of the attribution bias by all groups is a contributing factor to the highly sensationalized claims of "fake news," an attribute emerging from President Trump himself. Consequently, if something is printed that is viewed as disparaging to the in-group, it is attributed to "fake news." This is a reciprocal process with extremes of either group using this device to enhance their argument at the expense of their perceived out-group. Somewhere in between these polar extremes lie "actual facts."

"ACTUAL FACTS"—THE FERGUSON AND BALTIMORE REPORTS

On March 4, 2015, the U.S. Department of Justice, Civil Rights Division, made public its *Investigation of the Ferguson Police Department* (FPD). The following excerpts outline the findings:

> Ferguson's law enforcement practices are shaped by the City's focus on revenue rather than by public safety needs. This emphasis on revenue has compromised the institutional character of Ferguson's police department, contributing to a pattern of unconstitutional policing, and has also shaped its municipal court, leading to procedures that raise due process concerns and inflict unnecessary harm on members of the Ferguson community. Further, Ferguson's police and municipal court practices both reflect and exacerbate existing racial bias, including racial stereotypes. Ferguson's own data establish clear racial disparities that adversely impact African Americans. The evidence shows that discriminatory intent is part of the reason for these disparities. Over time, Ferguson's police and municipal court practices have sown deep mistrust between parts of the community and the police department, undermining law enforcement legitimacy among African Americans in particular.
>
> This culture within FPD influences officer activities in all areas of policing, beyond just ticketing. Officers expect and demand compliance even when they lack legal authority. They are inclined to interpret the exercise of free-speech rights as unlawful disobedience, innocent movements physical threats, indications of mental or physical illness as belligerence. Police supervisors and leadership do too little to ensure that officers act in accordance with law and policy, and rarely respond meaningfully to civilian complaints of officer misconduct. The result is a pattern of stops without reasonable suspicion and arrests without probable cause in violation of the Fourth Amendment; infringement on free expression, as well as retaliation for protected expression, in violation of the First Amendment; and excessive force in violation of the Fourth Amendment.

Racial Bias: Ferguson's approach to law enforcement both reflects and reinforces racial bias, including stereotyping. The harms of Ferguson's police and court practices are borne disproportionately by African Americans, and there is evidence that this is due in part of intentional discrimination on the basis of race.

Community Distrust: Since the August 2014 shooting death of Michael Brown, the lack of trust between the Ferguson Police Department and a significant portion of Ferguson's residents, especially African Americans, has become undeniable. The causes of this distrust and division, however, have been the subject of debate. Police and other City officials, as well as some Ferguson residents, have insisted to us that the public outcry is attributable to "outside agitators" who do not reflect the opinions of "real Ferguson residents." That view is at odds with the facts we have gathered during our investigation. Our investigation has shown that distrust of the Ferguson Police Department is longstanding and largely attributable to Ferguson's approach to law enforcement. This approach results in patterns of unnecessarily aggressive and at times unlawful policing; reinforces the harm of discriminatory stereotypes; discourages a culture of accountability; and neglects community engagement. . . . As a consequence of these practices, law enforcement is seen as illegitimate, and the partnership necessary for public safety are, in some areas, entirely absent.[9]

In August 2016, the U.S. Department of Justice, Office of Public Affairs, released its findings of the investigation into the Baltimore Police Department (BPD). The investigation was conducted by the Civil Rights Division's Special Litigation Section with the assistance of law enforcement professionals pursuant to provisions of the Violent Crime Control and Law Enforcement Act of 1994, an update of the 1968 Omnibus Crime Control and Safe Streets Act. A summary of the findings include what follows:

In May 2015, Attorney General Lynch announced the comprehensive investigation into the BPD after considering requests from city officials and hearing directly from community members about a potential pattern or practice of constitutional violations. The investigation focused on BPD's use of force, including deadly force, stops, searches and arrests, and discriminatory policing.

During the course of its investigation, the department found that the legacy of "zero tolerance" street enforcement, along with deficient policies, training and accountability systems, resulted in conduct that routinely violates the Constitution and federal anti-discrimination law. Throughout the investigation, the department heard consistently from both the community and law enforcement that BPD requires significant reforms to address problems that undermine its efforts to police constitutionally and effectively.

The department found reasonable cause to believe that BPD engages in a pattern or practice of:

- Conducting stops, searches and arrest without meeting the requirements of the Fourth Amendment;
- Focusing enforcement strategies on African Americans, leading to severe and unjustified racial disparities in violation of Title VI of the Civil Rights and the Safe Streets Act;
- Using unreasonable force in violation of the Fourth Amendment;
- Interacting with individuals with mental health disabilities in a manner that violates the Americans with Disabilities Act; and
- Interfering with the right to free expression in violation of the First Amendment.

The department also identified serious concerns about other BPD practices, including an inadequate response to reports of sexual assault, which may result, at least in part, from underlying gender bias. Another significant concern identified by the department was transport practices that place detainees at significant risk of harm.[10]

While U.S. Department of Justice recommendations were made in both the Ferguson and Baltimore consent decrees, there is little hope that these changes will be forthcoming or long lasting or that the federal government will provide adequate supervision and oversight for these agreed upon changes under the Trump administration and its attorney general, Jeff Sessions.

Assessing Law Enforcement Personnel

Few would argue that adequate law enforcement is a critical component of any viable society. The challenge is to provide a well-trained professional force that serves all members of society. Law enforcement, for the most part, is a routine, often boring profession throughout the country with the exception of "high crime areas." Training and professionalism is most critical in societies like the United States where law enforcement personnel are licensed to bear and use firearms. Both education (college or university degree) and professional training (police academy) are interrelated components of a professional police department regardless of level—federal, state, county, municipal, or local. The Omnibus Crime Control and Safe Streets Act served as the impetus for universal training standards, while the 9-11 terrorist attacks on the United States drew attention to the need for better channels of communication and information sharing. Modern technology and a larger number of recruits pursuing college-level degrees have addressed this major concern stemming from the problems endemic within the nation's highly decentralized law enforcement picture leading up to the turbulent era of the 1960s and 1970s. What is often lacking is adequate assessment of law enforcement personnel both at the entry level and continuing throughout this career lifespan. Today, we have a better understanding of the biology of human behavior, including impulse dysregulation, traumatic stress, and brain injuries. Reliable psychological assessments have also been present since the Second World War, techniques that provide the foundation of the behavioral profiling so popular in the forensic fields today. Thanks to new brain-imaging techniques over the past twenty-five years, new insights into the functioning of the brain have emerged and have addressed long-held misconceptions about human development and culpability. These insights have challenged judicial *cultural lags*, including such issues as treating juveniles or mentally deficient individuals as rational adults, hence deserving of society's harshest punishments, especially if they are members of the perceived minority out-groups. These major changes are as follows:

- 2002, in *Atkins v. Virginia*, the court outlawed the execution of the mentally retarded
- 2005, in *Roper v. Simmons,* the court prohibited the death sentence for offenders who committed their crime under age eighteen
- 2006, in *House v. Bell*, court ruled that post-conviction DNA evidence can be introduced
- 2012, in *Miller v. Alabama*, the court outlawed sentencing youth (under eighteen) to "life in prison without parole"

In *Roper v. Simmon*, the U.S. Supreme Court ruled that the Constitution forbids the execution of those convicted of murder who were under age eighteen at the time of the offense. This ruling ended this practice used in nineteen states, negating the death sentences of about seventy juvenile murderers at that time and barring states from executing minors in the future. In *Roper* the American Psychological Association (APA) acted as a "friend of the Court" and presented research on the development of the brain from childhood to young adulthood—notably the pruning of dendrites beginning at puberty and the slow process of myelination of the frontal lobe neurons (seven years following the cessation of physical growth $18 + 7 =$ age 25). The APA argued that the psychological consequences of this neurophysiological process included *impulsivity*, which is due to an immature frontal lobe capacity relevant to the central nervous system "executive functioning"—a critical factor regarding "mens rea" (rational intent and culpability). Moreover, a common outcome was group impulsivity, known as the *risky-shift phenomenon*, and that *substance use/abuse* merely exacerbated the individual's potential for self-control.

In *Miller v. Alabama*, these conditions were again presented before the high court when it was found that many states were doling out first degree murder sentences of "life without parole" for juvenile homicide offenders, ignoring these physiological and psychological processes whereby those under age eighteen (many clinicians would argue age twenty-five) should automatically fall into a special classification with these conditions constituting strong mitigating circumstances. *Miller* represented the practice of many states that automatically gave youth, once death qualified, sentences of "life without parole." The *Miller* case was actually a consolidation of two cases, *Miller v. Alabama* [no. 10-9646] and *Jackson v. Hobbs* [no. 10-9647]. In *Miller*, Evan Miller, age fourteen, was convicted of murder after he and another boy set fire to a trailer where they had bought drugs. In *Jackson*, Kuntrell Jackson, age fourteen, was with two other teens who went into a video store to rob it. Jackson was the outside lookout. One of his colleagues shot and killed the clerk. Jackson, like Miller, was charged as an adult and also given the maximum sentence of "life without any possibility of parole." Both youth were of African American descent. In the five to four decision, Justice Elena Kagan wrote: "*Miller* did not outlaw mandatory life sentences without possibility of parole for youth . . . it merely stated that this process could not be automatically assigned whenever the courts decide to adjudicate a juvenile as an adult for a crime related to a homicide—even if they did not commit the murder or intended to do so."[1]

Another consideration relevant to both offenders and law enforcement personnel is the prevalence of traumatic stress, including traumatic brain injuries. The first challenge in determining the presence of a mental disturbance is to attempt to discern between transitory and pervasive disorders. It is also important to attempt to separate personality disorders from clinical diagnoses, although this is not always an easy task, especially since baselines are not readily available. Also, a differential assessment needs to be made concerning substance-related disorders, which often complicates determining which diagnoses are primary and which are associated or comorbid features of the presenting mental problem. Transitory mental disorders include the adjustment disorders that are quite common for returning veterans or refugees. A serious consequence of untreated transitory disorders is anomic suicide. These disorders reflect conditions, if left untreated, that could manifest as a major clinical disorder. Fortunately, transitory mental conditions often lend themselves to effective treatments, namely psychopharmacology and cognitive behavioral therapies. The pervasive mental illnesses, notably those that are prone to be of a genetic or organic origin, such as major depression, bipolar depression, schizophrenia, delusional disorders, obsessive-compulsive disorder, and impulse control disorders, including paraphilia, are more complex to treat and often require a long-term treatment protocol. Included here are psychological outcomes from traumatic brain injuries (TBIs). Often diffuse (closed) head injuries are more difficult to identify than those injuries with a focal injury. Symptoms are associated with not only the type of TBI (diffuse of local) but are specific to the region of the brain insult. With mild TBIs, the person may remain conscious or only lose consciousness for a few seconds or minutes. These are often concussions and present with headache, vomiting, nausea, poor motor control, dizziness and balance problems, lightheadedness, blurred vision, ringing in the ears, fatigue/lethargy, and somatic difficulties. Behavioral problems include mood changes, confusion, memory problems, and difficulty concentrating or thinking. Moderate or severe TBIs, while more obvious, also present with a host of physiological and psychological problems, including persistent headaches, vomiting/nausea, convulsions, slurred speech, aphasia, weakness or numbness of limbs, poor motor coordination, confusion, and agitation or impulsive outbursts. Behavioral problems can include deficits in social judgment, inappropriate social interactions, and cognitive problems associated with memory, attention, and executive functioning. The treatment and rehabilitation needs of TBI patients include protocols that address: improving memory and problem-solving skills; managing stress and emotional problems, including temper and impulsive outbursts; and providing social and occupational skills.[2]

EXAMPLES OF POLICE
ASSESSMENT AND AGGREGATE PROFILING

Law enforcement assessments need to address both competency and suitability. A single measure is not adequate in addressing the issues of intelligence, education, personality, and aptitude. Thus, a battery of instruments is needed, with the interview driven by the Mental Status Exam, which will also highlight neurological deficits. Moreover, aptitude and suitability needs to include more than an interview with the hiring police official(s). Here, the strongest predictive instrument, and one widely used in police selection, is the Minnesota Multiphasic Personality Inventory (MMPI).

The Minnesota Multiphasic Personality Inventory

The MMPI is the most widely used tool for screening police candidates, mainly due to its capacity to satisfy two primary conditions: psychopathological (clinical) screening and the prediction of occupational success. Retrospective studies have led to a wealth of data relevant to both professional attitude and mental health status. This is one of the most studied psychological assessment tools with thousands of published reports. All versions—the MMPI, MMPI-2, and MMPI-A—provide a graphic profile based on a *t*-score distribution where fifty is the mean and the standard deviation is ten. Two standard deviations signify "statistical significance" within this format.

The MMPI consists of three validity scales (Lie, Validity, Corrections) and ten clinical scales. There are also a number of supplementary scales and critical items. Among the numerous predictive profile sets, the MMPI provides both forensic and police profiles, including those predicting: *Good Cop Profile, Bad Cop Profile, Mad Cop Profile*. The MMPI is one of the most widely used tools, along with the MSE, for screening for mental illness and is the leading assessment for predicting occupational success, including mental health professionals, law enforcement, and legal professionals. The

MMPI was first standardized in 1943 and readied for use. Its reliability and validity is not so much due to its original construction validation sample, which was poor by current standards, but to the numerous sets of predictive data generated by the MMPI during its more than seventy years of retrospective research relevant to both concurrent and predictive studies. Its predictive strength comes from the instrument being administered to all individuals entering academic and/or professional studies at the time of their entry into these programs. This represented the concurrent study data, whereby aggregate profiles were later developed reflecting those who were successful or unsuccessful in these professions, hence leading to the MMPI's predictive strength. These retrospective studies have led to a wealth of data in the areas of professional aptitude and mental health status. Clearly, this is one of the most studied assessment tools with thousands of published reports, including samples, worldwide.

The Validity Scales.   The original MMPI consists of three validity scales (Lie, Validity, and Corrections). The Lie scale (L) is based on a group of items that place the respondent in a favorable light but are unlikely to be truthfully answered as being true. The Validity scale (F) consisted of unfavorable items unlikely for any respondent to answer all as relevant to his or her life. Accordingly, high F scores reflect a number of responding errors: carelessness in responding, gross eccentricity, or deliberate malingering (faking bad). The Correction scale (K) again uses specifically chosen items that measure test-taking attitudes. A high K score most likely indicates defensiveness or an attempt to fake good. A low K score, on the other hand, may reflect frankness and self-analysis or yet another attempt to fake bad. The K score also provides a computed correction factor that is added to certain clinical scales in order to provide a weighted adjusted scale: scale 1 (Hs) = +0.5K; scale 4 (Pd) = +0.4K; scale 7 (Pt) = +1K; scale 8 (Sc) = +1K; and scale 9 (Ma) = +0.2K. These weighted factors are provided on the MMPI *Profile and Case Summary* sheet, which presents a graphic representation of the MMPI scores based on a *t*-score distribution.

The Clinical Scales.   The body of the original MMPI consists of ten clinical scales that correspond to the major clinical syndromes posited by the diagnostic and statistical manuals.

1. Hypochondriasis Scale (Hs). This scale measures the level of preoccupation with illnesses and health as well as long-term fears and worries about one's health.
2. Depressive Scale (D). This scale measures self-worth ranging from hopelessness (high *t*-score) to effortless optimism (low *t*-score). High scores, with suicidal ideations, represent a red flag for suicide potential.

3. Hysteria Scale (Hy). This scale measures one's preoccupation with body pain, including conversion disorders (psychosomatic illnesses with no biological basis). At the other end of the continuum, low *t*-scores indicate levels of trustfulness and a lack of hostility.

4. Psychopathic Deviant Scale (Pd). This scale is designed to measure amoral, asocial behavior and levels of empathy. Also measured are family conflicts, feelings of alienation, and problems with authority. This is a critical item when assessing law enforcement or military personnel. It is important to discern if a high score is indicative of a transitory event in the past or if the score reflects a pervasive characterological feature of one's personality.

5. Masculine-Feminine Interests Scales (Mf). This scale measures sexual identification and sexual occupational/professional identification. It focuses on contrasts of action versus feeling and expressions of aggression (verbal versus physical). This scale does not identify homosexuality or lesbianism. Instead it tends to identify certain personality traits, including competitiveness and aggressiveness as well as being outgoing, uninhibited, and self-confident.

6. Paranoia Scale (Pa). This scale measures ideas of mistreatment and persecution (higher *t*-scores) versus heightened interpersonal sensitivity and moral righteousness (lower *t*-scores). It combines with other scales to indicate critical personality disorders, including Paranoid Personality Disorder, and certain dangerous clinical disorders, such as Paranoid Schizophrenia and Paranoid Delusional Disorder.

7. Psychasthenia Scale (Pt). In contemporary terms, this scale measures obsessive and compulsive tendencies, including Obsessive Compulsive Personality Disorder and Obsessive Compulsive Anxiety Disorder. It also indicates excessive fears and other forms of rumination secondary to anxiety. It's a good index of psychological turmoil, discomfort, and agitation.

8. Schizophrenia Scale (Sc). This scale measures the degree of personal confusion, including serious thought disorders such as alienation from one's own feelings and from others, impaired concentration and attention, uncontrolled impulses, excitability, peculiar body experiences, delusions, depersonalization, and hallucinations. A number of personality disorders are indicated by elevated *t*-scores on this item (Schizoid, Schizotypal, Borderline, Antisocial, and so on) as well as Schizophrenia. Extremely high *t*-scores, however, are more likely to reflect transitory psychosis secondary to Substance-Use Disorders.

9. Hypomania Scale (Ma). This scale measures a person's activity from intense autonomic overactivity (high *t*-scores) to a markedly slow personal temperament (low *t*-scores). Autonomic endocrine/limbic dysregulation can result in an override of the executive functioning of the frontal lobe, thereby falsely presenting hypermania as a thought disorder or psychosis. The manias are associated with a number of disorders, including bipolar affective disorders, paraphilias, and impulse control disorders. They can also emerge as secondary features of substance-use disorders and organic brain damage, including dementia and TBIs.

10. Social Introversion-Extroversion Scale (Si). This scale indicates one's level of introversion versus extroversion. In Western societies where 75 percent of the people are extroverted and only about 25 percent introverted, extremes of the latter reflect pathology. However, extremely low *t*-scores can be problematic in that these individuals can be overly dependent on others for their social motivation and interaction. Indeed, being slightly socially introverted may prove to be a virtue for clinicians assessing and/or treating victims of traumatic stress.

Supplemental Scales. A number of additional scales, many outside the clinical criteria outlined in the DSM, are part of the more recent MMPI-2. Even with about twenty years of data available, most of these additional scales are not yet considered to have the reliability and validity of the original thirteen scales. However, four supplementary scales are common to both the MMPI and the MMPI-2. These scales appeared as a modification to the original MMPI and many practitioners used the expanded MMPI continue to draw on these items when using the MMPI-2.

A Scale. High *t*-score on this item reflects miserable and unhappy individuals.

R Scale. On the other hand, high scores on this scale reflect individuals who are careful and cautious.

Combined A/R Scales. U.S. Veterans Administration data profiled the A/R combinations among its patients. Depressive diagnoses were associated with the high A–high R profile, while personality disorders were mostly associated with the low A–low R profile.

Es Scale. High scores on this item are indicative of stability and good mental health.

MAC-R Scale. This scale does not measure if a person is a problem drinker as much as it indicates his or her potential to exhibit problems if he or she drinks. High *t*-scores on this item indicate individuals who present themselves as being socially extroverted, self-confident, and assertive but are also likely to be exhibitionistic and risk takers.

Two- and Three-Point Code Types Relevant to Police Profiles

Hs (1)/D(2) Code: High *t*-scores on these two clinical items indicate somatic discomfort and pain and can be considered as the "fatigue scale" for law enforcement personnel.

Hs(1)/Pd(4) Code: Although rare and mostly affecting males, individual with high *t*-scores on these clinical items can present with problems with the opposite sex and a drinking problem, despite the outward appearance of being social extroverts. This profile could point to officers likely to have family problems and who may be subject to sexual harassment complaints.

Hs(1)/Ma(9) Code: Persons with high *t*-scores on these clinical items present as being verbal, socially extroverted, aggressive, and belligerent, when, in fact, they are basically passive/dependent individuals trying to conceal their basic characterlogic tendencies.

D(2)/Pd(4) Code: High *t*-scores on these clinical items indicate an impulsive profile, including substance abuse, illicit behaviors, and family discord, features likely to be exacerbated by occupational stress and corresponding behaviors.

D(2)/Pt(7) Code: These officers would be tense, anxious, nervous, and excessively worried about the hazards of their job. Moreover, they tend to be rigid in their thinking and of the law. They may also be excessively religious and extremely moralistic, hence less tolerant to those they perceive as being deviant (out-groups).

Hy(3)/Pd(4) Code: Persons with a high *t*-score profile on these clinical items tend to harbor hostile and aggressive impulses and are unable to express their negative feelings appropriately. If scale three is the higher scale, indirect expression of anger is likely. Persons with a higher four scale are overcontrolled most of the time but have the potential for brief violent episodes, which can manifest themselves during a crisis situation.

Pd(4)/Pt(7) Code: High *t*-scores on these clinical items are indicative of episodes of acting out, including substance abuse and sexual promiscuity. Individuals with this profile may also report feeling tense, fatigued, and exhausted.

Hs(1)/Hy(3)/D(2) Code: Individuals with high *t*-score profiles on these clinical items have a tendency for conversion symptoms, where stress is often converted into physical symptoms. While presenting as sociable, they tend to be passive-dependent in their interactions. Look for an officer who pursues workmen's compensation following stressful duty.

D(2)/Pd(4)/Pt(7) Code: A high *t*-score profile on this clinical set indicates a passive-aggressive personality, which is often manifested by substance abuse and family and marital problems. Despite strong achievement needs, these individuals tend to be angry, hostile, and immature with undercontrolled impulses.

Political Correctiveness and MMPI Revisions.   The genesis of the current review of the predictive effectiveness of psychological testing was rooted in the U.S. Civil Rights Act of 1964, Section H of Title VII, which specifically makes reference to the use of nondiscriminatory tests for employment decisions. This, and other civil rights cases, led to the restructuring of the original MMPI. A major decision was the *Soroka v. Dayton-Hudson* case, better known as the Target case, which was filed as a class action on September 7, 1989. The case involved the use of a preemployment psychological screening device for security officers working for Target stores. The significance of the *Soroka* case was that it coincided with passage of the *Americans with Disabilities Act of 1990*, which underscored the importance of keeping the invasiveness of psychological inquiries in preemployment testing to a minimum. At that time, the Target stores used the Rodgers Condensed CPI-MMPI, which was developed in 1966. The California Psychological Inventory (CPI) augmented the MMPI by looking at attributes of one's personality using a twenty-scale format, compared to the MMPI's traditional ten clinical scales. However, the CPI also used 194 MMPI items in its 462-item measure. Security officer applicants screened out by Rodgers CPI-MMPI claimed that the inventory was not job related and was offensive and intrusive. Part of the problem with the Rodgers assessment tool was that no empirical data was available related to its administration, norming, standardization, and interpretation, even though such standards existed independently for the CPI and the MMPI. Hence, in August 1989, the MMPI-2 was introduced. This version came forty-six years after the original MMPI. The reason for a change in the MMPI was not that it needed re-norming (subsequent normings of the original has greatly increased its reliability and validity) but was to replace outdated items. Toward this end, the MMPI-2 omitted the sixteen repeat items, religious and sexual preference items, and what was felt to be outdated items. In all, 107 items were eliminated due to these reasons, but 108 items were added. Some of these new items pertain to revisions in the validity scales while others pertain to new scales and measures such as family dynamics, Type A behavior, eating disorders, substance abuse, and suicide.

The MMPI-2 is even longer (567 items) than the original MMPI (566 items). The norming sample for the MMPI-2 consisted of respondents who had higher educational levels than that of the general public, thereby contributing to a t-score distribution flaw where now $T = 65$ (a standard deviation and a half) indicates statistical significance instead of the traditional two standard deviations ($T = 70$ or more). In order to use the decades of reliability and validity associated with the original MMPI, the first 370 items of the revised MMPI-2 are said to correspond to the three validity and ten clinical scales of the MMPI, without of course the items measuring religiosity and sexuality.

Given the significant changes reflected in the MMPI-2, many clinicians question the transferability of the original MMPI's predictive validity, especially when measuring mental pathology and critical occupational suitability to the new versions. For one, hyperreligiosity and hypersexuality are common features of manic episodes.

A protocol used by forensic psychologists who prefer the greater reliability, validity, and predictability of the original MMPI is to alert those being tested as to archaic terms and the flexibility of tense (past or present). The authors found that 10 of the 566 items raised the most questions among those taking the MMPI:

Item 48: When I am with people I am bothered by hearing very *queer* things.

Item 57: I am a good *mixer*.

Item 70: I used to like *drop-the-handkerchief*.

Item 105: Sometimes when I am not feeling well I am *cross*.

Item 118: In school I was sometimes sent to the principal for *cutting up*.

Item 129: Often I can't understand why I have been so *cross* and *grouchy*.

Item 236: I *brood* a great deal.

Item 381: I am often said to be *hotheaded*.

Item 471: In school my marks in *deportment* were quite regularly bad.

Item 506: I am a *high-strung* person.

Being able to define these items in contemporary terms is the only adjustment that is required for the continued use of the original MMPI and its seventy years of post facto predictive validity. The original MMPI assessment, at the time of job entry, should be conducted along with a mental status exam, with the MMPI score constituting a baseline profile. Subsequently, the abbreviated MMPI assessment, consisting of the first 360 items covering the three validity scales and ten clinical scales, can then be administered as needed with these profiles compared with the initial MMPI baseline profile.

In 1992, the MMPI-A (adolescent version) was introduced based mainly on the items from the original MMPI. The MMPI-A comes in both a long form (478 items) and a short form (350 items). Most recently, the MMPI-2-RF (restructured form) is an attempt to give the MMPI-2 clinical scales the same validity of those in the original MMPI. Yet many clinicians see these efforts as further complicating the assessment role of the MMPI, especially regarding major clinical syndromes and personality disorders. The added content scales of the MMPI-2, such as the Dominance Scale, Addiction Potential Scale, Addiction Acknowledgement Scale, Social Discomfort Scale, Type A Scale, Overcontrolled Hostility Scale, Marital Distress Scale, and Psy-5 Scales, all seem to add to the original problem as to why the MMPI was changed in the first place—claiming intrusive attributes of human behavior that may not stand up in a court of law when their reliability and validity is challenged, let alone what they purport to measure.[3]

Mental Status Examination

The Mental Status Examination (MSE) covers six categories of mental status that are generally observed during the initial clinical consultation. There are various methods of conducting the MSE, with most trained clinicians using the casual conversational approach so as to not startle the interviewee and further elevate his or her stress level.

Appearance, Attitude, and Activity.   Appearance is the assessment of the physical characteristics of the client, including physical disabilities or abnormalities as well as the client's dress, hygiene, grooming. This observation needs to be in concert with the client's cultural norms and social class and not necessarily that of the clinician. Attitude is how the client reacts to the questions during the intake process—the factors here are cooperativeness, hostility, or overdependency. Activity looks at the client's physical demeanor during the interview. What is their activity level, especially that which seems abnormal for the situation—sitting rigidly, involuntary tics or tremors, fidgeting, unique mannerisms, and such.

Mood and Affect.   Mood and affect are sometimes difficult to distinguish from each other. Mood is how the person describes his or her feelings, while affect is the external manifestation of these feelings. The continuum for mood and affect runs from depression to mania. Generally speaking, mood and affect fall into six categories: euthymic (e.g., calm, friendly, pleasant); angry (e.g., belligerent, confrontational, hostile, irritable, oppositional, outraged); euphoric (e.g., cheerful, elated, ecstatic); apathetic (e.g., flat affect, dull, bland); dysphoric (e.g., despondent, grieving, hopeless, distraught, sad, overwhelmed); and apprehensive (e.g., anxious, fearful, nervous, tense, panicked, terrified).

Speech and Language.   Speech looks at fluency of the language spoken. Also, note if this is the client's original language or a second language. This category of the MSE looks at the following language functions: fluency of speech, repetition, comprehension, naming, writing, reading, prosody (variations in rate, rhythm, and stress in speech), and quality of speech. Portions of standardized intelligence tests such as the Wechsler batteries and the Stanford-Binet test can be used to determine many of these features. Disorders to look out for during this phase of the MSE include cluttering, dysgraphia, dyslexia, echolalia, mutism, palilalia, pressured speech, stuttering, and word salad, among others.

Thought Process, Thought Content, and Perception.   Thought process involves evaluating the organization, flow, and production of thought, looking for abnormalities such as flight of ideas, loose associations, tangentiality, clang associations, echolalia, perseveration, thought blocking, and word salad. Thought content and perception looks for delusions, homicidal or suicidal ideations, magical thinking, overvalued ideas, obsessions, paranoia, phobias, preoccupation, rumination, suspiciousness, depersonalization, derealization, hallucinations, and illusions.

Cognition.   Cognition is the ability to think using one's intellect, logic, reasoning, and memory. The cognitive testing sequence involves: 1) orientation × 4—person, place, time, and situation; 2) attention and concentration; 3) registration and short-term memory; 4) long-term memory (verbal and nonverbal); 5) constructional and visuospatial ability; and 6) abstraction and conceptualization. Standardized tests used for attention and concentration include the Trail-Making Tests, Symbol Digit Test, and the Stroop Color-Word Test, while the Digit Span (forward and backward) subtest of the Wechsler IQ batteries is used for attention. Short-term memory is usually tested by giving the client three common words (e.g., cat, blue, bike) at the beginning of the session and then having them repeat these words back to you at least fifteen minutes into the session. Visual memory and construction and visuospatial ability can be tested with the Bender-Gestalt, Draw-A-Clock, Rey-Osterrieth Complex Figure Test, or Trail-Making Tests.

Insight and Judgment.   Insightfulness includes the capacity for abstraction and the ability to communicate effectively with appropriate cognitive functioning while having a stable mood and affect and not manifesting any thought disorder. Insight and judgment are seen as being interrelated in that the ability to make sound judgments or decisions is dependent upon an adequate level of insight. Insight is the ability to be self-aware—being conscious of one's feelings, ideas, and motives. Intrusive defense mechanisms such as repression, displacement, dissociation, reaction formation, and intellectualization often arise during this portion of the MSE, as well as acting out, externalization, idealization, projection, and denial and distortions. These are features that impair one's insight and judgment.

The Mini-Mental Exam

This exam is an abbreviated form that is often used in hospital intakes. It consists of five categories: orientation; registration; attention and calculation; recall; and language. Under orientation, the client is asked the year, month, season, and day, as well as where he or she is at that time. Under registration, the client is asked to name three objects that you present and asked to repeat them back to you. In attention and calculation, have the client count back from one hundred by sevens. Stop after five answers. Under recall, ask for the three objects repeated earlier. With language, have the client name a pencil, and observe; have them repeat "No ifs, ands, or buts"; and then have them follow a three-stage command (take a paper in your right hand and fold it in half and put it on the floor). Then have them read a sentence and then write it followed with having the client copy a geometric design. These are usually scored and are used primarily with people suspected of brain damage, including those with TBIs.[4]

Other Assessments

While clearly the MMPI and MSE are the standard bearers of clinical assessment tools for a number of professions, including law enforcement, other instruments have surfaced that may supplement the MMPI and MSE. The Matrix-Predictive Uniform Law Enforcement Selection Evaluation Inventory (M-PULSE) (2004) is a relatively new instrument consisting of eighteen liability scales designed to predict officer misconduct; empirical scales to measure attitudes, values, and beliefs; and two validity scales to measure response bias. It consists of 455 statements and has mixed results regarding its validity in prescreening law enforcement and correctional officer candidates. Studies based on the M-PULSE liability scales found that the use of biographical information like this was not, in itself, predictive of police suitability on the job.[5]

Both the MMPI and MSE have the potential to address situational personality and/or mental disturbances such as suicide ideation, posttraumatic stress, substance abuse, potential for violence, and impulsive dysregulation secondary to brain trauma. This is especially relevant when military veterans are hired as civilian police officers. Quick assessment tools include those that address depression, anxiety, hopelessness, and suicide ideation. Screening instruments used for traumatic stress include the Impact of Events Scale (IES-R), General Health Questionnaire (GHQ 60), Symptom Checklist 90, Traumatic Symptom Inventory (TSI), Davidson Trauma Scale (DTS), Mississippi Scale for PTSD, Historical Clinical Risk Management (HCR-20), and the Detailed Assessment of Posttraumatic Stress (DAPS), to mention a few. For suspected brain injuries, use the McCormick TBI Interview, in addition to the neurological components of the MSE.[6]

· *14* ·

Politics and Policing

Even if we achieved a high level of well-trained, competent police personnel, they would still be subjected to political influences, especially those reflected in statutory laws. Federal and state legislatures make the laws that the police, judiciary, and corrections must enforce. Moreover, the top law enforcement official in both the federal and state system is the attorney general, who is either appointed or elected to this position. The U.S. president and governors can further influence the nature of law enforcement such as outlawing school desegregation or "sanctuary cities." Laws, especially federal laws, have the effect of legitimizing social and cultural norms, including determining class and racial differentials. The *Fugitive Slave Act of 1850* is a glaring example of congressional action requiring states to arrest and return black slaves who escaped to free states from slave state owners. This law mandated reluctant jurisdictions to participate regardless of existing state laws. The *Fugitive Slave Act* actually was vested in an earlier version established in 1793 as part of the U.S. Constitution (Article 4, Section 2):

> No Person held to Service or Labour in one State, under the Laws thereof, escaping into another, shall, in Consequence of any Law or Regulation therein, be discharged from such Service or Labour, but shall be delivered up on Claim of the Party to whom such Service or Labour may be due.[1]

Union officers refused to comply with the law during the Civil War, and it effectively ended with President Lincoln's *Emancipation Proclamation* on January 1, 1863.

In 1896, the U.S. Supreme Court, in its *Plessy v. Ferguson* decision, legitimized racial segregation and Jim Crow laws, which were prevalent in the post–Civil War South. This decision, in effect, sanctioned the often brutal enforcement of these laws by law enforcement. *Plessy v. Ferguson* also fueled the extralegal summary hanging and burning of blacks during this turbulent period. *Plessy* remained the "law of the land" until it was repudiated by the U.S. Supreme Court 1954 decision in *Brown v. Board of Education*. Despite the 1954 reversal, cultural lag throughout the South prevailed with Jim Crow laws remaining the de facto custom of many jurisdictions until passage of the U.S. Civil Rights Acts of the mid-1960s. Twenty-three years following the *Plessy* decision another nationwide order, the Eighteenth Amendment, Prohibition of Liquor, divided American society again, mandating police enforcement of this constitutional ruling by both federal and state authorities. The divisiveness created by Prohibition, coupled with the onset of the Great Depression, led to its repeal in 1933 (Twenty-First Amendment). Clearly, law enforcement, even at its best, is often challenged by political changes in the American landscape.[2]

Again, in the twenty-first century American society is divided along class and racial lines with citizens arguing that "black lives matter" in one camp versus those arguing that "blue lives matter," with each camp arguing their respective cases publicly. As can be expected, political influence has emerged from this often contentious and emotional national debate. The "Black Lives Matter" movement emerged following the death of armed black males by police officers, including incidents in New York City; Ferguson, Missouri; and Baltimore, Maryland. The "Blue Lives Matter" movement, along with its special adaptation of the American flag (with the white bar under the stars replaced with a blue stripe), emerged on December 20, 2014, following the execution-style killing of New York City police officers Rafael Ramos and Wenjian Liu. The organization was initially named Blue Lives Matter NYC, but soon became a nationwide movement.

This divide between law enforcement and minority communities intensified, leading to congressional actions that tend to enhance the status of police and other first responders to a special class deserving harsher penalties for actions perpetrated against them. Emotional arguments are presented supporting the *Thin Blue Line Act*, with U.S. Senator Thom Tillis (R-NC) in support of the *Thin Blue Line Act*, claiming that 2016 was one of the deadliest years for law enforcement. When "Fact Check" assessed this statement, it found that 2016 was actually one of the least deadly years in modern times; "In fact, fewer officers died in 2016 than most other years in the 20th and 21st centuries. More police officers died in 1916 (164) than in 2016 (143)."[3] Available data for 2017 show fifty police "line-of-duty deaths" with twenty due to assault (eighteen by gunfire) and twenty-one for vehicle-related incidents. As would be expected, the two most populous states had the highest incidents: (New York with five; California with four). The next highest incident involved Tribal Police with three deaths. These deaths also followed the gender differential within law enforcement with the vast majority of death being males (forty-eight) compared to two female police fatalities.[4]

House Resolution 814 was proposed in February 2015 and passed by the House of Representatives in June 2017. It is a bill "to amend title 18 of the United States Code, to provide additional aggravating factors for the imposition of the death penalty based on the status of the victim." The bill stipulates that the status referred to are law enforcement officers, firefighters, or other first responders. Some states already include these increased aggravating factors in their death penalty statutes, but even then, politics play a role in who is to be death qualified following a deadly assault on a police officer. Elevating the status of one citizen over another challenges the ideal of "equal justice for all," a major tenet in the 1976 U.S. Supreme Court decision to reinstate capital punishment. Giving greater legal weight to a particular type of victim greatly diminishes the status of the offender, essentially negating the provision requiring serious consideration be given to "mitigating" circumstances in order to mediate the "aggravating" circumstances justifying the use of the death penalty.

A recent case in New Hampshire illustrates this phenomenon. Former U.S. Senator Kelly Ayotte is a prime example of someone who used her political appointment as attorney general as a stage for national recognition as an ultra-conservative who used the death of a white police officers by a black man, Michael Addison, to get elected to the U.S. Senate. Clearly, Ayotte used the 2006 capital murder case of Michael Addison toward this end. The Addison case illustrates the dual standard of justice in New Hampshire, as well as its latent racial bias. Addison was prosecuted for killing Manchester police officer Michael Briggs. The shooting of officer Briggs rose to the level of a capital offense not because it was premeditated, since all indications are that it occurred as an impulsive act while Addison was attempting to flee apprehension, but due to the fact that the officer he shot subsequently died from these wounds.

Clearly, the race card was played in the Addison case. First, he was depicted as an "outsider" from Massachusetts. Attorney General Ayotte also made certain that he was charged with other assault and drug charges prior to his capital murder trial, hence, stacking the "aggravating" elements needed to off-set the "mitigating" circumstances required by the U.S. Supreme Court in capital cases heard since their ruling reinstating the death penalty in 1976. A disturbing element of the trial was the portrayal of Michael Briggs, a local white man, as a "more worthy" human being than an outsider, black man. Here, the attribution bias played a significant role in the trial. Addison's lawyer offered a plea to avoid the death penalty, but Ayotte insisted that this would be a death-penalty case. She later used the Briggs family in her Senate race political ads. More disturbing was the role that the Manchester Chief of Police David J. Mara played by having a significant presence of uniformed police officers during the entire Addison trial. This is reminiscent of Alabama, Mississippi, and Arkansas during the 1960s at the height of the civil rights turmoil. This clearly represents jury intimidation, something Attorney General Ayotte and Superior Court Judge Kathleen McGuire should not have allowed.

The death penalty issue regarding both a black defendant and the killing of a police officer is a contentious one in New Hampshire given that in 2008, multimillionaire John "Jay" Brooks was tried for capital murder in the premeditated death of handyman Jack Reid, who he wrongfully accused of stealing. Attorney General Ayotte chose not to participate in the prosecution in this case as she did in the Addison trial. White, wealthy John "Jay" Brooks was convicted of capital murder but spared the death sentence and instead is serving a life-without-parole sentence. In the required review of Addison's death sentence, New Hampshire Supreme Court Justice Robert Lynn raised the question whether the relative societal worth of a murder victim can be a factor in a jury's decision. Essentially, the high court examined the use of testimony of family members as to what an outstanding person Briggs was and then contrasted that to the "low life" status painted by the prosecution of Addison. The issue here is that if these statements were designed to appeal to the emotions of the jurors, the process could potentially prejudice the outcome of the trial and sentence. This tactic was not employed in the trial of two men involved in the 1997 killing of Epsom police officer, Jeremy Charron.

Both Briggs and Charron were white and grew up in the same rural community, Epsom, New Hampshire, and both joined the U.S. Marine Corps following high school. They later joined their hometown police force, a stepping stone for Briggs. Unfortunately, Charron was killed while serving as a rookie police officer. The suspects in Charron's killing had extensive criminal backgrounds and were apprehended later in Littleton, New Hampshire. Of the two suspects, Kevin Paul and Gordon Perry, Perry was tried for capital murder, but in the end Attorney General Philip McLaughlin approved a plea deal resulting in a life-without-parole sentence. Paul was given a minimum sentence of sixteen years for turning states evidence against Perry and is currently released on parole. Both Paul and Perry are white, as was Charron. Was Briggs considered a "more worthy victim" than Charron, or was it that the race of the offender was the critical, emotional deciding factor in the judicial outcomes? By the same token, was self-employed handyman, Jack Reid, considered less worthy of a victim than Briggs? The differences in these murder trials seem to indicate the variance in these judicial proceedings, raising questions on how the *Thin Blue Line Act* will be enacted.[5]

The Briggs case illustrates the *American Law Enforcement Heroes Act of 2017* (House Resolution 1428). This bill incentivizes state and local government to hire American veterans as new law enforcement officers. This bill amends the 1968 Omnibus Crime Control and Safe Streets Act to provide grant funds to hire military veterans as career law enforcement officers. While this has long been a practice throughout the country both at the federal, state, and local levels, this bill would provide monies to states to give veterans a preference in hiring. In this sense, the funding component is similar to the earlier LEAA program. This appears, on the surface, to be a viable approach to both hiring returning veterans as well as providing an available pool of potential law enforcement officers. The downside is the overuse of "heroes," which again implies special status for these members of society vis-à-vis others. Moreover, these potential law enforcement recruits need to be adequately screened for both meeting educational degree requirements and potential impulse control dysregulation secondary to traumatic stress, including traumatic brain injuries.[6]

Another current political controversy is the outlawing of "sanctuary cities"—a situation clearly exacerbated under the Trump administration. The president has threatened to cut federal funds to states that do not comply with federal immigration laws, doing so with his January 25 executive order. The country's top cop, U.S. Attorney General Jeff Sessions, stated that he will order the Justice Department to restrict federal grants to states that refuse to stop suspected undocumented individuals and turn them over to Homeland Security authorities—a decision that is currently being challenged by a number of states. This controversy has caused concern within law enforcement agencies, especially those within sanctuary cities like San Francisco and New York City. This action flies in the face of the "American Law Enforcement Heroes Act of 2017," again causing a rift between law enforcement agencies. Indeed, the Fraternal Order of Police warned President Trump and Attorney General Session that this was a bad idea—one that could jeopardize federal-state-local coordination during times of crises. Texas passed its own ban, ordering all police officers to question a person's immigration status and threatening officers who do not comply with arrest and jail.

Another concern is Attorney General Sessions's reversal of the Obama-era effort to reduce federal prison overcrowding by challenging the overly punitive drug-related convictions, a process that resulted in the disproportionate incarceration of minorities, notably African Americans and Hispanics. On May 12, 2017, the day following his recommendation to the president that FBI Director James Comey be fired, Attorney General Sessions ordered all federal prosecutors to pursue the most serious possible charged in all criminal cases, no matter the circumstances. The outcry against this action may force the Congress to focus more on the social and medical implications of the nation's drug crisis, providing legislation that would emphasize treatment over incarceration.[7] Adding to this confusion is President Trump's firing of FBI Director James Comey on May 11, 2017. On June 7, 2017, President Trump nominated Christopher Wray, a former assistant attorney general in the Department of Justice (2003–2005), to head the FBI. Clearly, the FBI improved its image since the biased era of J. Edgar Hoover and the troubled tenure of William Sessions, emerging as the leading law enforcement agency in the United States. This image of objectivity and neutrality is currently being challenged with Comey's firing for dubious reasons. The only other FBI director to be fired was William S. Sessions, who was removed from his position in 1993 by President Clinton based on ethical violations.[8]

POLICING HATE GROUPS

The Southern Poverty Law Center (SPLC) has documented an increase of not only hate crimes but hate groups in the United States recently. While this increase began, in part, as a reaction to having a black president, the SPLC sees a further spike in hate crimes under the Trump administration. Many groups now feel emboldened by Trump's own negative rhetoric, seeing this as license to increase their own racial animus—a phenomenon termed, *The Trump Effect.*[9] The SPLC lists some nine hundred hate groups currently operating in the United States: Ku Klux Klan (130); Neo-Nazi (99); White Nationalists (100); Racist Skinheads (78); Christian Identity (21); Neo-Confederate (43); Black Separatist (193); Anti-LBGT (52); Anti-Muslim (101); and general hate (100). The general hate category included anti–immigrant groups (14); hate music groups (16), holocaust denial groups (10), and radical traditional Catholics (14), among others. The SPLC reported 623 active antigovernment groups, including militias.[10] These groups again put law enforcement personnel in peril much like the turbulent 1960s and 1970s, a factor that lends itself to better training and national coordination as recommended by the blue ribbon commissions following the civil rights and antiwar turmoil fifty years ago.

Clearly the issue goes beyond keeping police objective during these confrontations, especially when they become the target of the group's actions. The challenge is to weed out those law enforcement personnel who hold strong sentiments for or against the groups they may be confronting. What is especially problematic is the rise of paramilitary militia groups since the Y2K hysteria generated at the beginning of the twenty-first century. Today, many of these groups give the appearance of aiding in policing border security and apprehending illegal migrants. In the Western states, the appeal of these groups seems to be their mandate for greater local control over federal lands. At any rate, antigovernment and racist elements prevail within these organizations, sentiments shared by a sizeable minority of the population. Hence, these militia groups appear to have broader public support than other radical groups, either on the right of left of the political spectrum. Two incidents in the 1990s added fuel to the growth of these movements in the twenty-first century: the federal response to both the Ruby Ridge and Waco incidents. Clearly, the federal and local law enforcement response to these incidents added sympathy to these movements. Ruby Ridge was the standoff in rural Idaho where federal agents surrounded Randy Weaver's compound in August 1992. Sold an illegal cut-off shotgun by an undercover federal agent, which was later seen as entrapment by an agent provocateur, Weaver hid out at his mountain retreat with this family. The pursuit by the FBI and U.S. Marshals Service resulted in the death of a U.S. Marshal, Mrs. Weaver, and the Weavers' fourteen-year-old son. Months later, near Waco, Texas, federal agents (ATF, FBI, Alabama and Texan Army National Guard) laid siege to David Koresh's Branch Davidian compound (Mount Carmel Center) following concerns regarding illegal firearms and possible child abuse of its members. The fifty-one-day standoff (February–April 1993) resulted in the compound being burned to the ground and the loss of seventy-six lives, including four ATF agents.

On the other hand, the federal handling of New Hampshire tax protest movement surrounding the arrest and conviction of Edward and Elaine Brown illustrated how these situations can be defused by patience. The Browns were convicted in federal district court in Concord, New Hampshire, in January 2007 of tax evasion on income of over a million dollars. Sentenced to five years and three months prison terms in April, they instead sheltered themselves in their massive one-hundred-acre fortress in Plainfield, which drew militias from throughout the country to their cause. Heavily armed and fortified, the federal agents waited out the Browns and their supporters, finally infiltrating the group and arresting them in October of 2007. These tactics were again employed during the 2014 seizure and removal of Cliven Bundy's cattle from public lands for his failure to pay grazing fees. Armed militias quickly came to the Bundy's defense, resulting in a standoff with federal law enforcement agents. Again, federal agents avoided an armed confrontation by allowing the groups to release the impounded cattle. Unfortunately, this action emboldened the militias, resulting in the occupation of the Malheur National Wildlife Refuge in Oregon from January 2 to February 11, 2016, by the Citizens for Constitutional Freedom (aka Mormon Mafia) led by Ammon and Ryan Bundy from Nevada. In this instance, Robert "LaVoy" Finicum was killed by Oregon State Police officers. In June 2017, the first armed militiaman was convicted and sentenced to seven years for his role in the Bundy ranch stand-off: Gerald "Jerry" DeLemus, of New Hampshire, a former Marine, delegate to the Republican National Committee and co-chair of Veterans for Trump in New Hampshire, who once ran for county sheriff and mayor of Rochester and whose wife is a former state representative. Also involved in the Bundy ranch standoff and awaiting trial is Debra Carter Pope, a former sheriff's deputy and air force veteran. DeLemus and Carter Pope illustrate the blurred lines between politics and policing.[11]

In concert with many popular extralegal militias are sworn law enforcement officers who share similar views. Indeed, recent quick response laws allow for law enforcement officers to cross state lines when called upon during crisis situations. This action predated the September 11 terrorist attacks, which only served to strengthen these cross-jurisdiction responses. In 1996, President Bill Clinton signed the Emergency Management Assistance Compact (EMAC), an agreement that involves all fifty states. The EMAC allows states to share resources and coordinate emergency personnel during times of crisis, including community disorders, insurgency, or enemy attack. It was invoked during Hurricane Sandy (2012) and Hurricane Matthew (2016). Its unique and questionable use by North Dakota Governor Jack Dalrymple during the Standing Rock pipeline protest brings back memories of the Wounded Knee II protest of the 1970s. The use of the EMAC in order to control social unrest was also used by Maryland Governor Larry Hogan during the Black Lives Matter protests in Baltimore in April 2015 in the wake of the death of Freddie Gray while in police custody. Here, some 300 state troopers from Pennsylvania and another 150 from New Jersey responded to the governor's EMAC request. In the North Dakota EMAC request, police responded from twenty-four counties, sixteen cities, and ten different states, adding fuel to an already military-siege situation involving the deployment of military land-mine-resistant vehicles, armored personnel carriers, and assault weapons. This overreaction to a legitimate American Indian–led protest resulted in the Standing Rock Sioux tribe calling for a Justice Department investigation to civil rights abuses. The Standing Rock situation also drew attention to the use of a militarized law enforcement reaction for the purpose of protecting corporate interests at the expense of a minority group.[12]

What motivated police from hundreds of miles away to join the North Dakota cause? To what extent does racism factor into this equation? There are no clear answers readily available but certainly this would be an ideal post facto research project. Again, available information regarding the growing radicalization of law enforcement stems from the SPLC. The SPLC documents the phenomenon of "constitutional sheriffs" within the United States. The constitutional sheriffs view the county as being the supreme entity in American law enforcement, a view they share with the Posse Comitatus movement. Robert "LaVoy" Finicum was part of a group leaving the Malheur National Wildlife Refuge in order to meet with Glenn Palmer, the sheriff of a nearby county, a self-described "constitutional sheriff" and purported supporter of the Bundy group. Sheriff Palmer is part of the Constitutional Sheriffs and Peace Officers Association (CSPOA), a right-wing law enforcement organization that claims over four hundred high sheriffs in the United States. Indeed, in 2012 Palmer was the first to claim the "CSPOA Sheriff of the Year" award.[13]

The CSPOA emerged as part of the anti-Obama Patriot movement. Its racist base is shored up by its antigovernment stance. The organization gained notoriety with its founder, Arizona sheriff Richard Mack, part of the Mormon Mafia and Gun Owners of America, which are prevalent throughout the rural West. The SPLC noted that in 2013, twenty-eight of the twenty-nine sheriffs who make up the Utah Sheriffs Association wrote President Obama stating that: "no federal officials will be permitted to descend upon our constituents and take from them what the Bill of Rights—in particular Amendment II—has given them."[14] In 2014, the CSPOA published a list of 485 sheriffs who they claim have vowed to uphold and defend the Constitution against Obama's unconstitutional gun measures. The CSPOA also claims to have nearly 1,000 chapters today, which supported the Bundy ranch and Malheur conflicts. The CSPOA's appeal goes beyond the rural range lands of the West to include sympathizers through the country, especially the South. Another group of current and former law enforcement and military personnel is the *Oath Keepers* and their Community Preparedness teams—armed vigilante groups. They also trace their origin to the beginning of the Obama administration and their opposition to a black president. The Oath Keepers were also present at the Bundy Nevada ranch debacle, as well as Ferguson, Missouri—supposedly to protect businesses from the Black Lives Matters protest—and they were at the Oregon Malheur National Wildlife Refuge.[15]

· 15 ·

Recommendations for American Law Enforcement

The issue of policing is not a simple matter where a single solution would solve all the issues confronting America and other societies. All societies have rules and enforcement agents, whether it is a secular or sectarian dictatorship or some form of representative government (parliament, legislature, executive committee). Indeed, law enforcement, by its definition, compels police to enforce the laws and rules promulgated by societal leaders. Unfortunately, given human nature, these rules are often biases that favor the majority or the group in control. Consequently, discrimination needs to be addressed at the leadership level (U.S. Supreme Court, federal and state legislative levels) first before we can adequately train and better regulate enforcement agencies such as the police. These issues are more complex within multiethnic, multisectarian societies, including contemporary, developed societies such as the United States.

Good, viable solutions were offered by the numerous presidential blue ribbon commissions/committees that followed the riots of the 1960s and 1970s. They included such concepts as hiring police officers with a minimum of a four-year liberal arts college degree. Instead, police academies morphed into military-style boot camps (cop shops) providing the mindset of an occupation force ready to face the perceived "enemies" of society. This was the antithesis of the concept of "community policing," whereby law enforcement is an integral component of the community within its jurisdiction (its patch or beat). Ideally, the police would be trained to be available to all members of the community regardless of race, ethnic origin, gender, or religion. And for this to be effective, the police would have to be attired for easy recognition without looking like a military occupational force.

Another recommendation at the time of the Omnibus Crime Control and Safe Streets Act was for civilian oversight in the form of "police commissions." Unfortunately, in many instances these positions became politicized with civilian commissions, like the prosecution, often automatically siding with law enforcement when issues of excessive force or blatant discrimination surfaced. Toward this end, the states and federal government need to provide professionally trained omnibus personnel that are independent of any political or ideological influence. Excessive force issues or pervasive corruption and discriminatory practices need to be reviewed by independent special prosecutors with officials in jurisdictions that target minorities or outsiders (e.g., Georgia speed traps) for financial gain (e.g., Ferguson, Missouri) to see if they have violated federal law under RICO or the Foreign Corrupt Practices Act. These are often premeditated acts and should not be dismissed as some civil infraction resulting in "cease-and-desist orders." If special aggravating circumstances are to apply to offenses against judges, prosecutors, law enforcement, and correctional personnel, then these same standards for aggressive prosecution need to be applied to judicial and police misconduct cases, resulting in independent prosecution and harsh sentences—not the "slap-on-the-wrist" sanctions currently in place. Using the Attorney General Ayotte case, uniformed police should be barred from petit jury trial audiences, especially if the case involves a law enforcement victim. Law enforcement's presence at jury trials, other than as witnesses, should be proportionate to their actual representation in the community at large, and then they should be compelled to wear civilian clothing like other members of society. Otherwise, this blatant abuse of intimidation should automatically signal a procedural cause for a mistrial, especially in capital cases like that of Michael Addison.

As stated earlier, law enforcement personnel, especially chiefs, sheriffs, and the like, need to lose the military attire that attempts to present the personnel as admirals and generals. Law enforcement personnel also need to align with their community and not with the *Blue Brotherhood* (aka *Bubbahood*). Clearly, this is a profession where unions should be exempt, if only because they instill a sense of "us versus them" within society, yet another factor is the polarization of police and segments of the public. Since the genesis of American law enforcement has its roots in the British system, we could follow their model. First and foremost, law enforcement needs to be identified by their attire, one that is markedly different from that that identifies the military. This is important so that communities do not feel that they are under siege or military occupation.

Unfortunately, with the advent of military equipment so readily available to police at all level of jurisdiction, a recent trend has been for law enforcement to wear "SWAT black" uniforms instead of the historically recognized blue. In order to end this trend and the confusion it causes, especially during this time of mutual aid and coordination across jurisdictions, a uniform code for police attire and shields needs to be adopted. For U.S. Marshals and county sheriffs, brown or tan uniforms along with a star signifying their status (U.S. Marshal, marshal deputy, high sheriff, sheriff deputy, and so on) should be worn. At the state level, the attorney general—the top law enforcement officer—should be the only "general" with that structure. The state police force could use gray or green uniforms and have their status indicated on their badge. Military-type rank could also adorn their uniform, with the head of the state police holding the rank of colonel. A similar standard should be used for municipal law enforcement agencies, including the largest—New York City, Los Angeles, and Chicago. They follow the British model to some extent in that there are patrol personnel (constables in England), followed by sergeant (same in England), lieutenant (inspector in England), captain (chief inspector in England), major (superintendent in England), and lieutenant colonel (chief superintendent), with the colonel (chief constable in England) at the head of the unit. Large municipal forces follow this model up to the rank of captain. From there, they usually jump to general rank, with a single star for commanders, two stars for assistant chiefs, and three stars for the deputy chief, with the chief of police holding the rank of a four-star general. Unfortunately, many local jurisdictions, including sheriffs, now wear general insignia on their uniforms, many adorning four and even five stars. Even small-town chiefs, those in command of only a few full-time officers, have the audacity to wear general stars on their uniform. This is wrong for a number of reasons. First and foremost is that it gives the impression of a military presence in the community. Secondly, it most likely violates the provisions of the "stolen valor" act. Lastly, black uniforms need to be restricted to special SWAT teams, and only worn when they are actively engaged in a crisis situation. Whenever interviewing "chiefs," or other law enforcement officers who present as having held high-ranks, for potential positions, educational credentials need to be reality tested, especially if they claim a graduate degree. Was it from a legitimate program or from a "cop shop" like the programs perpetrated under the Quinn Act in Massachusetts? Any claim to a graduate degree as justification for an enhanced salary should require looking at both the transcript and the Graduate Record Exam (GRE) score or its equivalent. Any GRE score on verbal reasoning and quantitative reasoning needs to be within at least one standard deviation from the norm (mean score). If there are questions, then have the candidates retake the GRE prior to their hire. On this note, there should be a standardized national exam that is taken by all law enforcement candidates, much like there is for entry into law school, medical school, or graduate psychology. Correspondingly, there should be pertinent ethical standards that are also tested, with acceptable scores being clustered around the national mean.

Military-type equipment needs to be restricted to those few engagements that warrant their use and not used as a form of intimidation like at the Native

American protest over the Keystone pipeline. Instead of giving more lethal weapons to law enforcement, the federal government should provide nonlethal equipment, along with training for these devices. Instead of every patrol car having a riot-shotgun and M-16s or M4s, they need beanbag and rubber bullet rounds. Pistols should have a sear check that automatically pauses the firing sequence after the first three rounds so that the officer can reassess his or her situation before emptying the thirteen- to fifteen-round magazine during an adrenaline high. Officers need to quickly designate an initial shooter when more than one of them is at a scene with a potentially armed offender. They need to be trained to only fire when there is an active shooter, using other nonlethal methods for situations where the person may be armed, or thought to be armed, but has not yet engaged in a firefight. Virtual reality scenarios can be used to test the likely reaction of officers to potential crisis situations. Their response can be recorded. Officers who cannot disengage from an autonomic adrenaline response need further training and/or psychological assessment. Moreover, body cams need to be used by all law enforcement at all times. Failure to do so should trigger a serious investigation with charges pending. If a pattern of such abuse is evident, then a special prosecutor needs to assess the department's policies and potential coverups of abuses.

Another critical factor is the screening process. Psychological scales can determine, to a fair accuracy, not only mental suitability (*mad cop*) but also problematic characterlogic flaws, including serious personality disorders (*bad cop*). The machismo/macho image also needs to be addressed, especially if steroids are involved. At minimum, psychological reassessments need to be administered if a clique of officers falls into this group. This can be seen as a form of intimidation (bullying) among members of society, notably minority members of the community. As previously stated, training needs to focus on the use of nonlethal approaches to crisis situations where the subject does not have a viable weapon (firearm, machete, or the like). Psychological protocols can train officers to control their level of adrenal response to crisis situations, such as those situations where officers empty their clip of fifteen to seventeen rounds in their response to a perceived threat, including reactions to the provocations by unstable individuals seeking death through a phenomenon known as "suicide by cop." These options have been available for over forty years, yet seldom employed. Law enforcement is an integral part of any viable society. How it is used is often a political factor, and as long as divisions are allowed and fostered within a society, police abuses will continue.

Prejudice is often associated with a rigid personality type. If someone appears to show indications of prejudices against a perceived out-group based on gender, race, ethnicity, religion, or age, then additional psychological assessments need to be administered. Personal crisis can also trigger bias outbursts or behaviors. Psychological reassessments are warranted during any severe adjust-ment period, during or following a significant change in the law enforcement officer's life circumstances, such as divorce or separation, death of someone close to them, or other unanticipated major changes in their life. I added the Authoritarian Personality (*F*) scale, forms 45 and 40 in my assessment of police candidates who came from seemingly rigid family and/or social orientations.[1]

Studies also show that by increasing the number of minorities within the criminal justice system does not, in itself, necessarily reduce the incidence of abuse. There is a strong incidence of intragroup prejudices, whereby minority officials, judges, prosecutors, and police treat defendants of color as harshly or even more harshly than white offenders. This may be in order to gain more respect from their white counterparts within the criminal justice system or be-cause they place excessive blame on minority offenders for fueling the negative stereotypes associated with minorities in general. A recent (2017) book on this phenomenon was written by James Forman Jr., entitled: *Locking Up Our Own: Crime and Punishment in Black America.*[2] The abused within Indian Country are also well documented, extending back over a century. Time and again, Indian police were selected to assassinate problematic Indians, often ordered to do so by their white supervisors. A more recent example was the police abuses at the Pine Ridge Sioux Reservation by tribal leaders against traditional Indians and AIM followers at Wounded Knee II. While there are few studies that quantify the level of intraracial or interracial abuses by law enforcement, a recent study used the Police and Law Enforcement (PLE) Scale in order to assess black men's police-based discrimination. Here, the authors found the PLE is a reliable and valid measure of black men's experiences of discrimina-tion with law enforcement. This could be a model for other studies involving police abuses within minority communities.[3] Law enforcement agencies have a powerful mandate—one that allows them to use deadly force on members of society. The police's ability to radically change one's life circumstances (arrest, conviction, incarceration, even death) gives them license only equaled by the medical professions. The major difference is that the latter (American Medical Association, American Psychiatric Association, American Psychological Asso-ciation) have promulgated strict "Principles of Ethical Standards" in an attempt to regulate practitioner's behaviors. The law enforcement profession needs similar standards, as well as impartial boards to implement these standards.

Postscript

An Ethno-Methodological Note

An interesting question for scholars is: "what motivated you to study this field of inquiry?" Max Weber noted two major influences in our lives: our family socialization and our life experiences as an adult. For some, their lives are planned out by their parents, so there is continuity between their family values and those acquired once they leave the family circle. Many academicians come from families that supported their educational pursuits, allowing them to go straight from prep-school to college, earning their undergraduate degree and graduate degrees while still in their twenties, and then to continue on with careers at a college or university. Others came into academia not by some predetermined parental plan but from a more indirect route, often by accident—serendipity.

A disadvantage of this route is being ill-prepared relevant to college preparation, while the advantage is seeing things in the raw, without the values and norms held by many from the privileged elite. Raised an ethnic Catholic (French Canadian) in a northern New England parish in the 1940s and 1950s, my early socialization was quite parochial. It was only when I joined the U.S. Marine Corps in 1959 at age seventeen that I began to experience different cultures and the marked divide in America relevant to class, caste race, gender, regionalism, and sectarianism. Parris Island was my prep school, as was the shock of living in the segregated Jim Crow South during the time of the civil rights protests. In retrospect, I was fortunate to be assigned to a 105-howitzer gun crew with African American noncommissioned officers. They showed me how the blacks had to live in North Carolina at this time, taking me to their homes and communities. Indeed, the marine corps was a safer and more equitable world for them than the rest of the South during the Jim Crow era.

Tours with the Sixth Fleet during the Algerian and Congo crises, and later in 1961 in Cuba during Detachment Alpha, exposed me to other cultures and conflicts at this time. This was followed by a tour with the Third Marine Division on occupied Okinawa, with deployments to the Philippines, Taiwan, Japan, and, later, Hawaii while in the reserves. It was while in Hawaii that I was processed for college under the disabled component of the GI Bill, which coincided with my honorable discharge in February 1965. Since it was mid-term for the academic year, the Veterans Administration (VA) sent me to the Church College of Hawaii (now Brigham Young University–Hawaii campus). This was fortuitous for me in that I really needed the one-on-one supervision and orientation provided by the Church College faculty given that I was not part of the college-prep curriculum while in high school. A requirement for non-Mormons was taking a course on the Mormon religion—a course that did not transfer to either the University of Hawaii or the University of New Hampshire. Nonetheless, it was intriguing for me to learn another sectarian worldview, even if it was one that blatantly discriminated against blacks and American Indians (I received an *A* in the course). Later experiences in Indian Country led me to rephrase the term LDS (Latter Day Saints) to LDP (Latter Day Puritans) due to the intensity of their efforts at cultural genocide among American Indian groups, one that matched the intensity of colonial New England. The VA then transferred me to the University of Hawaii for the following academic year. This experience exposed me to the East-West Center at the University of Hawaii, as well as with the Fijians, Samoans, and Tongans at the Polynesian Cultural Center at the Church College.

I took this cultural orientation back home with me when I transferred to the University of New Hampshire in 1966. Although a predominately white university, I was fortunate to be mentored by Stuart Hunter Palmer, a noted criminologist and social psychologist with his doctorate from Yale, who exposed me to the Human Relations Area File. Palmer was widely recognized for his cross-cultural studies, especially on the psychology of aggression. John (Jack) A. Humphrey and I became graduate assistants for Palmer, who introduced us to some of the leading criminologists at the time, including Gresham Sykes and Thorsten Sellin. Dr. Palmer was a member of the NH Governor's Crime Commission that distributed LEAA funds to local law enforcement agencies. He had both Jack and I assisting in the evaluations of these projects. Jack and I both got teaching positions as criminologists within the University of North Carolina system beginning in 1972—Jack at UNC–Greensboro and me at Western Carolina University (WCU). WCU was only twenty-six miles from the Eastern Band of Cherokee Indian, Qualla Boundary reservation, offering me opportunities for mentoring, research, and community service with the Cherokees. Soon after my arrival, Cherokee students encouraged me to represent them as the faculty advisor to the WCU Cherokee Native American Student Organization. During this time, an influx of Vietnam veterans was enrolled at WCU, and given my USMC experience, they requested that I be the faculty advisor to the Veteran's Organization. I later became the co-faculty advisor for the WCU Organization of Ebony Students and served as a mental health consultant to both the Cherokee Mental Health and Alcohol Program and the North Carolina Department of Mental Health.

My research grew from these experiences, including attending the 1974 East Coast Conference of Socialist Sociologists. It was here that I met Richard Quinney. Four of us drove from North Carolina to New Jersey during the gas crisis to attend the conference. I was later notified by the WCU provost that this activity was frowned upon and that it would be a mark against future tenure considerations. Adding to this situation was my participation in the 1975 Second Annual Conference on Blacks and the Criminal Justice System held at the University of Alabama. Governor George Wallace, confined to a wheelchair, personally welcomed us to the conference. I was fortunate to have Jack introduce me to Dr. Joseph Sandy Himes, the noted black (blind) sociologist at the University of North Carolina–Greensboro, who soon became my mentor relevant to social injustices afflicting both African Americans and American Indians at this time (1972–1977). Dr. Himes was instrumental in getting me the position of organizer and presider for the "American Indian Session" at the 71st American Sociological Association (ASA) conference held in New York City in 1976. Jack also introduced me to Dr. Harriet J. Kupferer, also on the UNC–Greensboro faculty, who had conducted research with Indians of the southeast. She also got Jack and me involved with the Southern Anthropological Society, which became a welcomed venue for our research, presentations, and publications.

In addition to presenting at the American Sociological Association (ASA) conferences (1974, 1975, 1976, 1977) and the Southern Anthropological Society (SAS) meetings, I made my initial presentation with the Academy of Criminal Justice Sciences (ACJS) in 1978 and joined the American Society of Criminology (ASC) in 1975, becoming a life member in 1976. During my time at WCU, I became involved in a tribal police issue involving the deaths of returning Cherokee Vietnam veterans who were arrested on the reservation for public drunkenness but incarcerated in the white county jail. Our Cherokee student organization sought and received the assistance of the leaders of the American Indian Historical Society, Rupert Costo and Jeannette Henry-Costo, who got the U.S. Civil Right Commission to investigate these three deaths. This inquiry resulted in the tribal police being cross-deputized with the U.S. Marshals, ending the need to transport Indian offenders off the reservation into often hostile white jurisdictions. Also, at this time I became involved in the plight of black female inmates incarcerated in North Carolina, including the Joann Little case. This involvement, coupled with the dismantling of the sociology and anthropology department at WCU in favor of the Reagan-style "cop shop" format, resulted in the termination of my employment within the University of North Carolina system.

Nonetheless, Dr. Himes was influential in getting me connected with an emerging group of minority scholars, the National Association of Interdisciplinary Ethnic Studies (NAIES) for Native American, Black, Chicano, Puerto Rican, and Asian groups, where I was fortunate to interact with Dennis Banks, Vine Deloria Jr, his aunt, Bea Medicine, and Angela Davis, among others, in an attempt to provide a voice, often absent, within the mainstream academic disciplines like sociology, psychology, anthropology, history, criminology, and criminal justice. Dr. Himes also introduced me to the emerging Southern Poverty Law Center, which became a major vehicle for litigating minority social injustices, especially in the South. I took these influences with me to my new appointment as an assistant professor of criminal justice at the University of Nebraska–Omaha (UNO), on the Lincoln campus (1977–1980).

In 1978, I shared an office with Chris Eskridge, who had just finished his PhD at Ohio State University. Also on the Lincoln campus was Julie Horney. The chair of the department, Vincent (Vince) Webb, and his close associate, Samuel (Sam) Walker, resided on the Omaha campus. This was the time of Wounded Knee II and the most intense white–Indian relations in Nebraska and the Dakotas since the end of the Indian Wars in the 1890s. My involvement with NAIES and the American Indian Historical Society resulted in my continued work within Indian Country, this time with the Sioux nations battling social injustices and police brutality (e.g., Wilson's GOONS, local white sheriffs). My work with the Nebraska Indian Commission also introduced me to the Native American Rights Fund (NARF) and the suit against the Nebraska penal system relevant to adequate access to cultural and religious resources for incarcerated Indian inmates. Here the consent decree allowed the Indian inmates to practice their traditional ways, including dress and hair style as well as having sweat lodges constructed on the prison grounds and having medicine men attend to their spiritual needs. The University of Nebraska–Lincoln (UNL) campus had a small core of activists interested in these issues, including several American Indian faculty, notably, Webster Robbins and Teresa LaFromboise, both in the educational psychology department. A number of white faculty members were also involved in the development of a new Lincoln Indian Center, most notably Elizabeth S. Grobsmith in the anthropology department. At this time, the Omaha campus hired a black attorney, Carolyn Watkins Marsh, and an American Indian professor, John Cross (Western Seminole tribe). These intense times coincided with the 1978 U.S.

Department of Justice's LEAA efforts to develop a minority curriculum within criminal justice programs, known as the SUNY Project. I became a member of the project, representing American Indians independent of Vince Webb's involvement as a "core major faculty." The Hoover/Anslinger/Wolfgang racist "cop shop" perspective became readily evident as the meetings proceeded at the State University of New York at Albany, resulting in a backlash among the minority faculty. Clearly, Vince Webb was part of the Wolfgang camp where elitist whites condescended to the Black, Hispanic, and Asian faculty. This rebellion resulted in a major challenge to the long-standing criminal justice perspective on minority justice.

Nonetheless, the Hoover/Anslinger/Wolfgang racist perspective continued to dominate both the ACJS and ASC for years to come. Carolyn Marsh, John Cross, and I challenged Webb's "good-ole boy" white autocratic dominance in the UNO Department of Criminal Justice program, filing a complaint with the Office of Civil Rights (OCR), Department of Education, in 1980 resulting in a sixteen-point corrective action "voluntary compliant agreement" consent decree. And although item four of the agreement stated that "The Recipient agrees that there shall be no discriminations or retaliation against any person affected by or involved in filing the complaint," Professors Marsh, Cross, and I were nonetheless terminated, and Dr. Webb continued to run the criminal justice program at UNO, including its Lincoln campus where Dr. Eskridge and Horney were located.

Seeking support from other faculty, notably Christ Eskridge, Julie Horney, and Samuel Walker, none was forthcoming. In retrospect, this became an excellent career move for all three. Chris Eskridge continued his move within the American Society of Criminology by ingratiating himself with Sarah Hall, the ASC executive administrator, becoming indispensable and later moving up to the ASC director position where he was able to impose some of his Mormon values on the organization, such as replacing "wine socials" with "ice-cream socials." And by avoiding getting involved in the American Indian Movement controversy playing out in his academic patch, Chris was able to use his ex-official ASC position to promote the Wolfgang/Webb perspective internationally. Indeed, Eskridge proudly proclaims himself, "the jet-setting UNL professor promoting criminology internationally." Julie Horney, brought up among the white elite during North Carolina's Jim Crow era, divorced and married Vince Webb, and later became dean of the same SUNY-A program that sponsored the failed LEAA minority justice program. She also became fellow and president of the ASC. Dr. Horney died unexpectedly while vacationing in Mexico in October 2016. Sam Walker's academic career also blossomed with his close association with Vince Webb, gaining recognition for his expertise in policing. Ironically, among his awards is the "W. E. B.

Du Bois Award for contributions to the field of Criminal Justice on race and ethnicity" from the Western Society of Criminology in 2011. However, the person who benefitted the most from his strong adherence to the Hoover/Anslinger/Wolfgang perspective was Vincent J. Webb, who, despite the consent decree reflective of the racial biases in the program he directed, received the "UNO Chancellor's Medal for Outstanding Service" in 1993. He remained chairman of the UNO criminal justice program until 1996 and went on to head other criminal justice programs: Department of Administration of Justice, Arizona State University–West (1996–2003), and most recently, dean of the College of Criminal Justice at Sam Houston State University in Texas. He also served a term as president of the Academy of Criminal Justice Sciences. Marsh, French, and Cross were effectively black listed within criminal justice. Carolyn Marsh went back to her legal practice working with federal prisoners in California, while John Cross joined the sociology faculty at Oklahoma State University where he served as editor of *Free Inquiry in Creative Sociology*. I retrained in the clinical field, earning a doctorate from UNL in educational psychology and measurement majoring in cultural psychology.

The battle for getting minority and gender recognition within the ASC and ACJS was a long and difficult process, one that Sloan Letman and I pursued despite our status as "outsiders." Sloan Letman came from a noted family of black ministers. When we met in the 1970s, he was the dean and member of the faculty at Loyola University of Chicago. He later went on to teach at the University of Illinois, Chicago–Circle. Sloan and I represented a small core of faculty interested in better promoting the minority perspective within the criminal justice system at both the academic and practitioner levels. Another organization that promoted this cause was the Society of Police and Criminal Psychology and book publisher Michael (Mickey) C. Braswell, who published our 1981 manuscript, *Contemporary Issues in Corrections*. Sloan T. Letman III died in 2015.

My retraining in psychology took me back to New Hampshire where I worked for nine years (1980–1989) as a staff psychologist for the state of New Hampshire, including that as a forensic psychologist. Part of these duties was training law enforcement in how to handle the growing population of de-institutionalized mental patients, including those with a potential for violent impulse behaviors. My duties also involved forensic assessments, conducted with Dr. Paul Emery, a forensic psychiatrist. We tested clients relevant to their competency to stand trial and/or to their degree of dangerousness, including dangerous sexual offenders. We had the advantage of current research and protocols being developed at Dartmouth Medical School in conjunction with other prominent universities in the region, including the work on paraphilics being done at Johns Hopkins University.

I went back to academia in the fall of 1989 with a psychology teaching and research position at Western New Mexico University (WNMU), where I also served as the police psychologist for the police academy. The challenge here was fitting the MMPI to the three major sectarian or cultural groups represented in the state and region—Protestant/Mormon Anglos, Catholic Hispanics of Mexican heritage, and American Indians (e.g., Pueblos, Navajos, and Apache). Sorting the aggregate MMPI profiles by ethnicity and gender, I was able to develop an adaptive cultural profile with strong predictive features (the results were published in a number of journals). Awareness of unique cultural and/or sectarian variances was also a helpful teaching and clinical tool in that I also had a clinical practice in Arizona in a region that also included the San Carlos Indian Reservation. My clinical practice with the Arizona Department of Economic Security often lead to sectarian challenges from LDS leaders and officials, including testing clients in Sheriff Richard Mack's jail. Many officials I encountered were adamant that Mormon men did not harbor aberrant sexual thoughts let alone behaviors. And despite a seemingly high percentage of bulimic girls and teens, church officials and family members often claimed that the problem within LDS families was colitis and not a clinical syndrome like bulimia or anorexia. These cultural barriers forced me to conduct thorough neurological, forensic, and clinical assessments that could easily be verified and replicated by other competent clinicians. Cultural testing was also needed to discern when test results indicated low intelligence when, in fact, this may have been a language barrier relevant to the test norms. This was the case especially with Hispanic and American Indian clients where English was not their primary language.

I continued to be involved in criminal and social justice issues during my tenure at WNMU, including being the program committee chair for Native American sessions and local arrangements chair at the 1998 Academy of Criminal Justice Sciences annual meeting held in Albuquerque, New Mexico, during Dr. "Gerry" Vito's term as ACJS president. We had sixteen American Indian sessions, a first within the ACJS or ASC conferences to date. This success was due to Dr. Vito's efforts to bring minority issues into the criminal justice academic arena. Also, during this time, Professors Frank (Trey) P. Williams and Marilyn McShane were developing a unique juvenile justice doctoral program at Prairie View A&M University in Texas, one with a viable minority perspective producing quality minority graduates. This change came about due to a legal challenge with Texas A&M University located a mere forty miles away, which long established itself as the "flag ship" institution for the entire Texas A&M system when, in fact, both facilities at College Station and Prairie View were created on the same date in 1876 as land-grant institutions, one for whites and the other for "freedmen." The resulting "consent decree" established Prairie View as the "co-flag ship" institution with resources now allocated for the development of viable doctorate programs. Dr. Williams and McShane were instrumental in developing the doctoral program in juvenile justice.

Another change within academic justice programs was the fall of the Soviet Union in 1989 with newly liberated countries vying for Western attention. Patrick Lynch at John Jay College in NYC quickly filled this void with his biennial international conferences. My WNMU colleague, Magdaleno Manzanarez, and I were fortunate to attend the fourth (Budapest, Hungry, 1998), fifth (Bologna, Italy, 2000), and sixth (London, England, 2002) of these conferences. At the same time, the International Police Executive Symposium (IPES) was convening international conferences. I participated in the ones in Szcytno, Poland (2001); Prague, Czech Republic (2005); Ohrid, Macedonia (2009); and Sofia, Bulgaria (2014). There was also the first Key Issues Conference, Societies of Criminology held in Paris, France, in 2004. A common theme at these international conferences is the challenges surrounding policing, including adequate community policing and the fair treatment of minority members of society. These challenges continue today, not only in former communist countries (Society Union, Yugoslavia) and emerging democracies, but in the United States; thus, the need for works like this one that address these issues from more than the "cop shop" academic perspective.

Laurence Armand French, PhD
Professor Emeritus of Psychology, Western New Mexico University
Affiliate Professor, Justice Studies, University of New Hampshire

Notes

CHAPTER 1

1. Max Weber, *The Protestant Ethic and the Spirit of Capitalism*, trans. T. Parsons (London: Allen & Unwin, 1930).

2. A. Stephanson, *Manifest Destiny* (New York: Hill and Wang, 1995).

3. A. Smith, *An Inquiry into the Nature and Causes of Wealth of Nations*, 2 vols. (London: Strahan Cadell, 1776).

4. M. Weber, *The Protestant Ethic*, 52.

5. K. T. Ericson, *Wayward Puritans: A Study in the Sociology of Deviance* (New York: John Wiley & Sons, 1966), 36.

6. Ibid.

7. K. C. Davis, "God and Country," *Smithsonian* (October 2010): 86–96.

8. Ibid., 91.

9. L. A. French, *Psychocultural Change and the American Indian: An Ethnohistorical Analysis* (New York: Garland Publishing, Inc., 1987).

10. J. Conway, "Perspectives on the History of Women's Education in the United States," *History of Education Quarterly* 14 (Spring 1974): 1–12.

11. J. Best and R. Sidwell, *The American Legacy of Learning* (Philadelphia: J. B. Lippincott, 1967).

12. G. Nash, *Red, White, and Black* (Englewood Cliffs, NJ: Prentice-Hall, 1974); T. Perdue, *Slavery and the Evolution of Cherokee Society, 1840–1866* (Knoxville, TN: University of Tennessee Press, 1979).

13. H. Bullock, *A History of Negro Education in the South* (Cambridge, MA: Harvard University Press, 1967); M. Carnoy, *Education as Cultural Imperialism* (New York: David McKay, 1974); D. Ravitch, "On the History of Minority Group Education in the US," *Teachers College Record* 1 (December 1976): 213–28; C. Woodson. *The Education of the Negro prior to 1881* (New York: Putnam's, 1915).

14. M. Beschloss, *The Presidents: Every Leader from Washington to Bush* (New York: American Heritage/Simon & Schuster, Inc., 2003).

15. L. A. French, "Militarization of the Police." In *Police Use of Force*, ed. M. J. Palmiotto (Boca Raton, FL: CRC Press, 2017), 65–80.

16. G. A. Rawlyk, *Yankees at Louisburg: The Story of the First Siege, 1745* (Montreal: Breton Books, 1999), 47.

17. Colin G. Calloway, *North Country Captives* (Hanover, NH: University Press of New England, 1992), viii.

18. J. M. Faragher, *A Great and Noble Scheme: The Tragic Story of the Expulsion of the French Acadians from Their American Homeland* (New York: W. W. Norton, 2005), x.

19. V. Pareto, "The Circulation of Elites." In *Theories of Society: Foundations of Modern Sociological Theory*, eds. T. Parsons et al. (New York: The Free Press, 1961) 551–58.

20. E. Speare, "New Hampshire Loyalists," *Stories of New Hampshire: Living History of the Granite State* (Chelsea, MI: Sheridan Books, 2000), 106–8.

21. C. Moore, *The Loyalists: Revolution, Exile, Settlement* (Toronto: McCelland & Stewart, 1994); G. G. Campbell, *A History of Nova Scotia* (Toronto: The Ryerson Press, 1948).

22. C. G. Calloway, *The American Revolution in Indian Country: Crisis and Diversity in Native American Communities* (New York: Cambridge University Press, 1995), xv.

CHAPTER 2

1. *The Constitution of the United States of America.* (Washington, DC: Library of Congress, 2015), 1.

2. J. Isbister, *The Immigration Debate: Remaking America* (West Hartford, CT: Kumarian Press, 1996).

3. M. Beschloss, *The Presidents: Every Leader from Washington to Bush* (New York: American Heritage/Simon & Schuster, Inc., 2003); J. Durant and A. Durant, *Pictorial History of American Presidents* (New York: A. S. Barnes & Company, 1955).

4. *1917 Immigration Ace: An Act to Regulate the Immigration of Aliens to, and the Residence of Aliens in, the United States*, H.R. 10384; Pub.L. 301; Stat. 874 (64th Congress, February 5, 1917).

5. N. Abrams and S. S. Beale, "Federal, State and Local Criminal Enforcement Resources," in *Federal Criminal Law and Its Enforcement*, 2nd edition (St. Paul, MN: West Publishing, Company, 1993), 5–15.

6. W. G. Bell, *Commanding Generals and Chiefs of Staff, 1775–2005: Portraits and Biographical Sketches* (Washington, DC: United States Army Center of Military History, 2005).

7. *U.S. Constitution*, Article II.

8. J. K. Mahon, *History of the Militia and the National Guard* (College Park, MD: The Potowmack Institute, 1983); B. M. Stentiford, "The Meaning of a Name: The Rise of the National Guard and the End of the Town Militia," *Journal of Military History* 72 (2008): 724–54.

9. *U.S. Constitution*, Article I; Section 9, paragraph 2.

10. H. A. Gailey, *Historical Encyclopedia of the United States Marine Corps* (Lanham, MD: The Scarecrow Press, 1998).

11. "The Problem of Equal Protection," in *American Constitutional Interpretation*, eds. W. F. Murphy, J. E. Fleming, and S. A. Barber (Westbury, NY: The Foundation Press, 1995), 235–46.

12. L. A. French, "Jim Crow America," in *Running the Border Gauntlet* (Santa Barbara, CA: Praeger, 2010), 15–19.

13. A. Schiffrin, *Dr. Seuss & Co. Go to War* (New York: The New Press, 2009), 16.

14. *Posse Comitatus Act* (Knott Amendment). 20 Stat. 152, 18 USC.; 1385 (June 18, 1878); L. W. Yackle, "Historical Introduction," in *Federal Courts: Habeas Corpus* (New York: Foundation Press, 2003), 1–58.

15. P. S. Foner, *History of the Labor Movement in the United States: From Colonial Times to the Founding of the American Federation of Labor* (New York: International Publisher, 1947); J. D. Horan, *The Pinkertons: The Detective Dynasty That Made History* (New York: Crown Publishers, Inc., 1967); B. Burrough, *Public Enemies: America's Greatest Crime Wave and the Birth of the FBI, 1933–34* (New York: Penguin Books, 2004).

CHAPTER 3

1. R. M. Brown, "Historical Patterns of Violence in America," in *Violence in America: Historical and Comparative Perspectives*, eds., H. D. Graham and T. R. Gurr, Special Report Submitted to the National Commission on the Causes and Prevention of Violence (New York: Bantam Books, 1969), 62–64.

2. M. Beschloss, *The Presidents*.

3. B. W. Sheehan, *Seeds of Extinction: Jeffersonian Philanthropy and the American Indian* (New York: W. W. Norton, 1974), 54.

4. Ibid., 4–5.

5. W. Nugent, *Habit of Empire: A History of American Expansion* (New York: Alfred A. Knopf, 2008).

6. *Johnson and Granham's Lessee v. William McIntosh*, 21 U.S., 543, 5 L.Ed. 681 (1823).

7. *Cherokee Nation v. Georgia*, 30 U.S. 1, 5Pet. 1, 81 L.Ed. 25 (1831).

8. W. C. Canby Jr., *The Cherokee Cases and Indian Removal: 1820–1850, American Indian Law in a Nutshell*, 2nd ed. (St. Paul, MN: West Publishing, 1988), 16–17.

9. M. Feldberg, *The Turbulent Era: Riot and Disorder in Jacksonian America* (New York: Oxford University Press, 1980), 3.

10. G. Jahoda, *The Trail of Tears: The Story of the American Indian Removals 1813–1855* (New York: Wings Books, 1975), 36.

11. H. D. Graham and T. R. Gurr, *Violence in America: Historical and Comparatives* (*Eisenhower Report*) (New York: Bantam Books, 1969), 64–66.

CHAPTER 4

1. R. M. Brown, "Historical Patterns of Violence in America," in *Violence in America: Historical and Comparative Perspectives*., eds. H. D. Graham and T. R. Gurr,

154–58; *Special Report Submitted to the National Commission on the Causes and Prevention of Violence*. New York: Bantam Books, 1969: 62–64.

2. R. M. Brown, "Historical Patterns of Violence in America," *Police Violence*, 60–62; neovigilantism, 69; The Problem of Frontier Law Enforcement and Justice, 178–83.

3. Plessy v. Ferguson, 163 U.S. 537: 283–88 (1896).

4. Brown, "Lynch Mob Violence," 50–51.

5. R. Ginzburg, *100 Years of Lynching: The Shocking Record Behind Today's Black Militancy* (New York: A Lancer Book, 1962), 64–65.

6. H. E. Barnes and N. K. Teeters, *New Horizons in Criminology*, 3rd edition (Englewood Cliffs, NJ: Prentice-Hall, 1959), 378–81.

7. J. F. Steiner and R. M. Brown, *The North Carolina Chain Gang: A Study of County Convict Road Work* (Chapel Hill, NC: University of North Carolina Press, 1927; London: Oxford University Press, 1927), 55–56.

8. Ibid., 81–101.

9. T. Horwitz, "November 29, 1864/Sand Creek, Colorado: Hundreds of Women and Children Were Coming Toward Us, and Getting on Their Knees for Mercy," *Smithsonian* 45, no. 8 (2014): 50–57.

10. P. Cozzens, "Grant's Uncivil War: The President Promised Peace with Indians—and Covertly Hatched the Plot That Provoked One of the Bloodiest Conflicts on the Plains," *Smithsonian* 47, no. 7 (November 2016): 48–59.

11. R. W. Stewart, ed., "Winning the West: The Army in the Indian Wars, 1865–1890," in *The United States Army and the Forging of a Nation, 1775–1917*, Vol. 1 (Army Historical Series) (Washington, DC: U.S. Government Printing Office, 2001).

12. D. Brown, *The Galvanized Yankees* (Lincoln, NE: University of Nebraska Press, 1963/1985).

13. L. A. French, *Jurisprudence and Cultural Genocide: Outlawing Traditionalism, Legislating Indian Country: Significant Milestones in Transforming Tribalism* (New York: Peter Lang, 2007), 65–69.

14. L. Standing Bear, *My People the Sioux* (Lincoln, NE: University of Nebraska Press, 1975); *Standing Bear v. Crook* (Indians are people declaration), 25 Federal Cases, 695, 697, 700–701 (May 12, 1879).

15. W. C. Canby Jr. "Movement to the Reservations: 1860 to 1887," 17–19. *American Indian Law in a Nutshell* (2nd ed.) (St. Paul, MN: West Publishing, 1988).

16. W. T. Hagan, *Indian Police and Judges: Experiments in Acculturation and Control* (New Haven, CT: Yale University Press, 1966).

17. W. Clum, *Apache Agent* (New York: Houghton Mifflin, 1936); A. H. Kneale, *Indian Agent* (Caldwell, ID: Caxton Printers, 1950).

18. W. T. Hagan, *Indian Police and Judges*.

19. Hagan, ibid.; F. H. Harrison, *Hanging Judge* (Caldwell, ID: Caxton Printers, 1951).

20. Harrison, ibid.; H. Croy, *He Hanged Them High* (New York: Duell, Sloan, and Pearce, 1952).

21. G. Shirley, *Law West of Fort Smith* (New York: Collier Books, 1961), 139.

22. L. D. Ball, *The United States Marshalls of New Mexico and Arizona Territories, 1846–1912* (Albuquerque, NM: University of New Mexico Press, 1978).

23. S. J. Brakel, *American Indian Tribal Courts: The Cost of Separate Justice* (Chicago: American Bar Foundation, 1978).

24. S. L. Harring, *Crow Dog's Case: American Indian Sovereignty, Tribal Laws, and United States Law in the 19th Century* (New York: Cambridge University Press, 1994); W. C. Canby Jr., *The Cherokee Cases and Indian Removal*, 17–19.

25. Ex parte Crow Dog, 109 U.S. Reports, 557, 571–72 (1883); Major Crimes Act. U.S. Statutes at Large, 23: 385(18 USC, 1153) (1885); and *United States v. Kagama*, 118 U.S. 375, 382–85 (1886).

26. L. A. French, *Jurisprudence and Cultural Genocide*, 65–69.

27. Ibid.

28. R. M. Utley and W. E. Washburn, *Indian Wars* (Boston: Houghton Mifflin Company, 1977), 290–91.

CHAPTER 5

1. F. W. Marks III, *Velvet on Iron: The Diplomacy of Theodore Roosevelt* (Lincoln, NE: University of Nebraska Press, 1970).

2. L. A. French, Asia, Southeast, *Religion and Violence: An Encyclopedia of Faith and Conflict from Antiquity to the Present*, Vol. 1, ed. J. I. Ross (Armonk, NY: M. E. Sharpe, 2011), 69–78.

3. M. Boot, "'Attractions' and 'Chastisement'—The Philippine War, 1899–1902," in *The Savage Wars of Peace: Small Wars and the Rise of American Power* (New York: Basic Books, 2003), 99–100.

4. M. V. Henderson, "Minor Empresario Contracts for the Colonization of Texas, 1825–1834," *The Southwestern Historical Quarterly* 31, no. 4 (1928): 295–32.

5. C. L. Dufour, *The Mexican War: A Compact History, 1846–1848* (New York: Hawthorn Books, 1968); S. V. Connor and O. B. Faulk, *North America Divided: The Mexican War, 1846–1848* (New York: Oxford University Press, 1971).

6. W. P. Webb, *The Texas Rangers: A Century of Frontier Defense* (Boston: Houghton Mifflin Company, 1935).

7. C. T. Haven and F. A. Belden, *A History of the Colt Revolver* (New York: Morrow, 1940); J. E. Parsons, *The Peacemaker and Its Rivals: An Account of the Single Action Colt* (New York: Morrow, 1950).

8. C. H. Harris III and L. R. Sadler, *The Texas Rangers and the Mexican Revolution: The Bloodiest Decade, 1910–1920* (Albuquerque, NM: University of New Mexico Press, 2004), 15.

9. B. H. Johnson, *Revolution in Texas: How a Forgotten Rebellion and Its Bloody Suppression Turned Mexicans into Americans* (New Haven, CT: Yale University Press, 2003).

10. B. H. Procter. *Just One Riot: Episodes of Texas Rangers in the 20th Century* (Austin, TX: Eakin Press, 1991); L. A. French, "Militarization of the Police," in *Police*

Use of Force: Important Issues Facing the Police and the Community They Serve, ed. M. J. Palmiotto (Boca Raton, FL: CRC Press/Taylor & Francis Group, 2017).

11. P. Gardner, *Porfirio Diaz: Profiles in Power* (Harlow, England: Pearson Education Limited, 2001), 37.

12. Ibid.

13. A. Camp, *Politics in Mexico* (New York: Oxford University Press, 1993).

14. A. Brenner, *The Winds That Swept Mexico* (Meridian, CT: The Meridian Gravure Company, 1971).

15. C. C. Clendenen, *The United States and Pancho Villa: A Study in Unconventional Diplomacy* (Ithaca, NY: American Historical Association, Cornell University Press, 1961).

16. B. H. Johnson, *Revolution in Texas*; C. H. Harris and L. R. Sadler, *The Texas Rangers and the Mexican Revolution*; J. Sandos, *Rebellion in the Borderlands: Anarchism and the Plan de San Diego—1904–1923* (Norman, OK: University of Oklahoma Press, 1992).

17. B. H. Johnson, *Revolution in Texas*, 113.

18. Ibid., 120.

19. D. M. Coerver and L. B. Hall, *Texas and the Mexican Revolution: A Study in State and National Border Policy, 1910–1920* (San Antonio, TX: Trinity University Press, 1984).

20. Ibid.

21. J. W. Hurst, *The Villista Prisoners, 1916–1917* (Las Cruces, NM: Yucca Tree Press, 2000).

22. Ibid.

23. A. Knight, *U.S.-Mexican Relations, 1910–1940. An Interpretation*, Monograph Series 28 (San Diego, CA: Tinker Foundation, 1987).

24. Hurst, *The Villista Prisoners 1916–1917*; F. Tompkins, *Chasing Villa: The Last Campaign of the U.S. Cavalry* (Harrisburg, PA: Military Service Publishing Company, 1934).

25. J. A. Crutchfield, *Revolt at Taos: The New Mexican and Indian Insurrection of 1847* (Yardley, PA: Westholme Publishing, 2015), 111–12; *Fleming v. Page* (50 U.S. ((9 How.) 603 (1850).

26. Treaty of Peace, Friendship, Limits, and Settlement between the United States of America and the United Mexican States, Concluded at Guadalupe Hidalgo, February 2, 1848.

CHAPTER 6

1. W. E. B. Du Bois, "Education and Work," *Journal of Negro Education* 1 (April 1931): 15–18; E. F. Frazier, *Black Bourgeois* (New York: Free Press, 1962); A. Hacker, *Two Nations: Black and White, Separate, Hostile, Unequal* (New York: Ballentine/Random House, 1995).

2. F. Galton. *Hereditary Genius: An Inquiry into Its Laws and Consequences* (London: Macmillan, 1869).

3. L. M. Terman, *The Measurement of Intelligence* (Boston: Houghton Mifflin, 1916); *Buck v. Bell,* 274 U.S. 200, 205, No. 292, U.S. Supreme Ct. (1927).

4. Terman, *The Measurement of Intelligence.*

5. Ibid., 26.

6. E. Black, *War Against the Weak: Eugenics and America's Campaign to Create a Master Race* (New York: Four Walls Eight Windows, 2003); E. Brantlinger, *Sterilization of People with Mental Disabilities: Issues, Perspectives, and Cases* (Westport, CT: Auburn House, 1995).

7. H. E. Barnes and N. K. Teeters, *New Horizons in Criminology*, 3rd edition (Englewood Cliffs, NJ: Prentice-Hall, Inc., 1959).

8. *Larry P. v. Riles,* 343 F Supp. 1308 (N.D. Cal.) (1972) *Preliminary Injunction*; 502 Fed. 963 (9th Cir.) (1979; 1984) *Affirmed; Final Order,* Terman.

9. R. Campbell, *In Darkest Alaska: Travel and Empire along the Inside Passage* (Philadelphia, PA: University of Pennsylvania Press, 2007), 88–89.

10. Ibid., 153.

11. G. Simmel, *Conflict,* trans. K. A. Wolf (New York: The Free Press, 1955); H. E. Barnes and N. K. Teeters, *New Horizons in Criminology,* 13.

12. P. Taft and P. Ross, "American Labor Violence, Its Causes, Character, and Outcome," *The History of Violence in America: A Report to the National Commission on the Causes and Prevention of Violence,* eds. H. D. Graham and T. R. Gurr (New York: Bantam Books, 1969), 281–395.

13. Ibid., 410, 415–17.

14. D. Whitehead, *The FBI Story* (New York: Random House, 1956), 41.

15. Ibid., 43.

16. P. Taft and P. Ross, "American Labor Violence, Its Causes, Character, and Outcome," *Lynching of Frank Little,* 333–36.

17. *Indian Intercourse Act,* U.S. Statutes at Large, 4: 564, July 9, 1832.

18. R. Snake Jr., Snyder Act of 1921, *Report on Alcohol and Drug Abuse* (Task Force Eleven: Alcohol and Drug Abuse) (Washington, DC: American Indian Police Review Commission, Government Printing Office, 1976), 27–32.

19. Barnes and Teeters, 14.

20. A. E. Alcock, *History of the International Labor Organization* (New York: Octagon Books, 1971); R. L. Filippelli, *Labor in the USA: A History* (New York: Alfred A. Knopf, 1984).

21. National Firearm Act of 1934; Public Law, 73-474; 48 Stat. 1236; *Miller v. United States,* 307 U.S. 174, 59 S.Ct. (1939); *The Constitution of the United States of America,* Amendment II, 1791.

22. J. A. S. Grenville, "The Depression, 1929–1939," *A History of the World in the Twentieth Century* (Cambridge, MA: The Belknap Press of Harvard University Press, 1980), 161–78.

23. J. A. Salmond, *The Civilian Conservation Corps, 1933–1942: A New Deal Case Study* (Durham, NC: Duke University Press, 1967).

24. B. Burrough, *Public Enemies: America's Greatest Wave and the Birth of the FBI, 1933–34* (New York: Penguin Books, 2004), 8–9.

25. B. Denenberg, *The True Story of J. Edgar Hoover and the FBI* (New York: Scholastic, Inc, 1993), 59.

26. B. Burrough, *Public Enemies.*

27. R. Unger, *The Union Station Massacre: The Original Sin of J. Edgar Hoover's FBI* (Kansas City, KS: Andrew McMeel Publishing, 1997), 236.

28. L. Sloman, *Reefer Madness: A History of Marijuana in America* (Indianapolis, IN: Bobbs-Merrill, 1979); J. C. McWilliams, *The Protectors: Anslinger and the Federal Bureau of Narcotics (1930–1962).* (Newark, DE: University of Delaware Press, 1990).

29. Barnes and Teeters, 381–82.

30. H. A. Gailey, *Historical Encyclopedia of the United States Marine Corps* (Lanham, MD: The Scarecrow Press, Inc., 1998), 7.

31. P. N. Pierce and F. O. Hough, *The Compact History of the United States Marine Corp* (New York: Hawthorn Books, Inc., 1960), 153, 155, 160.

32. H. A. Gailey, *Historical Encyclopedia of the United States Marine Corps*, 38–39.

33. S. D. Butler, *War Is a Racket* (New York: Round Table Press, 1935), 30–34.

34. W. Manchester, *American Caesar: Douglas MacArthur, 1880–1964* (Boston: Little, Brown & Company, 1978), 152.

35. J. Archer, *The Plot to Seize the White House* (New York: Hawthorn Books, 1973), 118–19.

36. C. Daniel, editorial director, "Japanese-Americans Are Imprisoned," in *Year by Year from 1900 to 2000: American Century* (New York: Dorling Kindersley Publishing, Inc., 2000), 142.

37. S. Taylor, "The Internment of Americans of Japanese Ancestry," in *When Sorry Isn't Enough: The Controversy over Apologies and Reparations for Human Injustice*, ed. R. L. Brooks (New York: New York University Press, 1999), 165–76.

CHAPTER 7

1. C. Clinton, *The Black Soldier: 1492 to the Present* (Boston: Houghton Mifflin, 2000), 75.

2. Ibid., 65.

3. *The Constitution of the United States of America*, Amendment XIV.

4. J. G. Quinones, *Chicano Politics: Realities & Promise 1940–1990* (Albuquerque, NM: University of New Mexico Press, 1990); E. R. Stoddard, Mexican American Education, *Mexican Americans* (New York: Random House, 1973), 1223–34.

5. *Mendez v. Westminster School District*, 64 F. Supp 544 (C.D. Cal. 1946).

6. *Hernandez v. Driscoll CISD*, Civil Action (Civ.A.) 1384, U.S. District Court of the Southern District of Texas (S. D. Tex.), 1957.

7. J. Meacham, "Do Business Leaders Make Good Presidents?" *Time* (January 30, 2017): 36–37.

8. B. Denenberg, "Hoover and the Civil Rights Movement," in *The True Story of J. Edgar Hoover and the FBI* (New York: Scholastic, Inc., 1993), 138–39.

9. N. Cullather, *Secret History: The CIA's Classified Account of Its Operations in Guatemala, 1952–1954* (Palo Alto, CA: Stanford University Press, 1999); P. Gleijeses, *Shattered Hope: The Guatemala Revolution and the United States, 1944–1954* (New Haven, CT; Princeton University Press, 1992); R. H. Immerman, *The CIA in Guatemala: The Foreign Policy of Intervention* (Austin, TX: University of Texas Press, 1982); J. Handy, *Revolution in the Countryside: Rural Conflict and Agrarian Reform in Guatemala 1944–54* (Chapel Hill, NC: University of North Carolina Press, 1994); S. Kinzer and S. Schlesinger, *Bitter Fruit: The Story of the American Coup in Guatemala* (Cambridge, MA: Harvard University Press, 1999).

10. G. Lesley, *The School of the Americas: Military Training and Political Violence in the Americas* (Durham, NC: Duke University Press, 2004).

11. *Mexican Labor Agreement of 1951, 1961, 1963* (Public Law 78); Senate Agriculture Committee Hearing, 1951; House Agriculture Committee Hearing, 1963; and R. B. Craig, *The Bracero Program: Interest Groups and Foreign Policy* (Austin, TX: University of Texas Press, 1971).

12. J. R. Garcia, *Operation Wetback: The Mass Deportation of Mexican Undocumented Workers in 1954* (Westport, CT: Greenwood Press, 1980).

13. D. L. Fixico, *Termination and Relocation: Federal Indian Policy, 1945–1960* (Albuquerque, NM: University of New Mexico Press, 1986); Public Law 83-280 (August 15, 1953), U.S. Statutes at Large, 67: 588–90.

14. Ibid., R. Drinnon, *Keeper of Concentration Camps: Dillon S. Myer and American Racism* (Berkeley, CA: University of California Press, 1987).

15. R. Costo and J. Henry-Costo, *Indian Treaties: Two Centuries of Dishonor* (San Francisco, CA: Indian Historian Press, 1977), 36.

16. American Indian Policy Commission. "Off-Reservation Indians," in *American Indian Policy Review Commission. Finial Report* (Washington, DC: U.S. Government Printing Office, 1977), 431–32.

17. J. W. Kirshon, editor in chief, "The Eagle Ascendant 1946–1999," in *American Century: Year by Year from 1900–2000* (New York/London: Dorling Kindersley Publishing, Inc., 2000), 266–81.

18. A. Stephason, *Manifest Destiny: American Expansion and the Empire of Right* (New York: Hill and Wang, 1995), 125–29.

19. J. W. Kirshon, "The Eagle Ascendant 1946–1999."

20. H. D. Graham and T. R. Gurr, *Violence in America: Historical and Comparatives* (Eisenhower Report) (New York: Bantam Books, 1969), 419–20, 424, 427.

21. J. W. Kirshon, "Chicago: The Whole World's Watching," in *American Century*, 302.

22. D. Farber, *Chicago '68* (Chicago: University of Chicago Press, 1988); J. Schultz, *No One Was Killed: The Democratic National Convention, August 1968* (Chicago: University of Chicago Press, 2009).

23. R. B. McKay, chairman, *Attica: The Complete Story of the Events Leading to the Bloodiest One-Day Encounter between Americans in This Century*, The Official Report of the New York State Special Commission on Attica (New York: Bantam Books, 1972), xi, xv.

24. Ibid.

25. B. Denenberg, "Hoover and the Civil Rights Movement," 165–68.

26. T. Weiner, *Enemies: A History of the FBI* (New York: Random House, 2012).

27. B. Denenberg, 165–68.

28. B. Denenberg, 169–72.

29. 421 F2d, *Bucher v. Selective Service System Local Boards Nos. Etc.,* No. 17414 (January 2, 1970).

30. L. Lader, *Power on the Left* (New York: W.W. Norton, 1979).

31. B. Denenberg, 186; M. Marqusee, *Redemption Song: Muhammad Ali and the Spirit of the Sixties* (Brooklyn, NY: Verso Books, 2017).

32. B. W. Wheeler and S. D. Becker, "A Nation of Immigrants: The Fourth Wave in California," *Discovering the American Past: A Look at the Evidence* (Boston: Houghton Mifflin Company, 2002), 290–307.

33. J. Quinones, *Chicano Politics: Reality & Promise 1940–1990*; R. Rosaldo, et al. *Chicano: The Beginnings of Bronze Power* (New York, NY: William Morrow & Company, 1974).

34. E. Poniatowska, *Massacre in Mexico*, trans. H. R. Lane (New York: Viking, 1975).

35. J. G. Quinones, *Chicano Politics*.

36. Y. Bushyhead, "In the Spirit of Crazy Horse: Leonard Peltier and the AIM Uprising," in *The Winds of Injustice: American Indians and the U.S. Government*, L. A. French (New York: Garland Publishing, 1994), 81–82.

37. Ibid.

38. Ibid., 84–85.

39. Ibid.

40. Lyndon B. Johnson, President Johnson, Special Message to Congress, March 6, 1968, *Public Papers of the President of the United States: Lyndon B. Johnson 1968–69*, Vol. 1: 1068 (Washington, DC: U.S. Government Printing Office), 336–37, 343–44.

41. Opening Statement of Hon. James Abourezk, *Hearing before the Sub-Committee on Indian Affairs of the Committee on Interior and Insular Affairs,* United States Senate, 94th Congress, 1st Session, on S20105, December 3 and 4, 1975.

42. M. Thompson, Commissioner of Indian Affairs' Letter to Hon. Peter W. Rodino, Chairman, Committee on the Judiciary, House of Representatives, dated, May 20, 1975, *Criminal Jurisdiction in Indian Country*, Serial no. 33, 94th Congress, 2nd Session (1976), 25–26.

43. *Indian Crimes Act of 1976* (May 29, 1976), *U.S. Statutes at Large*, 90: 585–86.

44. Criminal Jurisdiction Over Indians, Public Law 102-137, *U.S. Statutes at Large*: 646 (October 28, 1991).

CHAPTER 8

1. A. Platt, "The Politics of Riot Commissions, 1917–1970: An Overview," in *The Politics of Riot Commissions* (New York: Macmillan, 1971), 8–34; also cited in R. Quin-

ney, *Critique of Legal Order: Crime Control in Capitalist Society* (Boston: Little, Brown and Company, 1973), 74.

2. F. P. Graham, "A Contemporary History of American Crime," in *The History of Violence in America: A Report to the National Commission on the Causes and Prevention of Violence* (New York: Bantam Books, 1969), 498–501.

3. J. W. Kirshon, *America's Century: Year by Year from 1900 to 2000* (New York: Dorling Kindersley Publishing, Inc. 2000), 326.

4. J. W. Kirshon, *America's Century*, 328.

5. W. Knapp, *Commission Report (With Summary and Principal Recommendations, Issues August 3, 1972)*, Commission to Investigate Allegations of Police Corruption and the City's Anti-Corruption Procedures (New York: George Braziller, Inc., 1972), foreword.

6. R. Daley, *Target Blue: An Insider's View of the NYPD* (New York: Delacorte Press, 1971), 49.

7. W. Knapp. *Commission Report*, 260.

8. L. A. French, "The Incarcerated Black Female: The Case of Social Double Jeopardy," *Journal of Black Studies* 8, no. 3 (1978): 321–35.

9. *Omnibus Crime Control and Safe Streets Act of 1968*, Public Law 90-351; 82 Stat. 197/42 USC.: ch. 46 (June 19, 1968).

10. *Gideon v. Wainwright* (372 U.S. 436, 1963); *Miranda v. Arizona* (384 U.S. 436, 1966).

11. *In re Gualt* (387 U.S. 1): 1967.

12. *Furman v. Georgia* (408 U.S. 238, 345, 1972); *Gregg v. Georgia* (428 U.S. 153, 96 S. Ct, 2912, 1976); *Jurek v. Texas* (428 U.S. 262, 96 S. Ct. 2950, 1976); *Proffit v. Florida* (428 U.S. 242, 252, 1976).

CHAPTER 9

1. R. Quinney, *Critique of Legal Order: Crime Control in Capitalist Society* (Boston: Little, Brown and Company, 1974), 119, 122.

2. G. M. Sykes, *Criminology* (New York: Harcourt Brace Jovanovich, Inc., 1978), 11.

3. M. Wolfgang, "The Philadelphia Study, Victim-Precipitated Criminal Homicide," in *Delinquency, Crime, and Social Process*, eds. D. R. Cressey and D. A. Ward (New York: Harper & Row, Publishers, 1969), 1032–33.

4. M. Wolfgang, "The Philadelphia Study, Victim-Precipitated Criminal Homicide"; M. Wolfgang and F. Ferracuti, *Subculture of Violence* (London: Tavistock Publishing, 1967); J. R. Daughen and P. Binzen, *The Cop Who Would Be King: Mayor Frank Rizzo* (Boston: Little, Brown and Company, 1977).

5. L. A. French, "Introduction—Minority Justice," *Quarterly Journal of Ideology: A Critique of Conventional Wisdom (Special Issue, Minority Justice)* 11, no. 4 (1987): i.

6. Education Project in Criminal Justice, Graduate School of Criminal Justice, State University of New York at Albany: Law Enforcement Assistance Administration (77CD-99-0004) (September 1, 1977).

7. S. Kurkjian and S. Greenberger, "Fewer College Sites for Quinn Bill Work," *The Boston Globe* (April 29, 2003): A20; Associated Press, UMass President Subpoenaed to Testify about Mobster Brother, *Concord Monitor* (December 1, 2002): A2.

8. *Criminology: An Interdisciplinary Journal* 55, no. 1 (February 2017).

9. P. G. Zimbardo, *The Stanford Prison Experiment*, slide/tape presentation produced by Philip G. Zombardo (Stanford, CA: 1971); R. K. Merton, *Social Theory and Social Structure* (Glencoe, IL: Free Press, 1957).

CHAPTER 10

1. *Indian Intercourse Act* (U.S. Statutes at Large, 4: 564, July 9, 1832).

2. R. Snake, *Report on Alcohol and Drug Abuse (Task Force Eleven: Alcohol and Drug Abuse)*, First Report to the American Indian Policy Review Commission (Washington, DC: U.S. Government Printing Office, 1976).

3. N. Abrams and S. S. Beale, "A History of Federal Drug Control Laws," in *Federal Criminal Law and Its Enforcement*, 2nd ed. (St. Paul, MN: West Publishing Company, 257).

4. Ibid., 257–58.

5. Ibid., 259.

6. Ibid., 259–60.

7. Public Law 106-120; 113 Stat. 1626 (December 3, 1999).

CHAPTER 11

1. N. deB. Katzenbach, *Task Force Report: The Police,* The President's Commission on Law Enforcement and Administration of Justice (Washington, DC: U.S. Printing Office, 1967), 3–5.

2. Ibid., 7.

3. Ibid., 38.

4. Ibid., 4, 5.

5. L. A. French, "Militarization of the Police," in *Police Use of Force: Important Issues Facing the Police and the Community They Serve*, ed. M. J. Palmiotto (Boca Raton, FL: CRC Press/Taylor & Francis Group, 201), 56–80.

6. R. Linton, *The Study of Man* (Appleton, WI: Appleton-Century-Croft, 1936).

7. L. A. French, "Militarization of the Police."

8. J. W. Kirshon, "Riots Ravage Los Angeles after King Verdict," in *American Century: Year by Year from 1900 to 2000* (London: Dorling Kindersley, 2000), 398.

9. P. Vercammen, "20-Years Ago, Gunbattle Terrorized North Hollywood—and Shocked America," CNN U.S.: Updated 2238 GMT (0638 HKT) (February 28, 2017).

10. R. Chuck Mason, *Securing America's Borders: The Role of the Military* (Washington, DC: Congressional Research Service (7-5700 R41286) (February 25, 2013). https://fas.org/sgp/crs/homesec/R41286.pdf.

11. M. Caruso, ed., "America Incarcerated," *Smithsonian* 47, no. 9 (January/February 2017): 79.

12. N. Pickler, "Obama Restricts Police Military Gear." *Associated Press, Concord Monitor* (May 19, 2015), A8.

13. Ibid.

CHAPTER 12

1. E. Durkheim, *The Rules of Sociological Methods*, trans. Sarah Solovay and John Mueller (Glencoe, IL: The Free Press, 1950); M. Weber, *The Theory of Social and Economic Organization*, trans. A. M. Henderson and Talcott Parsons (Glencoe, IL: The Free Press, 1947); G. Simmel, *Conflict*, trans. Kurt A. Wolff (Glencoe, IL: The Free Press, 1955).

2. A. L. Baldwin, "A Cognitive Theory of Socialization," in *Handbook of Socialization Theory and Research*, ed. D. A. Goslin (Chicago: Rand McNally and Company, 1969), 325–46; L. Festinger, *A Theory of Cognitive Dissonance* (Palo Alto, CA: Stanford University Press, 1957).

3. L. Coser, *The Function of Social Conflict* (Glencoe, IL: The Free Press, 1956); L. Coser, *Continuities in the Study of Social Conflict* (Glencoe, IL: The Free Press, 1962).

4. E. Durkheim, "On the Normality of Crime," in *Theories of Society: Foundations of Modern Sociological Theory*, eds. T. Parsons, et al. (Glencoe, IL: The Free Press, 1961), 872–75.

5. H. Becker, *Outsiders: Studies in the Sociology of Deviance* (Glencoe, IL: The Free Press, 1963).

6. W. F. Ogburn, *Social Change: With Respect to Cultural and Original Nature* (New York: Dell Publishing Company, 1966).

7. G. Simmel, *Conflict*.

8. S. Milgram, *Obedience to Authority* (New York: Harper & Row, 1974); N. E. Miller, "The Frustration-Aggression Hypothesis," *Psychological Review* 48 (1941): 337–42; S. Palmer, *The Psychology of Murder* (New York: Thomas Y. Crowell Company, 1960).

9. *Investigation of the Ferguson Police Department*, United States Department of Justice Civil Rights Division (March 4, 2015), 2–3, 4, 5–6.

10. "Justice Department Announces Findings of Investigation into Baltimore Police Department," *Justice News* (Washington, DC: Department of Justice, Office of Public Affairs, Wednesday, August 10, 2016), https://www.justice.gov/opa/pr/justice-department-announces-findings-investigation-baltimore-police-department.

CHAPTER 13

1. *Atkins v. Virginia,* 536 U.S. 304 (2002); *Roper v. Simmons,* 543 U.S. 551 (2005); *House v. Bell,* 547 U.S. 518 (2006); *Miller v. Alabama,* 567 U.S. 460 (2012).

2. L. A. French and B. deOca, "The Neuropsychology of Impulse Control: New Insights into Violent Behaviors," *Journal of Police and Criminal Psychology* 16 (2001): 25–32.

3. J. R. Graham, *MMPI-2: Assessing Personality and Psychopathology* (New York: Oxford University Press, 2000); R. L. Green, *The MMPI-2: An Interpretive Manual* (Boston: Allyn & Bacon, 2000); L. A. French, "Police Culture and the MMPI," *International Journal of Comparative Criminology* 3 (2003): 63–67; L. A. French, "Assessing Law Enforcement Personnel: Comparative Uses of the MMPIs," *Forensic Examiner* 11, nos. 3&4 (2002): 21–28.

4. P. T. Trzepacz and R. W. Baker, *The Psychiatric Mental Status Examination* (New York: Oxford University Press, 1993); R. L. Smith and W. F. Black, *The Mental Status Examination in Neurology* (New York: F. A. Davis, 2000).

5. R. D. Davis and C. D. Rostow, "Matrix-Predictive Uniform Law Enforcement Evaluation Selection," *Forensic Examiner* 11 (November/December 2002): 19–24.

6. J. M. Violanti, *Police Suicide: Epidemic in Blue* (Springfield, IL: Charles C Thomas, 1996); APA, *American Psychologist—Special Issue: Comprehensive Soldiers Fitness* 66 (2011): 1–86; W. B. Walsh and N. E. Betz, "The Assessment of Personality (Part II)," in *Tests and Assessments*, third ed. (Prentice-Hall, 1995), 87–148; National Center for Posttraumatic Stress Disorders—Assessments, United States Department of Veterans Affairs, https://www.ptsd.va.gov/professional/assessment/overview/index.asp.

CHAPTER 14

1. *The Constitution of the United States of America*, Article IV, Section 2 (3rd paragraph) (1793).

2. *Fugitive Slave Act of 1850: An Act or Amend, and Supplementary in the Act Entitled "An Act Respecting Fugitives from Justice, and Persons Escaping from the Service of Their Masters,"* 31st U.S. Congress, 9 Stat. 462 (1850); *Homer A. Plessy v. John H. Ferguson*, 163 U.S. 537 (May 18, 1896); *The Constitution of the United States of America*, Amendment XVIII, Prohibition of Liquor (1919); and Amendment XXI, Repeal of Prohibition (1933).

3. W. Doran, "Claim That 2016 Was One of the 'Deadliest Years' for Officers Is False," (PollitiFact staff), *Concord Monitor* (May 26, 2017), B1.

4. Officer Down Memorial Page. http://www.odmp.org/search/year/2017/printview.

5. H.R. 814 (114th): Thin Blue Line Act: *To Amend Title 18, United States Code, to Provide Additional Aggravating Factors for the Imposition of the Death Penalty Based on the Status of the Victim* (Washington, DC: Government Printing Office, February 9, 2015); L. A. French, "And Justice for Some," in *Frog Town: Portrait of a French Canadian Parish in New England* (Lanham, MD: University Press of America, 2014), 224–28.

6. H.R. 1428, American Law Enforcement Heroes Act of 2017.

7. "Nation: Sentencing Reversal Angers Both Sides." *Time* 189, no. 2 (May 29, 2017), 11.

8. *Today's FBI Facts and Figures, 2013–2014* (Washington, DC: U.S. Department of Justice, Federal Bureau of Investigation, Office of Public Affairs, 2015); Directors, Then and Now, https://www.fbi.gov/history/directors; D. Johnson, "Defiant F.B.I. Chief Removed from Job by the President," *New York Times* (July 20, 1993), http://www.nytimes.com/1993/07/20/us/defiant-fbi-chief-removed-from-job-by-the-president.html?mcubz=0; D. Von Drehle, "Nation: The Comey Misfire: Did Donald Trump Ax James Comey because He Mishandled the Clinton Email Investigation? Or Did He Have the FBI's Probe of His Campaign's Possible Links to Moscow in Mind?" *Time* 189, no. 19 (May 22, 2017): 20–26.

9. M. Potok, "The Trump Effect: The Campaign Language of the Man Who Would Become President Sparks Hate Violence, Bullying, Before and After the Election," *Intelligence Report* 162 (Spring 2017): 32–35; "SPLC Fights Back against Bigotry in White House," *SPLC Report* 47, no. 1 (Spring 2017): 1, 3.

10. M. Potok, "The Year in Hate and Extremism," *Intelligence Report* (Spring 2015): 36–62; "Hate Groups Rise, Fueled by Trump Campaign," *SPLC Report*: 13.

11. R. Lenz, "670 Days: The Bundy's of Nevada Orchestrated Two Armed Standoffs with the Government. After Almost Two Years, They Finally Face Justice." *Intelligence Report* 161 (Summer 2016): 22–29; K. Ritter (Associate Press), "N.H. Man Sentenced in Bundy Standoff—Judge: Organizer of Militia at Nevada Ranch a 'Bully Vigilante.'" *Concord Monitor* (Thursday, June 1, 2017): A1, A7.

12. A. Sammon and S. Keith, "How Did Police from All Over the Country End Up at Standing Rock? A Clinton-Era Directive Used Mainly for Natural Disaster Relief Has Drawn in Law Enforcement from Faraway States." *ZUMA* (December 4, 2016).

13. M. Potok and R. Lenz, "Line in the Sand: A Radical and Growing Organization of 'Constitutional Sheriffs' Is Promoting Defiance of Federal Laws It Doesn't Like," *Intelligence Report* 161 (Summer 2016): 30–36.

14. Ibid., 35.

15. Ibid.; R. Lenz and M. Potok, "Seeds of Sedition: The Oath Keepers Say They're Busy Forming Armed 'Preparedness Teams.' But What They're Preparing for Is Pure, Dystopian Fantasy," *Intelligence Report* 161 (Summer 2016): 37–39.

CHAPTER 15

1. D. C. Miller, Authoritarian Personality (*F*) Scale, Forms 45 and 40, *Handbook or Research Design and Social Measurement*, third ed. (New York: David McKay Company, 1977), 412–16.

2. J. Forman Jr., *Locking Up Our Own: Crime and Punishment in Black America* (New York: Farrar, Straus and Giroux, 2017).

3. D. English, L. Bowleg, J. M. Tschann, R. P. Agans, and D. J. Malebranche, "Measuring Black Men's Police-Based Discrimination Experiences: Development and Validation of the Police and Law Enforcement (PLE) Scale," *Cultural Diversity and Ethnic Minority Psychology* 23, no. 2 (2017): 185–99.

Index

About the Author

Laurence Armand French, PhD, is professor emeritus of psychology at Western New Mexico University and senior researcher and affiliate professor of Justice Studies at the Justiceworks Institute at the University of New Hampshire, Durham. He has taught criminology, criminal justice, sociology, and psychology at various universities, including minority-serving universities, and has won awards for this minority-based research. He was Senior Fulbright Scholar assigned to the University of Sarajevo in Bosnia and Herzegovina for the 2009–2010 academic year. He has written many articles and books, including *Frog Town: Portrait of a French Canadian Parish in New England*, *Running the Border Gauntlet*, and *Native American Justice*. He received the 1999 National Institute on Drug Abuse (NIDA) research award for his work in assessing substance abuse among minorities in the U.S. Southwest.